Pentateuch

SCM CORE TEXT

Pentateuch

Walter J. Houston

scm press

© Walter J. Houston 2013

Published in 2013 by SCM Press
Editorial office
3rd Floor
Invicta House
108–114 Golden Lane,
London EC1Y 0TG

SCM Press is an imprint of Hymns Ancient & Modern Ltd
(a registered charity)
13A Hellesdon Park Road
Norwich NR6 5DR, UK
www.scmpress.co.uk

British Library Cataloguing in Publication data

A catalogue record for this book is available
from the British Library

978-0-334-04385-0

Typeset by Regent Typesetting, London
Printed and bound by
CPI Group (UK) Croydon

Contents

Part C

Preface

This is not a book-by-book survey. It is an introduction to scholarship on the Pentateuch as a whole, in three main areas, concerning the text in itself, its historical origins and the ways in which it has been and is being read. Where there is no existing work to draw on, I have offered my own observations. I hope that the material for reflection and exercise and the suggestions for further reading, which are reasonably comprehensive, will make it suitable for use both by the individual student and the general reader, and in class. I assume readers will have a basic knowledge of the history of ancient Israel and Judah and of the Old Testament generally, but scholarly approaches are explained as required.

The Bibliography is intended partly for reference – the works given by author and abbreviated title in the footnotes refer to it – and partly to back up the sections on further reading with general works and commentaries. Only works in English are listed; of course, that includes articles in foreign-language periodicals and collections.

The book should be used with the Bible open beside it. References are to the English versions, where the numbering of verses in the Hebrew text differs. However, quotations, unless otherwise stated, are given in my own translation from the Hebrew. I do not want to privilege any particular English version of the text.

A word on language and gender. Human beings are always referred to in inclusive language, where appropriate – so 'the ancestors' rather than 'the patriarchs', unless the reference is exclusively to Abraham, Isaac and Jacob. However, God will frequently be found referred to with masculine pronouns. Most references to 'God', and all references to 'YHWH', which is how I render the divine name, occur in discussion of the text of the Pentateuch, where Israel's God is treated as masculine, so it is realistic to follow this usage. But I have tried, particularly when discussing the theology of the Pentateuch in Chapter 10, to be sparing in the use of pronouns.

This work has occupied the bulk of my time for the past three years, and the road has been harder going than I expected. The work still has its defects, but they would have been far more numerous than they are without the generously given advice of several friends and colleagues, including the two anonymous peer reviewers, who saw a sample chapter as well as the outline of my proposed work. Those whose names I know are Graham

Davies, Cheryl Exum, Walter Moberly, John Sawyer and the late and much missed Roger Tomes. I warmly express my gratitude to them all. I am also grateful to the SCM Press commissioning editor, Natalie Watson, who gave me the opportunity of writing the book and was very patient in waiting for it. My wife Fleur, as always, has been constant in her interest and encouragement. Without her this would have been a much harder and more lonely road to travel.

Walter J. Houston

Abbreviations

This list does not include abbreviations of the names of books of the Bible, or of states of the USA, or the best-known general abbreviations.

AB	Anchor Bible
ABD	*Anchor Bible Dictionary*
ACCS	Ancient Christian Commentary on Scripture
BASOR	*Bulletin of the American Schools of Oriental Research*
BCE	before the Common Era (= BC)
CBQ	*Catholic Biblical Quarterly*
CE	of the Common Era (= AD)
ECC	Eerdmans Critical Commentary
EQ	*Evangelical Quarterly*
HBOT	Sæbø (ed.), *Hebrew Bible/Old Testament: The History of its Interpretation*
HCOT	Historical Commentary on the Old Testament
ICC	International Critical Commentary
IDB	*Interpreter's Dictionary of the Bible*
JAAR	*Journal of the American Academy of Religion*
JBL	*Journal of Biblical Literature*
JSOT	*Journal for the Study of the Old Testament*
JTS	*Journal of Theological Studies*
KJV	King James Version
LCL	Loeb Classical Library
NCB	New Century Bible
NEB	New English Bible
NICOT	New International Commentary on the Old Testament
NIV	New International Version
NRSV	New Revised Standard Version
OTC	Old Testament Commentary
OTL	Old Testament Library
REB	Revised English Bible
VT	*Vetus Testamentum*
ZAR	*Zeitschrift für die altorientalische und biblische Rechtsgeschichte*
ZAW	*Zeitschrift für die alttestamentliche Wissenschaft*

1

Approaching the Text

What is the Pentateuch and why is it worth reading?

The first five books of the Old Testament or Hebrew Bible, Genesis, Exodus, Leviticus, Numbers and Deuteronomy, have always been recognized as a distinct unit, often known as the 'five books of Moses' or as the Pentateuch, from the Greek, meaning 'the five scrolls'. For Jews it is the 'Torah' or 'teaching'.

Why is it worth reading? That depends on the reader. I am assuming that the majority of readers of this book will be Christians. Many of the foundations of the Christian faith are found here, foundations that are taken for granted in the New Testament. It speaks of creation, of sin and the fall, of God's promise, of the calling of God's people, of liberation and of hope. Many readers, it is true, are put off by the numerous pages of laws and cultic regulations. But they should persevere. After all, the 'Law' includes the Ten Commandments, and the two 'great commandments' identified by Jesus: 'You shall love the Lord your God' and 'You shall love your neighbour as yourself.' And those are by no means the only passages of moral value in these pages. That is to say nothing of the stories – Adam and Eve, Jacob and Laban, Joseph, Moses and the burning bush ...

For Jews this text has an even greater importance. It is this text and no other that is written to this day by hand on a great scroll and kept in the Ark in prominent view at the end of every Orthodox synagogue. It is this text, this scroll, that once a year is carried with high rejoicing round the synagogue. It is this text that is taken out to be read through, Sabbath after Sabbath, right through from beginning to end every year, with no exceptions for the duller parts of Leviticus. No other part of the Hebrew Bible is treated in this way, only selected portions of the prophets being read alongside the allotted passage of the Torah.

This central place of the Torah in the Jewish community is already illustrated in the Bible itself, when in Nehemiah 8 Ezra reads from it for an entire morning to the people gathered in the square in front of the Water Gate, with the Levites assisting the people to understand it. The narrator implies that this was the first time the people here gathered had heard it. It makes a tremendous impression on them: they weep when they hear the words, but the Levites encourage them to rejoice instead.

In the light of this, we might describe the Torah as the foundation document of a community. We could compare it to the Gospels in Christianity, to the Qur'an in Islam or in a different way to the US Declaration of Independence. It enables the Jewish community to understand themselves and their place in the purposes of God: it gives them their identity and their meaning, tells them where they have come from and where, in the purposes of God, they are going and prescribes their way of life and behaviour.

Not only the Jewish community: the Samaritans also recognize the Torah as Scripture and use it in similar ways. The Samaritans are today a very small community, only a few hundred strong. But it is likely that at one time they were more numerous. For them it is their only Scripture, and it is their foundation document as much as that of the Jews. Jews and Samaritans dispute the claim between them to be the inheritors of the tradition of Israel.

Is there any reason why non-religious people should be interested in these books? If they are interested in knowing something of the roots of western civilization, yes, of course there is. It is simply not possible to understand western art and literature without knowing the Bible, and that means above all the Pentateuch and the Gospels.

So don't go beyond this chapter without setting to and reading the Pentateuch itself. Read it fast. It's no longer than a modern novel. Don't stop to puzzle over difficulties. Read a book at a sitting, or half a book, depending on the time you have available: Genesis one evening, Exodus the next, and so on. And when you carry on with this book, have the Bible open beside it. I quote some important texts in full, but usually I just give a reference.

The significance of the Pentateuch

The significance of the Torah for Israel is far more than what is conveyed by the name 'law', which is used to refer to it in the New Testament (see Chapter 3, p. 42), precisely because it is basically a story. According to this story, Israel was chosen and called by God, through their ancestors Abraham, Isaac and Jacob, to be God's peculiar possession or 'special treasure' (Exod. 19.6; Deut. 7.6), and God delivered them from state slavery in Egypt. With them God made a covenant, by which they committed themselves to observe the commands for their life, national and individual, which God gave them, which are set out in the Torah.

It is this last feature that may be thought to justify the name 'law', and much of traditional Jewish scholarship is devoted to elucidating these commandments and working out how precisely they should be observed. It is the conviction of many Jews that it is Israel that has taught the world justice and compassion, which are taught in the Torah and are the essence of the character of God (Exod. 34.6–7).

Christians also regard the Pentateuch as part of Scripture, and Christians too claim the name 'Israel' (see Gal. 6.16). It does not on its own play the foundational part in their traditions that it does in those of the Jews and Samaritans. But it is indispensable, furnishing the basis of such central doctrines as those of creation and the fall. As for the story of Israel, the promises to the patriarchs, the exodus from Egypt and the covenant of Sinai, these have often been seen as the first stage in a 'history of salvation', leading eventually to the coming of Christ (see below, pp. 172–6). The way the Pentateuch is understood by Jews and by Christians is the subject of Chapter 8 in this book.

The foundational function served by the Pentateuch for 'Israel' enables us to begin to understand why it contains such diverse materials. For both story and law or moral instruction are relevant to this function: both origins and custom or moral ethos help to define a community.

The shape of the Pentateuch

All the same, this only enables us to understand it in the most general terms. It does not elucidate the precise shape that confronts us, let alone explain the details. It is divided into five 'books', originally scrolls, hence the Greek name Pentateuch. The writing of the entire Torah on one scroll is a more recent development, subsequent to the biblical period. There is a fairly new start at the beginning of each book, although the breaks before the beginning of Exodus and Deuteronomy are much more pronounced than those at the beginnings of Leviticus and Numbers, where the narrative is more directly connected to what has gone before.

The structure of the content is that of a story, which begins in Genesis with the creation of the world, with the failure of the first humans and the world's narrow escape from un-creation in the Flood. Genesis goes on to the story of the promises made by God to Israel's ancestors, to be their God and to give them a country to live in. It ends with their migration to Egypt. Exodus relates the story of Israel's deliverance from slavery in Egypt through the agency of Moses and their arrival at Mount Sinai. There God makes a covenant with them and gives them commandments and laws, and instructions for the erection of a movable sanctuary in which God may dwell with them. In Leviticus God speaks from this 'Tabernacle' or 'Dwelling' to give cultic regulations and moral laws; and in this book the sacrificial cult is initiated. In Numbers we have further laws and an account of the wandering of the Israelites after they have failed to take the opportunity to enter the promised land. In Deuteronomy, standing once more on the borders of that land 40 years later, they hear Moses give them a very long sermon including more laws and moral exhortation, concluding with the announcement of another covenant; Deuteronomy and the Torah as a whole ends with Moses' death. Israel's taking possession of the land is left to the book of Joshua, which is not part of the Torah, though there is no radical break in the narrative.

Questions

Summarizing the contents of the Torah in that way draws attention to some of its unusual features. There is not only the combination of narrative and law, which I have already pointed out. The points where the text begins and ends raise questions. If this story is the foundation story of Israel, why does it begin with the creation of the world and ten more chapters concerning the early history of humanity? And why does it end where it does, without relating the fulfilment of one of the promises God had made to God's people far back in the text? These questions suggest the basic question 'What is the Torah about?', 'What is its theme?'

Closer examination raises questions of different kinds: why are there two accounts of creation? Was the divine name revealed in primeval times, as Genesis 4.26 suggests, or only to Moses, as Exodus 3.15 suggests and Exodus 6.3 more definitely asserts? Are the Israelites permitted to sacrifice in many places, as Exodus 20.24 suggests, or only in one, as Deuteronomy 12 commands?

The questions raised suggest two different kinds of answer. Some can only be answered by investigating the history of the text. Others demand that we try to understand its present meaning. And many can be answered in different ways as the reader changes stance. As with other biblical texts, the scholarly study of the Pentateuch includes 'synchronic' study, which treats the text in its final form (or forms), as a literary text; 'diachronic' study, which attempts to discover the circumstances and motives of its writing, the historical process by which the text has come into being; and the study of 'reception history', the study of how it has been read and understood and responded to by actual readers, past or present. One common way in which these three aspects are described is as, respectively, 'the world of the text', that is, the world which is created in the reader's mind by reading it, 'the world behind the text', and 'the world in front of the text'.

The task ahead

The three parts of this book correspond to these three modes of reading or study. I am not offering studies of the individual books in this guide. I aim to enable an understanding of the Pentateuch as a whole. We shall start in the synchronic mode, with the world of the text, because we should start with what is known before we move on to what is unsure, and with that text which we are required to understand before we can form hypotheses about its origin. Then we shall tackle some approaches to the historical study of this text, before returning to look in more detail at what it has meant to its readers through the ages and today.

Part A

Here we shall try to form as clear a picture as we can of the Pentateuch as it stands, of what it appears to convey as a finished work and the genres, methods and forms it uses to convey it.

There are two fundamentally different types of material in the Pentateuch, using different styles, structures and literary forms, and requiring different approaches and methods in their study: that is, narrative and 'law'. But I want to suggest that these are not simply two separate parts of the Pentateuch as a whole. Rather, the *whole* Pentateuch is a narrative, which includes laws and instructions as part of the story, spoken by characters in the story (God and Moses) and helping to drive the plot. And at the same time the *whole* Pentateuch is Torah, commonly translated 'Law': part of the purpose of the story is to validate the commandments and instructions as obligations on the hearers. Therefore Chapters 2 and 3 are 'The Pentateuch *as* Narrative' and 'The Pentateuch *as* Torah'.

The overall structure of the Pentateuch is narrative, so we deal with the Pentateuch as narrative first, in Chapter 2. Modern literary study has developed concepts and methods for the analysis of narrative. Much work of this kind has been done on various parts and passages of the Pentateuch, but biblical scholars seem generally to have fought shy of the ambitious task of applying it to the Pentateuch as a whole. An exception is David Clines's work on the theme of the Pentateuch.[1]

In Chapter 3 we ask how the Pentateuch functions as Torah, and we look in detail at passages of commandment and instruction. One question that arises here is whether 'law' is indeed the right description for much of this material, or, if it is, how its function differs from that of written law in modern society. Recent scholarship on law in ancient Near Eastern societies will be drawn on to illuminate the issue. But the primary question is how the Torah defines the identity and responsibility of Israel, in relation to God and to each other, or in other words the religious and moral commitments demanded of them. In the chapter I will show how this is done both narratively, as the body of covenant commandments builds up, introduced by the Ten Commandments, and thematically, as many areas of life are addressed in widely separated parts of the Pentateuch.

We shall move next, in Chapter 4, to that key feature of the text which relates and links narrative and law, the promises of God and his commandments, and thus makes the genre of Torah comprehensible to the reader. This feature is the series of *covenants* between God and humanity which occur throughout the story. A great deal of work has been done on the concept of a covenant in the Hebrew Bible. Simply understood, a covenant is a solemn promise made in the context of a relationship – we shall go into the definition in more detail in the chapter. It is certainly significant that the

---

1 Clines, *Theme*.

making of a covenant is an action, and so it is the natural way of presenting a relationship of commitment in narrative form.

Part B

Here we move into the realm of historical criticism, and the historical criticism of the Pentateuch is a dominant and indeed foundational aspect of modern Old Testament scholarship. One of the difficulties in introducing people to this aspect is the 'so what?' question. Suppose – to take the example of the best-known and still dominant conception of the literary history of the Pentateuch – the hypothetical documents J, E, D and P existed (see below, p. 94), what difference would that make, either to the way we read the Pentateuch, which remains the same Pentateuch regardless of what hypothesis we may adopt about its origin, or to the scriptural authority that may be ascribed to it, or to the theological teaching drawn from it? If the Torah functions in the hearers' present as a world of reality, its own past must surely be an irrelevance.

From one point of view that is true; but that answer will not satisfy you if you are interested not just in the world created by the text but in the world that produced the text, and particularly if you believe, as many readers of this book will, that this world, the world of ancient Israel, was confronted by a revelation of God. If that really happened, it is important to know when and how it did.

Apart from the obvious problems of contradictions and inconsistencies, which I referred to above, and which were the initial stimulus for forming hypotheses about the origins of the Pentateuch, the mainspring of Pentateuchal criticism has always been a historical one. Julius Wellhausen, renowned as the scholar who set the classic source hypothesis of the Pentateuch on a firm foundation, was interested in the question only because of its bearing on the history of Israel's religion, and the epoch-making work of 1878 in which he argued for his theory is called *Prolegomena to the History of Israel* (the Greek word prolegomena means 'things which have to be said beforehand'). On almost the first page of this book he describes how as a young student in the 1860s he felt dissatisfied with the standard view at the time (it has been revived again since) that the Torah was the foundation of the whole Old Testament: he just could not see the evidence for this in the prophets and historical books. So when he discovered in a casual conversation that a certain scholar believed that in fact the preaching of the Prophets came before the writing of the Law, he seized on the idea, and set himself to argue the case in detail. The main thesis of his work is that the Torah is the starting point for Judaism, not for the history of monarchic Israel.

For anyone who believes in divine revelation, it must be a question of critical importance whether the account of the origin of Israel's life with God that we find in the Torah is (a) based on ancient tradition, however embellished, or (b) expresses in story form a theological insight of prophets and writers of a much later time. If (a) is true, that key revelation which placed Israel under obedience to a single sovereign transcendent God took place at the beginning of their history. If (b) is true, the key revelation, however it may have been prepared for, took place in the course of Israel's history and in part as a response to historical events. Many believers will be disturbed by the implication that some of the key episodes in the Torah's story must be more or less inventions. The issue is most serious as regards the covenant, because of the central significance of the covenant in the story, structurally and theologically.

The historical criticism of the Pentateuch is therefore of serious importance historically and so possibly theologically, depending on one's theological assumptions. In this book I shall deal with it in three chapters.

The first two of these, Chapters 5 and 6, deal with the historical process by which the Pentateuch came into being. Since we have no direct evidence, we are wholly reliant on hypothesis about it, and much of the chapters will necessarily consist in the review of competing theories. Chapter 5 is concerned with the composition and redaction of the text, and when and why this may have taken place. 'Composition' refers to the hypothetical elements – sources, documents, editorial comments, whatever they may be – from which the text has been *composed* or put together. 'Redaction' means the process of editing that has produced the present text or a hypothetical earlier text.

The word 'redacted' in the media tends to mean 'deleted' or 'censored'. This is not what biblical scholars mean by it. Redaction may involve among other moves the deletion of parts of a source text, but adding material is probably much more frequent.

We shall not be able to look at all the theories about these processes, but I shall try to identify the main points of divergence and run a few test cases which may indicate how one might decide between them. In this chapter I also touch briefly on theories about the origins of the material; but scholars today recognize that we know next to nothing about this.

If Chapter 5 is concerned with the coming to be of the Pentateuch, Chapter 6 asks about the circumstances in which it was finally redacted and accepted as Torah. What were the social, religious and political situations in which this occurred? What were the motives which led community leaders to produce the texts? In what way were their own interests involved? How did the Pentateuch become authoritative Scripture for the Jewish and Samaritan communities? The questions have attracted a good deal of attention in recent years, and recent theories will require evaluation.

Chapter 7 asks: given the complex history of the Pentateuch, how much, if anything, of it has some chance of being historical fact? Although the discussions in the previous two chapters will have made it difficult to be sanguine about this, I shall look first at what it would have meant as history for its first readers and then at serious scholarly arguments for its historicity or that of individual narratives in it, and ask how convincing they are and whether it is possible to disengage a kernel (or more) of historical fact from the narratives.

Part C

The final section of the book looks at our text from the point of view of the reader. The study of the way in which the text has been interpreted in the course of history is known as 'reception history', and it is a fast-growing branch of biblical study. The whole field of reception history is enormous, and we are only able to look at three restricted aspects here which may be the most important for readers of this book. Chapter 8 is concerned with the traditional reader, Jewish or Christian, and the way in which their communities have understood the text and related it to their lives. In previous chapters we shall sometimes have referred to traditional readings of the text, but here I shall approach the matter more systematically. The aim will be to show how the same text in the context of different traditions and different situations has been taken to authorize very different theologies and practices. We shall try to select examples that serve to illustrate attitudes towards and understanding of the whole Pentateuch, although much premodern exegesis tends to be atomistic.

Chapter 9, in contrast, deals with the growing mass of readings in recent times representing the responses of modern readers with their own secular concerns or influenced by secular ideologies: feminist, liberation-theological, ecological and other readings of the kind. Again, it will only be possible to bring forward a very few examples in the space available.

The final aspect, in Chapter 10, is an approach to an understanding of the theology of the Pentateuch taken as a whole: how it presents the character and actions of God and God's relationship with humanity, particularly Israel. I argue here that it is right to put this in the section dealing with the response of the reader because that is essentially what any biblical theology is. The way in which we systematize the varied theological material of the Bible, or the Pentateuch, reflects our own commitments and our larger theological framework; that is why works of biblical theology differ so much. I explore some of these differences before offering my own outline of the theology of the Pentateuch in the context of my own concerns. Hence this chapter has a more personal aspect than any of the previous ones.

The Pentateuch stands at the fountain-head of what is often referred to as the 'Judaeo-Christian' tradition, and is the source of many of its sometimes acclaimed and sometimes reviled values. It is my hope that the material studied in this book will enable the reader to understand how and why that tradition originated and view it with sympathy as well as critical attention.

Part A

2

The Pentateuch as Narrative

The title of this chapter is 'The Pentateuch as Narrative', not 'The Narrative of the Pentateuch'. The Pentateuch as a whole is a narrative, and the blocks of law or instruction are integrated into it as speeches of characters in the story, rather than being mere interruptions. The aim is to explain the narrative as a structure *including* these sections, rather than *excluding* them in order to explain it. In Chapter 3 we shall reverse the procedure and explain the Pentateuch as Torah, instruction or 'law', with the narrative parts supporting and validating the commandments. We shall tackle the work under four main headings: genre, plot, narrative discourse (including the narrator and the characters), and overall theme. See the following table for these and other technical terms.

Terms used in the study of narrative[1,2]

characterization	The means used by the *narrator to give an impression of a *character.
characters	The entities that take part in the action of a narrative, either actively or passively, provided that they have human characteristics – they do not have to be actually human.
closure	A narrative has closure if the reader is left without unfulfilled expectations or unanswered questions at the end. 'So they lived happily ever after' is a typical *closing* as well as finishing sentence in a fairy tale.
genre	A type of writing, recognized in a culture, with definite characteristics. Narrative genres we would recognize include history, biography, novel, detective story.

---

1 Derived mainly from Abbott, *Introduction*.

2 When a word defined in this table is used for the first time in the following text, an *asterisk refers to the definition here.

implied author	The picture of the author built up by the reader from the evidence of the work, excluding any external information there may be. In some narrative works, the implied author may merge with the *narrator.
implied reader	The reader or audience that the work appears to be addressed to; the ideal reader, who is in possession of all the information the work assumes and in *sympathy with its values.
motif	A repeated element in the narrative, generally either a phrase or an object or symbol; not always distinguishable from a *theme, but it tends to be concrete rather than abstract.
narrator	The voice that the reader perceives as telling the story, whether a character or an anonymous voice. Not the same as the author: the author is the historical person who actually wrote the story, the narrator is an impression created by the text itself.
narrative discourse	The *story as narrated, as it is presented in a particular narrative.
plot	The course of events in the narrative, understood as structured in a particular way through *tension and resolution.
point of view	This may refer to the position (physical and emotional) from which we 'see' the events in a narrative; or to the way in which the narration reflects the interests and values of a particular *character.
reliable and unreliable	A *narrator or a *character is reliable if what he or she says is in harmony with the values of the work (the implied author) and does not misdirect or confuse the reader.
resolution	See *tension.
rhetoric	Essentially the art of persuasion. The term has a variety of applications in literary study. I am using it (following Booth) to refer to the various means used to persuade the reader of the (factual or moral) truth of the story and the values of the work.
story	In a technical sense, refers to the action of the narrative, or *plot, as distinct from the *narrative discourse. I also use it for narrative in the style of fiction in distinction from other means of telling history, for example lists, laws.
sympathy	The feeling a reader develops in favour of a particular character. A sympathetic character is one who attracts the reader's sympathy.

tension and resolution	A plot as it develops creates interest or excitement by posing questions about how it will turn out: this is tension. As it concludes, the questions are answered and the excitement relaxes: this is resolution.
theme	Any issue, question or subject that recurs in a narrative. As distinct from a *motif, it is generally abstract. In this chapter, 'overall theme' means the main narrative issue of the whole Pentateuch.

Genre

Central to the interpretation of any piece of writing, not only literature and not only narrative, is to decide its *genre, the kind of writing that it is. Damrosch defines genre as 'the framework of norms and expectations shaping both the composition and the reception of a text'.[3] If we know a work's genre, we know roughly what to expect; conversely what we find in a text by way of form, content and style helps us to establish its genre, so there is bound to be some to-and-fro on the question as we read and reflect on it. Part of reading an ancient text successfully is learning to recognize what the ancient reader would have known of 'the framework of norms and expectations' shaping a particular genre.

The Pentateuch as history writing

The obvious question here is whether the Pentateuch should be understood as history, as Christians and Jews traditionally have always done. This question has two sides to it, which are easily confused: whether the events related are historical, that is, factual, and whether the text itself is historiographical, that is, whether it belongs to a genre of historical writing. The question of the historicity of the Pentateuch, that is, the extent to which its accounts can be deemed factual, will be dealt with in Chapter 7. Here we are concerned with its genre.

That it is in some sense historiographical is widely agreed, and emphasized by some, for example Sternberg.[4] But there are many historiographical genres, including annals, royal inscriptions, victory odes and so forth. Among them all Van Seters distinguishes 'history writing' by the historian J. Huizinga's definition, that 'History is the intellectual form in which a civilization renders account to itself of its past'.[5] Van Seters, however, imports a national emphasis into his use of this definition; so that an Israelite history

---

3 Damrosch, *Covenant*, p. 2.
4 Sternberg, *Poetics*, pp. 23–35 and passim.
5 Van Seters, *In Search of History*, p. 1.

would be one that renders account of Israel's past. As the Pentateuch clearly does this, it qualifies as *history writing*.[6] It gives an account of Israel's past which is plainly intended to define and govern them in the present. There are several features of the Pentateuch that point to its character as a history book, among them the genealogies and chronology that link the personalities and events of the narrative through time with nations, tribes and clans and events of the time of writing. Again, there are references to names, customs and so on that survive 'until today', for example Genesis 26.33 and 32.32. There is no break between the narrative of the Pentateuch and that of Joshua to Kings, which ends with events that everyone recognizes as historical, which can be verified from the Assyrian and Babylonian records. If it is a history book, it is only the first part of a continuous history from creation to the fall of Jerusalem. The whole Genesis to Kings story is sometimes called the 'Primary History' (to distinguish it from Chronicles, Ezra and Nehemiah as the Secondary History).[7]

But unlike Kings, there is no event in the Pentateuch that can be verified from contemporary records. What if much of it is myth or legend, as has been widely believed in the modern era? If we come to the Pentateuch with 'norms and expectations' derived from *modern* history writing, we would then find it difficult to call it history writing. We do not expect historians in our culture to include myths and legends in their works. For this reason many scholars until recently avoided the description 'history' for the Pentateuch's genre. Words like 'saga' or 'legend' might be used instead. But Van Seters's survey shows that this kind of material was normal in *ancient* history writing. We should therefore express the genre of the Pentateuch more precisely as *ancient history writing*.

Story?

Are there competitors to 'history' for a definition of the genre of the Pentateuch? Clines may appear to set one up, when he asserts, in relation to the Pentateuch, that '*story* and not history [is] the primary mode of communication of religious truth'.[8] But there is no real contradiction here. Clines defines the Pentateuch as a *story in the sense familiar to us through modern fiction, an account of action that moves purposively through time towards a goal.[9] But this is how history is generally told. Most historians aim to shape a coherent, intelligible story from the mass of events that they know of.[10] The Pentateuch is no different in this respect.

---

6 Blenkinsopp agrees: *Pentateuch*, p. 34.

7 Blenkinsopp, *Pentateuch*, p. 34.

8 Clines, *Theme*, p. 109.

9 Clines, *Theme*, p. 112.

10 See Abbott, *Introduction*, p. 155.

Biography?

There is a case for seeing at least Exodus to Deuteronomy as biography. Van Seters sees the Pentateuchal historian as casting this part of his work in the form of a life of Moses, but 'presented entirely in terms of the concerns and destiny of the people';[11] this kind of biography is a sub-genre of history. More systematically, but too briefly, Knierim mounts a case for seeing the whole Pentateuch as a life of Moses, as 'fundamental for the beginnings of Israel's history', with a prelude in Genesis setting his life and work in the context of world history.[12] To see the life of Moses as the primary focus of the narrative would have the advantage of being able to explain why it ends where it does, with the death of Moses. However, Moses is not the leading character in the Pentateuch; God is.

But is it narrative at all?

James W. Watts argues that the Pentateuch, taken as a whole, does not belong to a narrative genre at all, neither history nor biography.[13] The mixture of genres, narrative, law, instruction and others such as genealogy and song, argues that it belongs to a unique genre of its own. It is simply Torah. But as the title of Watts's book hints, this puts the emphasis on the teaching aspects of the Pentateuch, rather than the narrative. It takes the form it does in order to persuade its hearers of its claims upon their lives.

That is true. But the claims made by the Pentateuch include narrative claims. It teaches that God has chosen Israel, and it is because of this that God can give Israel laws. It is only because the readers are able to identify themselves with the Israel of the *story* that they can accept the laws for themselves. And in that its overall structure is narrative, it must be possible to make overall sense of it as narrative, and if narrative, then history, even though it is not written in the way we would expect history to be written. Watts effectively accepts that it is a narrative by suggesting that the hearers, that is, Israel, have to decide for themselves how it ends.[14]

The conventions of the genre

So how is it written? What are the conventions of the genre of history as it is instanced in the Pentateuch? How does it narrate history, in its selection of materials, its presentation of historical causality and its narrative method? It shares these features with other biblical histories (Joshua to

---

11 Van Seters, *Moses*, p. 2.
12 Knierim, 'Composition', pp. 369–79; p. 372.
13 Watts, *Reading Law*, esp. pp. 154–7.
14 Watts, *Reading Law*, p. 154. See below.

Kings, Chronicles and Ezra–Nehemiah), which suggests that they all belong to a common genre.

The selection of materials

Most critics – all, until recently – think that the various materials of the Pentateuch are for the most part traditional and transmitted orally until they were put in writing, either in the Pentateuch itself or in predecessor documents. Form critics have identified various categories of traditional stories as elements in the biblical historical works, at least in the Pentateuch and in Joshua and Judges, and to some extent elsewhere.[15] Some stories can be traced to a foreign origin; the story of the Flood in Genesis 6—8 is the classic example. The legal materials included in the narrative are also often regarded as existing law 'codes' added to the narrative editorially.

However, there has been an increasing tendency in recent work to argue for the free composition of some or much of the narrative material and even of laws. The most consistent argument in this respect comes in Van Seters's three books on the Pentateuch.[16] Few would follow Van Seters in this wholesale attribution of the Pentateuchal narrative to pure invention. But it is generally recognized that it would have required a good deal of creative imagination to develop a connected story from the vast and varied array of traditional material which the writers drew on. This is a question addressed long ago in a key essay by Gerhard von Rad. He concluded that the first Pentateuchal historian was developing and expanding a traditional confession of faith.[17] As most scholars today do not follow him in this, our impression of the creativity of the historical writers who developed the Pentateuch is considerably heightened.

Divine causality

The most immediately obvious way in which biblical histories differ from modern ones is their open appeal to divine causality. God makes things happen; this is specifically stated again and again, only less frequently in Samuel and Kings than in earlier books. In the Pentateuch the activity of God within history is all-pervasive. One way of expressing the subject of the Pentateuch is that it is the story of what God has done for Israel. True, human beings are presented as acting freely, and even influencing the way in which God acts. But it is God who is responsible for the decisive events: creation, the choice of Abram, the deliverance of Israel from Egypt. Moreover, God constantly

---

15 See Coats, *Genesis*.
16 Van Seters, *Prologue; Moses; Law Book*.
17 Von Rad, 'Form-critical Problem'.

appears as a character in the narrative, and makes speeches, including very lengthy ones giving laws and instructions. This divine involvement imparts a quite distinctive colour to the Pentateuchal narrative, and it also gives decisive authority to the laws and instructions.

Narrative method

Biblical historical narrative in general is rendered by an anonymous *narrator,[18] largely in vivid scenes with dialogue in direct speech. Alter describes it as 'historicized prose fiction', or alternatively 'fictionalized history'.[19] The term 'fiction' risks confusion with the idea mentioned above that events may have been simply invented, or that the genre of the narrative is fiction. The Pentateuch does appear to claim to be telling of real events, and so its genre is history. But it often reads like fiction. To avoid such a misunderstanding, I shall not use the word 'fiction' to refer to the imaginative way in which the biblical history is presented, and speak instead of *story-like* narrative method.

Non-story-like elements

But story-like narrative is not the only way in which history is told in the Pentateuch. Large amounts of legal or instructional material are integrated with the narrative, and there are other types of non-story material as well, such as genealogies and lists. Some of these have important functions in maintaining the continuity and chronology of the narrative, such as the genealogies in Genesis 5 and 11. There are also poems embedded in the narrative, by being said or sung by characters, for example Genesis 4.23–24, Genesis 49.3–27 or Exodus 15.1–18.

How does the legal material work as part of the narrative? Watts shows that there are other ancient writings which combine narrative and command, and argues that this is a common rhetorical strategy, which appears in a variety of genres, such as law codes and treaties. It is always aimed at persuading, but the objects of persuasion may vary.[20] In the case of the Pentateuch, the narrative of what God has done serves to persuade Israel to obey the laws (see Deut. 6.20–25).

But the laws are spoken by characters in the narrative, either God or Moses: thus the laws are *part* of the narrative in a way they are not in Watts's examples. T. W. Mann argues that they have a narrative function: they serve to render the character of YHWH in much the same way as his

---

18 Ezra (in part) and most of Nehemiah are the only exceptions.
19 Alter, *Art*, pp. 24–6.
20 Watts, *Reading Law*, pp. 40–52.

actions. 'Words and deeds belong together, and only together do they fully render the person of Yahweh as represented in the Pentateuchal narrative.'[21]

But it is not only the *giving* of laws and instructions that are part of the narrative. In many cases, the narrative relates the fulfilment of instructions, and in others it tells of how Israel, or many in Israel, ignored or violated them. Exodus 12 relates both the instructions for the observance of Passover and the Israelites' first observance (v. 28). The instructions in Exodus 25—31 for setting up the wilderness sanctuary and for ordaining Aaron and his sons as priests to serve it are carried out respectively in Exodus 35—40 and Leviticus 8—9; and the sacrifices offered in the latter narrative are offered according to the instructions in Leviticus 1—7. On the other hand, one of the major drivers of *plot in the Pentateuch is the Israelites' constant disobedience to YHWH's commandments and directions, as in the worship of the golden calf (Exod. 32.1–6), or the refusal to enter the promised land in Numbers 13.31 – 14.4. Whatever the importance of the laws for the Pentateuch's readers, they are also an indispensable element of the narrative.

Plot

What is the story that the Pentateuch tells? I am using the word 'story' here in the way it is used by Abbott: the 'sequence of events', what is often called the 'plot', as contrasted with '*narrative discourse': 'those events as represented', the way in which the story is told, which we shall think about in the next section.[22] In this section we are concerned with the story in itself. There are of course a large number of plots or stories in the Pentateuch. They could be called sub-plots, but here we are concerned with the story of the Pentateuch as a whole, on the assumption that it really has a single overall plot, however complicated. The essence of plot is conflict. We can analyse the action by noting its points of *tension, where conflict emerges and escalates, and resolution, where one party is victorious or there is reconciliation.[23] Tension raises questions about how the narrative will proceed, which resolution may answer. Only the very widest arcs of tension can be sketched here.

As we have seen, God is active almost throughout. The conflicts of broadest reach in the Pentateuch are between God and another party. This may be humanity as a whole, as in much of Genesis 3—11, Pharaoh, in Exodus 1—15, or the Israelites, who are in conflict with God at the same time as God is protecting and teaching them, in Exodus 15 to Numbers 26.

---

21 Mann, *Book*, p. 116.

22 Abbott, *Introduction*, p. 19. Walsh, *Narrative* (p. 6), has three levels of interpretation rather than two (cf. Bal, *Narratology*, pp. 5–6 and elsewhere), but this is unnecessary here.

23 As in Walsh, *Narrative*, pp. 13–22.

The Pentateuch begins with creation, but this does not involve conflict. Conflict begins with the presence of creatures capable of independent action, such as disobedience to God (Gen. 3), or violence to each other (Gen. 4; 6.11). God regrets that he[24] made them at all (Gen. 6.6). How will this extreme tension be resolved? God sweeps all the creatures of earth away bar Noah and the minimal selection of creatures that enters the ark with him.

God then adopts a different strategy. He chooses one of Noah's progeny, Abram, a childless man, and makes him promises. The fulfilment of these promises occurs over the entire action of the Pentateuch and beyond, so that at this point the most extensive arc of tension begins.[25] Within Genesis, where there is no consistent opposition to God, God himself raises tension by announcing plans that appear impossible to fulfil, and resolves it by fulfilling them, as in the birth of Isaac (Gen. 17.15–21; 18.10; 21.1–2); and notoriously at one point (Gen. 22.1–19) by demanding action (the sacrifice of Isaac) that would nullify the promise; again, he resolves it himself (this episode is studied below, pp. 32–5). Genesis 12—50 also relates many cases of inter-human conflict, some of which turn out to further and some to hinder God's intentions.[26] An elaborate sub-plot of this kind brings Jacob and his family to Egypt (Genesis 37—50). By the end of Genesis it is clear that the first part of the promise, that Abraham will have many descendants, has been fulfilled, and in the opening of Exodus they have become a people.

The highest degree of tension in the plot is reached when the Pharaoh and his Egyptians emerge as the opponents of God, and put the Israelites in Egypt to forced labour (Exod. 1.8–14). Where does this leave God's plan? The possibility of resolution only begins to be visible when God 'remembers his covenant' with Abraham, Isaac and Jacob (2.24). He reveals himself and his name YHWH[27] to Moses, promises to bring the Israelites out of Egypt and lead them to the land of Canaan and commissions Moses to act as his agent (3.1—4.17; 6.2—7.7); he also repeats his promise that he will be their God, and they his people (6.7). There ensues a long-drawn-out conflict between YHWH, represented by Moses (and Aaron), and Pharaoh, in which tension, resolution and renewed tension follow each other swiftly until YHWH's final victory, when Pharaoh and his army are drowned in the Red Sea (7.8—15.17).

However, the resolution created by the removal of YHWH's great enemy is not a resolution to the longer-range tension generated by YHWH's promises. The commitment to be Israel's God appears on the face of it to be already in operation. But it becomes evident that it is YHWH's will to have this relationship expressed in a body of legal and moral teaching and

---

24 Here, and elsewhere, I reproduce the gendered language of the text I am speaking of.

25 Cf. Clines, *Theme*.

26 See Turner, *Announcements*.

27 This is how I represent the sacred name of God, which Jews traditionally avoid pronouncing, and which is represented in most English versions as 'LORD' in small capitals.

embodied in a cultic system. A delay of nearly a year at Mount Sinai (Exod. 19.1 to Num. 10.11) is required for the establishment of the cult, including the building of a mobile sanctuary, the giving of a large body of teaching, and military preparations. YHWH makes obedience to the teaching the sign that Israel belongs to him, as in Exodus 19.5: 'Now therefore, if you will obey my voice and keep my covenant, you shall be my special possession out of all peoples ...' By making the covenant in Exodus 24.3–8, they express their faithfulness and commit themselves to obey the commandments.

But does this make the people securely YHWH's? Repeated complaints and rebellions (Exodus 32—34; Numbers 11—25) drive a series of plot complications. The questions regularly raised in the plot episodes are, from the *point of view of YHWH, whether Israel will trust him, and from the point of view of Israel, whether YHWH will care for his people. Two types of resolution appear in these episodes, often together: YHWH does show his material care for them, but he punishes them for refusing to trust or to obey him. Twice, an extreme of tension is reached with YHWH's threat to destroy them. He only forgives and spares them in response to Moses' pleas (Exod. 32.9–14; Num. 14.11–20). The resolution of the latter complication (the episode of the spies) is that the fulfilment of the promise of the land is delayed for 40 years and totally denied to the current generation of adults.

From Numbers 26, at the end of the 40 years,[28] there are no further rebellions and the only issues still delaying entry into the land are proper preparation, and conflict, including war, with obstructive nations. The preparations include the very lengthy series of speeches by Moses giving further and updated teaching and laws for life in the land (the book of Deuteronomy). The Pentateuch breaks off before the crossing of the Jordan, but no doubt it is raised that it will happen. But whether Israel will keep the land they have been granted, by being faithful and obedient, remains a question. The question dominates both Leviticus 26 and most of the last seven chapters of Deuteronomy. Israel is given the choice, expressed most memorably by Moses in Deuteronomy 30.15: 'I set before you today life and good on the one hand, death and disaster on the other.'

The Pentateuch ends without *closure.[29] It ends with an as yet unfulfilled expectation that Israel will enter the land, and with questions unanswered, especially the questions whether Israel is capable of being faithful to their God and whether their God will permit them to keep the land. Even if we read on to the end of Kings, we gain no final assurance on either point. Watts emphasizes that the Pentateuch leaves it up to its readers to 'decide its ending by their own actions'. 'Will Israel live by this Torah or not?'[30]

---

28 Olson, *Death*.
29 See Abbott, *Introduction*, pp. 55–66, who distinguishes between closure 'at the level of expectations' and at 'the level of questions'.
30 Watts, *Reading Law*, p. 154.

Sketch the arcs of tension, and the moments of resolution, in some of the stories in Genesis, for example Genesis 16; or 19.1–29; or 21.9–19; or (a more complex undertaking), in 37+39—45.

Narrative discourse

As Abbott points out, the same story may be told in many different ways, and in different media: as a novel, a play, a film and so on. This is certainly true of the stories of the Bible, which have been retold again and again in diverse ways. Many of us will have first been introduced to parts of the story of the Pentateuch by way of a book of children's Bible stories, and will also have seen films such as *The Ten Commandments*. Each of these will have its particular take on the story expressed in its narrative discourse, and this will differ from the take of the Pentateuch itself (for some theological attempts to do the same thing, see Chapter 10). Any serious narrative work engages its readers or audience at a moral or intellectual level, to attempt to persuade them of its values, beliefs and ideology, not primarily through the story in itself, but through its *rhetoric.*[31] It would be a mistake to assume that it is only through law that the Pentateuch achieves its rhetorical purpose. The *narrative* discourse, the way in which the *story* is told, also expresses this. It encourages us to look at the story from the point of view of God, who appears as the author of all the main initiatives. How does the narrative achieve this effect?

I intend to answer this question in two ways, first of all by looking at some of the rhetorical tools used on the level of the entire work to shape the attitudes of the reader, and then by studying an important passage where the reader's *sympathy with YHWH may be problematic, to see how the narrator exercises persuasion. The rhetorical tools I have selected are the *narrator, the *characters, and repeated elements, that is, *themes and *motifs. But first we must briefly look at who the *implied readers are, for this determines how the rhetoric is intended to work.

The implied reader

It might be better to speak of the 'implied hearers', since texts like Deuteronomy 31.9–13 and Nehemiah 8 show that public reading was the way in which the text was expected to be made known.[32] Clearly the implied

---

31 Abbott, *Introduction*, pp. 40–55; Booth, *Rhetoric*, on modern fiction; Sternberg, *Poetics*, on biblical narrative; Watts, *Reading Law* and *Ritual*, on law in the Pentateuch; all focusing on different aspects of narrative.

32 See Watts, *Reading Law*, pp. 15–31.

hearers are Israelites, living in their own land at some time much later than the events of the narrative. The laws are obviously addressed to the situation of a settled people. Texts like Genesis 12.6 or Leviticus 18.28 assume the Canaanites have already disappeared. The hearers know themselves as descendants of the 'children of Israel' who are directly addressed in the speech of Moses, and they are therefore included in the covenant: Deuteronomy 29.14–15. On the other hand, Leviticus 26.40–45 and Deuteronomy 30.1–10, which assure them that YHWH will bring them back from exile, imply that at some point the hearers will be in exile.

The narrator[33]

Frequently in modern literature the author consciously invents a character to tell the story, who may or may not take part in the action. This is not the case in the Pentateuch, but here the concept of the narrator is useful, in that, despite the likelihood that many authors have contributed to the text, the reader still has the sense of being addressed by a single voice. So even if there is no narrator constructed by the author, there is one constructed by the reader. We might say that while *historically* we speak of authors (as on p. 92 below), as readers of *literature* we find it simpler to think of a narrator, as a way of speaking about how the narration is done.

The 'narrator' in biblical narrative is impersonal, unidentified, never saying 'I'; amazingly, never even identified with the Israelites by saying 'we'.[34] It is common to call such a narrator 'omniscient'. What this means is that the point of view of the narration is not that of an observer alongside the characters, but as it were that of a superhuman person who can observe normally inaccessible things, such as people's intimate thoughts.[35] So we often learn things in the biblical narrative that could not be observed in real life, such as the act of creation, or Abraham's thoughts when asked by Sarah to expel Hagar and Ishmael (Gen. 21.11). But rather more often we are not told people's thoughts and motivations. The 'narrator' leaves us to infer them, and in this way raises the narrative interest, whether or not they are later revealed.[36] For example, in the Joseph story, what is Joseph's motive for stringing his brothers along, tormenting them with the demand to bring Benjamin and then framing Benjamin for theft? We are left with our own deductions. An issue that affects the entire plot of the Pentateuch is God's reason for choosing Abram for particular blessing (and then Isaac

---

33 Abbott, *Introduction*, pp. 67–82.

34 There are two exceptions, but neither of them is in the Pentateuch.

35 See the argument between Sternberg, *Poetics*, pp. 181–5, and Gunn, 'Reading Right', pp. 58–60.

36 Much of Sternberg's book is concerned with the biblical narrator's manipulation of the reader's knowledge, 'maneuvering between the truth and the whole truth' (*Poetics*, p. 51).

and Jacob, each time more surprisingly), rather than anyone else (see further below in Chapter 10, pp. 218–20).

The telling of the story in this fashion is the first important rhetorical tool by which the reader is induced to accept the authority of the text. The narrator appears to be independent, not involved in the narrative, even neutral from the standpoint of the implied readers. Students of narrative distinguish between *reliable and unreliable narrators, and normally an unreliable one will be a character in the narrative. Hence this impersonal narration appears to be authoritative and reliable. Sternberg accepts its authority; he asserts without qualification: 'The Bible always tells the truth in that its narrator is absolutely and straightforwardly reliable.' If you simply follow what the narrator says, you will not go far wrong in unravelling the story.[37] Gunn points out that this needs a lot of qualification.[38] The Pentateuch contains contradictions in points of fact, which historical critics have settled by postulating separate sources (see below, pp. 89–90). How does the literary critic deal with them, unless by saying that the narrator is *not* reliable, but inclined to be self-contradictory?

Reliability is not just a matter of the facts. Booth's original definition of a 'reliable narrator', when he invented the term, was one who 'speaks or acts in accordance with the norms of the work'.[39] We should consider whether the values and commitments called for by the work as a whole are significantly different from those implied by the narrator. The question raised by Israel's rebellions concerns only their trust in YHWH and loyalty to him. But the laws cover a vast range of other issues, not least justice in society. The narrator of Exodus 16 to Numbers 25 gives YHWH's teaching on the inter-human, social dimension of life no role in the plot, making the issue of life or death for Israel turn solely on the question of their submission, trust and obedience towards YHWH and his agent Moses (and Aaron). So, do the 'norms of the work' include the social justice taught in the laws or not? And if so why does it play no role in the plot here? (Genesis is different in this respect.)

Characters and *characterization

Both plot and characters are essential to a story.[40] They react on each other: the characters make the plot, and the plot reveals (and often in part changes) the characters. This is certainly the case in the Pentateuch. The plot is not determined by God in advance, whatever his intentions: it is the

---

37 Sternberg, *Poetics*, p. 51.

38 Gunn, 'New Directions', pp. 70–2; 'Reading Right', pp. 56–7; Gunn and Fewell, *Narrative*, pp. 53–6.

39 Booth, *Rhetoric*, pp. 158–9.

40 Abbott, *Introduction*, pp. 130–3.

result of human reactions to God's initiatives and God's reactions to human initiatives.[41]

Characterization

There are two possible means of creating character open to a narrator: either describing the character for us ('telling'), or showing him or her in speech and action. The Bible's strong inclination is towards showing. It is rare for people to be described in any way. The remarkable exceptions in the Pentateuch are the two comments on Moses in Numbers 12.3 and in Deuteronomy 34.10–12; and even the latter is largely a summary of the action in which he had been involved. But things are different when it comes to God. The character of YHWH is a significant theme in the Pentateuch. However, the narrator does not 'tell' us of his character. The descriptions of his character in Exodus 20.5–6 (=Deut. 5.9–10) and Exodus 34.6–7 are *self*-descriptions. Normally in narrative we would treat a character's description of himself with great caution, knowing people's propensity for deception and self-deception. But these descriptions are in accord with what we are *shown* of YHWH's character, and are sufficiently double-sided to cover most (not all) of what we are shown. Moses also describes YHWH's character (Deut. 10.17–18; 32.4), and for the most part he appears to be reliable,[42] but again, these descriptions should be tested against what we are shown.

Reliable and unreliable characters

Like narrators, characters may be reliable or unreliable.[43] They either represent the *implied author's viewpoint on fact and value, or in one or other respect they represent a different point of view, which the reader who accepts the implied author's authority (that is, the implied reader) will see as false. YHWH is seen as reliable by most readers of the Pentateuch, so that his view of any other character tends to carry the day for them. But it is not too difficult or remarkable for a reader to turn against this authority because of the apparent immorality of one or more actions of YHWH, and thus some readers will find themselves taking the side of another character.[44] On the other hand, when the Israelites act as if Moses is never going to come down from the mountain (Exod. 32.1), or object to the food on offer in the wilderness and say things were better in Egypt (for example, Num. 11.4–6), they are plainly contradicting the authority of the narrator, and so the reader learns to mistrust them.

---

41 See Turner, *Announcements*.
42 Kissling, *Characters*, pp. 32–68.
43 Kissling, *Characters*, esp. pp. 20–1.
44 Fewell and Gunn, *Gender*.

Characters

The 'entities' who take part in the story of the Pentateuch are not all human: we have a talking snake (Gen. 3.1–6) and a talking donkey (Num. 22.28–30); and, of course, the one character who is on stage almost throughout and responsible for much of what goes on: God, under various names, most frequently YHWH. It is also necessary (as I have done above) to speak of the Israelites as a single character, since they are so frequently depicted as acting collectively and with a single mind. But all of these are portrayed with human characteristics (Balaam's donkey only for the few verses in which God 'opens her mouth'), and therefore deserve to be called characters. There are just two, apart from YHWH, who take part in the action of the greater part of the Pentateuch: Moses and the Israelites. It is these three that we shall consider individually.

Few characters in the Pentateuch are at all complex, but one or two, such as Abraham or Joseph, are more rounded. Select one of these prominent characters and try to describe him or her for yourself.

YHWH[45]

The various names under which God is named in Genesis, as well as the general word Elohim, 'God', used in narrative especially before Exodus 6 but also sometimes afterwards, are clearly all names of YHWH: see Genesis 16.13; 17.1; Exodus 6.3.

1 YHWH, the only God worthy of the name (see below, pp. 215–16), is creator and world ruler, and exercises impartial justice. In exercise of this role he destroys the corrupt world in the Flood, and later comes down to inquire into the 'cry' sent up by those oppressed in Sodom, and responds to the concern of Abraham that he might destroy the innocent along with the guilty (Gen. 18.16–33). And he appears in the laws of social morality as the defender of the oppressed poor (for example, Exod. 22.23–24).

2 A strongly marked feature of YHWH's character is his concern for his own reputation ('glory' is the standard translation), and this motive is uppermost in a great deal of the destruction that he causes. This is particularly clear in the story of the plagues of Egypt and at the Red Sea, where in one of the strands of the narrative YHWH insistently announces that he is acting 'that you/they may know that I am YHWH'.[46] Moses successfully

---

45 See Houston, 'Character', which has detailed argument I have no space for here.

46 Gunn, 'Hardening'; Gowan, *Theology*, pp. 127–67; Houston, 'Character', pp. 20–5.

appeals to this side of his character (among others) against his threat to destroy the disobedient people. 'Why should the Egyptians say, "He intended evil when he brought them out – to kill them in the mountains and to wipe them off the face of the earth"?' (Exod. 32.12).

3 Most of what YHWH does in Exodus to Numbers, and in much of Genesis as well, he does as the God of Israel rather than as the universal God. Indeed, he uses his power as creator quite unashamedly to benefit Israel, as at the Red Sea. YHWH's self-descriptions in Exodus 20 and 34 are strongly relational,[47] concerned not with God's relation with the world in general, but with his people. The more comprehensive is Exodus 34.6–7: 'YHWH, YHWH, a God merciful and gracious, patient and rich in loving loyalty (*hesed*) and faithfulness, who maintains his loyalty with thousands, who forgives evil, rebellion and offence, but does not cancel guilt, and visits the evil of fathers on sons and grandsons, down to the third and fourth generation.' He is concerned with those who are involved with YHWH, as the God of Israel, sufficiently closely to be seen as 'loving' or 'hating' him (Exod. 20.6). As a 'jealous God' (Exod. 20.5; 34.14; Deut. 4.24; 5.9; 6.15) YHWH is angry with *Israelites* who are seduced to 'other gods', but is not concerned with others, unless they are in a position to entice Israelites (Deut. 7.1–6). However, precisely because they are his people, he is able and (ultimately) willing to forgive them. This is the point of the placing of Exodus 34.6–7 to introduce the resolution of the golden calf story. Although Moses has had to plead with him, he would not be able to persuade him to do something contrary to his character. Thus we see that these descriptions have two sides to them: YHWH's loving faithfulness to his people who love him and maintain their loyalty, *or* whom he chooses to forgive, and his terrifying wrath against those who 'hate' him, that is, who desert their loyalty.

While these are self-descriptions, they are borne out by the events of the story. The occasions when God makes promises have a high profile in the narrative, and many can be seen as having structural significance. The promises to Abraham, Isaac and Jacob are repeatedly referred to later in the story.[48] The way in which the ancestors of Israel are provided with offspring, preserved in famine and led down to Egypt, dominates Genesis. The high point of the Pentateuch is the defeat of the oppressor Pharaoh with 'great signs and wonders' and the deliverance of the Israelites out of Egypt: again repeatedly referred to later. Then in the wilderness there are repeated stories of the preservation of the people, at YHWH's direction, by the miraculous supply of food or water. The reverse side of this, of course, is his destruction of those who are disobedient or disbelieving in a whole series of incidents in the wilderness. Equally rooted in his commitment to the Israelites is his brutal treatment of Israel's enemies, beginning with the

---

47 Houston, 'Character', pp. 16–17.
48 For a convenient list, see Clines, *Theme*, pp. 32–47.

Egyptians who suffered in the 'plagues' and ending with the commands to destroy entire peoples for Israel to settle in their land, or because of the religious threat they offered (Num. 21.34–35; 31; Deut. 7.1–5; 20.16–18).

Moses

From the moment that Moses accepts YHWH's commission in Exodus 3.1—4.17 his role is virtually exclusively that of a mediator. He represents the will of YHWH to Pharaoh and to the Israelites. Less often, but crucially, he represents the interests of the Israelites to YHWH, and at those points turns the plot in decisively new directions, as we have seen. But how is he qualified for this role? As the story proceeds, his successful exercise of it reassures the reader not only that he is worthy of his position, but that YHWH's own plan, carried out through Moses, is right. But even before he is commissioned, the narrator persuades us that he is worthy of it. First, the story of his birth and adoption (Exod. 2.1–10) is so marvellous that he is surely marked out for greatness. Without saying so, the narrator suggests that there is a divine hand behind these events. Then Moses' actions when he grows up (Exod. 2.11–17) reveal a vital aspect of his character. He is angered by injustice and concerned for those he knows to be his own people; what is more, he is fierce and impulsive in vindicating them.

We are thus confident that YHWH has made the right choice, even if Moses himself is not. His long-drawn-out resistance to YHWH's call shows that he is an independent character, not a mere pawn of YHWH, capable of thinking for himself, and soon enough he is complaining to YHWH again when the work appears to be going awry (Exod. 5.22–23). Even though in the long narrative of the exodus (Exod. 6.1—15.21) he appears to fade into a simple agent without a will of his own, once the victory is won his character emerges once more. He is utterly loyal to YHWH, and easily angered by disobedience and mistrust on the part of Israelites (for example, Exod. 16.6–8, 20), even to the point of exemplary terror (Exod. 32.19–29). Note that he is not executing any sentence of YHWH in this massacre.

But he is also capable of being angry with YHWH (Num. 11.11–15), and most impressively he has the guts to stand up to YHWH on Israel's behalf when he perceives him to be proposing to act unjustly or unmercifully towards his people. See Exodus 32.11–14 and Numbers 14.13–19; also Numbers 12.13, where he prays for Miriam at Aaron's plea. But he acts in these instances not as an opponent of YHWH in general, but as what Coats calls 'the king's loyal opposition'.[49] It is because of his loyalty, exemplified again and again, that he has the influence to be able to turn YHWH away from his initial purpose.

---

49 Coats, 'Opposition'.

The Israelites

I am concerned here with the Israelites when they act as a whole people, not with any individuals or smaller groups. In the story of the exodus they are largely passive, except for the key point when they cry out against their harsh treatment and their cry reaches the ears of YHWH, who then acts to deliver them (Exod. 2.23–25). The only issue is whether they are going to put their trust in Moses and in YHWH, and on this they are uncertain: initially they believe on the evidence of the signs YHWH had given Moses (4.31), but after the reverses of Exodus 5 they no longer do so 'because of their broken spirit and their harsh slavery' (6.9). From that point on they stand on the sidelines while YHWH pursues his battle with Pharaoh, but they leave Egypt when they are told to do so (12.34–39). Only when the final victory has been won do they 'put their trust in YHWH and in Moses his servant' (14.31).

In the wilderness they display a stronger spirit, but their reactions are again ambivalent. On the one hand, they accept the invitation to covenant: 'All that YHWH has commanded we shall do' (Exod. 19.8; cf. 24.3); and they normally submit to the leadership of YHWH and Moses and do all that is required of them. On the other, they display a persistent rebellious tendency. This is most often displayed over the question of food or water, or the lack of them; but more serious, both for their leaders and for themselves, are the two great episodes of idolatry in Exodus 32 and Numbers 25, and the refusal to enter the land in Numbers 13—14. They are portrayed as fickle, lacking in trust in YHWH and in Moses and Aaron, reluctant to accept hardship, nostalgic for the material comforts of Egypt, but easily terrified into submission. It is not a flattering portrait. It is made clear that their ultimate good fortune does not come to them because of their virtue and heroism, but because of YHWH's favour and blessing; and this message is driven home to them by Moses in Deuteronomy 9.

Repetition: themes and motifs

One of the most important ways in which a narrator brings home the desired interpretation of the narrative is through the repetition of themes and motifs.[50] These terms are often used interchangeably, but according to Abbott a rough working distinction is that themes are abstract and motifs are concrete. A theme may be expressed as an idea, such as faith or obedience or forgiveness. A motif is an object such as the staff with which Moses is instructed to perform signs, or a phrase such as 'a land flowing with milk and honey'. Motifs may encapsulate or point to themes – the latter phrase points to God's potential blessing of Israel in the land – but not the other way round. Still, it is not easy to decide in many cases whether a

---

50 Abbott, *Introduction*, p. 95.

repeated element should be classified as a theme or a motif. The themes of
the Pentateuch express its theology, so we shall come back to some of them
in Chapter 10.

> The survey of themes and motifs here is very incomplete. See how many
> more you can find. What themes do the motifs you have discovered point
> to? One way of developing a list, if you have read the whole Pentateuch, is
> to go back again to the beginning and, moving through Genesis, to note the
> ideas, plot structures and images that recur in the rest of the Pentateuch.

Blessing

Even in Genesis 1 we come across the theme of God's blessing, which is
invoked repeatedly in the Pentateuch. In Genesis 1.28 part of the content of
the blessing of human beings is 'be fruitful and multiply; fill the earth and
subdue it'. This is thematically similar to God's promise to Abram in Genesis 13.15–17, etc. – the same Hebrew word is translated 'earth' in Genesis
1.28 and 'land' in Genesis 13.15 and elsewhere in the patriarchal blessings.
Much of the Pentateuch is concerned with the fulfilment of these blessings
(see further below, pp. 36–7).

God's choice

Noah is chosen as the father of the renewed human race when the rest are
to be destroyed. As the story proceeds, God's successive choices of Abram,
Isaac and Jacob guide it towards the emergence of the people of Israel.
God also chooses Moses as the deliverer of Israel (Exod. 3.10), Aaron as
high priest (Exod. 28.1), and Joshua as Moses' successor in the leadership
(Num. 27.18). The key choice of Abraham is entirely unexplained. Noah
and Joshua appear to be chosen on merit (Gen. 6.9; Num. 27.18), Isaac
is chosen over Ishmael because of his mother (Gen. 17.19), and there is
contextual justification for the choice of Moses, as we have seen. But the
choices of Jacob (Gen. 28.13–14), who had cheated his brother out of his
inheritance and his paternal blessing, and of Aaron, who sets up the golden
calf, are surprising. The lesson is clear enough that God's choice is sovereign
and unconstrained by human desires or moral judgements. The issue will be
revisited from a theological point of view in Chapter 10.

Promise

After the Flood is over, God promises all creatures of the earth through
Noah that he will not repeat it, describing his words as a covenant: Genesis

9.8–17. (In Gen. 8.21–22 God is speaking to himself, not to Noah.) The ancestral narratives are structured by God's promises to the ancestors, beginning with Genesis 12.1–3. In Genesis 15.18 and Genesis 17 the promises are portrayed as covenants, and in 22.16–18 as an oath. The promises are repeated finally to Moses in Exodus 3.7–10 and 6.2–8, and in this last passage God recalls the covenant of Genesis 17. According to Clines the promises to the ancestors may be conveniently classified as promises of posterity, land and relationship with God. He argues, with the use of a formidable list of references, that much of the Pentateuch speaks explicitly or, more often, implicitly of the fulfilment of these three categories of promise.[51]

Commandment and law

The first words of God in Genesis 1 are a command: 'Let there be light', and much of the creative work of God here is achieved by words of command, including the blessings 'Be fruitful and multiply'. More significant for the future is the first command, in fact a prohibition, that creatures have a choice to obey or not, in Genesis 2.17, and disobedience to this command sets the action in train. Divine commands are obviously very frequent throughout the Pentateuch, and whether they are obeyed or not determines much of the action. We should distinguish, however, between commands to be carried out immediately, such as those given to Moses in Exodus 25—31, for the establishment of the Dwelling, and moral commands or laws of permanent validity: the first of these is in Genesis 9.4–6. This is the prototype of the more extensive moral or legal speeches that meet us later in the Pentateuch. The motif of covenant is also involved with these: Exodus 19.4; 24.7–8; 34.10; Deuteronomy 5.2–3; 29.1.

Covenant

The motif of covenant, as we have seen, is used in a most complex variety of contexts. It may be regarded as a motif sometimes dramatizing, but always making more vivid, the fundamental theme of commitment. It dramatizes the commitment of YHWH to his creatures, and specifically to Israel since the time of the ancestors, and the requirement from Israel of answering commitment and obedience to YHWH. It is not merely a motif, but a means of structuring the account and bringing promise and fulfilment, commandment and obedience, narrative and law, into relation. For this reason it is given a chapter of its own (Chapter 4).

The proper response to a promise is trust, or faith, assuming that the one who promises can be trusted – and the narrator takes for granted that God

51 Clines, *Theme*, pp. 38–47.

can be trusted. The proper response to commandment is obedience, if the one who commands has the right to do so – and the narrator takes for granted that God does have that right.

Faith

In Genesis 15.6, in response to YHWH's promise of descendants, we are told 'He [Abram] believed YHWH.' Although the theme of faith is not very often explicitly mentioned in the Pentateuch, the occasions when this is done are significant. Here it sums up Abram's response to God's promise. The question whether the Israelites will believe Moses when he comes to them with a purported message from YHWH occupies part of the dialogue between YHWH and Moses in Exodus 3—4: Exod. 4.1–9. As we have noted, they are ambiguous about it (above, p. 28). The issue for YHWH in the wilderness is whether the Israelites trust him (Num.14.11; 20.12).

Obedience

Whenever God gives a command, the issue of obedience and disobedience arises. Obedience is closely related to faith, indeed the major episodes of disobedience in the Pentateuch arise because of lack of trust: this is clear enough with Eve in Genesis 3.1–7, and the Israelites in Exodus 32.1–6, who think Moses is never going to come back, and in Numbers 14.1–4, when they trust the spies rather than YHWH. In all these cases the disobedient people run a great risk of immediate death, and only avoid it by the gracious forgiveness of YHWH. Even so, many die in Exodus 32, and in Numbers 14 all of the adults are condemned to die without seeing the promised land. Disobedience is thus an important driver of plot, and reveals a great deal about the implied author's values.

But obedience is far more important, since it is the way in which God's blessing and salvation are achieved. The obedience of Noah in Genesis 6.22 delivers the world from final destruction, the obedience of Moses in Exodus 4.18–20 and onwards delivers his people from the 'house of slaves' to serve YHWH, and the obedience of Moses again in Exodus 35—40 enables the presence of YHWH to be experienced by Israel in their midst. The obedience of Abraham in Genesis 22 will be explored at length below.

Forgiveness

Disobedience would on several occasions have brought the story to a premature end, were it not for God's forgiveness or mitigation of the punishment. The first human couple are not condemned 'to die on the day' that they eat of the forbidden tree (Gen. 3; cf. 2.17). Humans and other creatures are not all wiped out in the Flood. YHWH responds to Moses' pleas not to destroy the people altogether in Exodus 32.11–14 and Numbers 14.13–25. A number of scholars have pointed out a distinctive plot structure in Genesis 1—11 that embodies this theme: Clines defines it as 'sin–speech–mitigation–punishment'.[52]

Rhetoric in the episode: the binding of Isaac (Gen. 22.1–19)[53]

This famous story has fascinated readers and attracted the attention of theologians for 2,000 years. It has generated commentary and reflection among both Jews and Christians. For Christians it foreshadows the crucifixion understood as the voluntary sacrifice of Jesus, while for Jews it prefigures the sufferings undergone by Jews through the centuries, mostly at the hands of Christians. For both it has enabled those undergoing suffering to make sense of their experience.[54] Here we shall be looking at the story in its Old Testament context, to examine how the narrator guides us to understand the rightness of God's initially puzzling and shocking command.

The command to sacrifice Isaac must be seen in the context of the whole Abraham story, in which Isaac is the long-awaited son, born to his parents in old age and the bearer of God's covenantal promise to Abraham of descendants to occupy the land where Abraham has pitched his tent. He is therefore being asked to give up not only his beloved son (v. 2), but all his hopes, while God appears to be undermining his own plan. And the rhetoric of the passage, restrained as it is, emphasizes the fearfulness of the demand. How then can it be right for God (up to v. 11 the deity is consistently referred to as Elohim) to make it, or possible for Abraham to accede to it?

In the first verse, what God is doing is defined: 'God *tested* Abraham.' Moberly studies the usage of this word (Heb. *nissah*) elsewhere in the Hebrew Bible.[55] There will be echoes of such passages as Deuteronomy 8.2: 'You shall remember all the way that YHWH your God has led you these forty years in the wilderness, to humble you and to *test* you, to know what was in your heart, whether you would keep his commandments or not.' Not only God, but also they themselves learn from their testing: it is a means of character formation and spiritual growth. In Exodus 20.20, where the people are terrified at the theophany, Moses reassures them by telling them that God has come to test them, 'so that the fear of God may be before your eyes', and the theme of 'fear of God' emerges here at verse 12. For a reader

---

52 Von Rad, *Genesis*, pp. 152–3; Westermann, *Genesis 1—11*, p. 47; Clines, *Theme*, pp. 66–70.

53 Besides the commentaries, among which von Rad's and Wenham's are interesting in different ways, see Moberly, *Bible*, pp. 71–131 (also 132–83); Levenson, *Death*, pp. 125–42; Gunn and Fewell, *Narrative*, pp. 98–100; Delaney, 'Abraham'.

54 See Levenson, *Death*, pp. 173–232, and works cited on p. 245, n. 2, especially Spiegel, *Last Trial*; and see below, Chapter 8.

55 Moberly, *Bible*, pp. 97–107.

attuned to these echoes, the narrator has set down a marker at the start that
what Abraham will experience will be for his good, even if it is not a good
experience.

There is a tendency (seen, for example, in von Rad[56]) to attach the word
'only' to the word 'test' – 'only a test', implying that it is only Abraham's
ignorance of God's real intentions that makes the experience as grim as it is.
Of course, that ignorance is necessary to the test; but it is not necessary to
the idea of a test that it should not be real. Abraham has no reason to suppose at the beginning of the story that the sacrifice will not be carried out.[57]

Most English versions begin God's speech simply, 'Take your son'. In
the Hebrew, God qualifies his command with the particle *na*, which expresses politeness; the best translation of it in most places is 'please'. But
you do not need to say 'please' to your inferiors. *Na* is not usual in divine
speech to humans. God knows that what he asks will be deeply distressing
to Abraham, and recognizes this by the unusual politeness of his speech. According to Moberly, Abraham has a choice, and grows through making the
choice to obey. But what of Isaac? Has he any choice?

Abraham does not reply to God. Some have wanted him to object as he
objected in chapter 18, when he feared the Sodomites would be indiscrimin-
ately destroyed.[58] Was Isaac less dear to him than Lot? But this point, from
the perspective of the implied reader, is misconceived.[59] Sodom was subject
to punishment, and it was right that the innocent should not be included in
the punishment. But Isaac was not going to be punished, but sacrificed, and
a sacrificial victim should be perfect and unblemished. It could be argued
that sacrifice was an honour. Again, in chapter 18 Abraham asks God to
stick to his own principles. But Levenson points out that some texts (especially Exod. 22.29) may suggest that in early times in Israel the sacrifice of
the firstborn son to YHWH was acceptable.[60] However, other texts direct a
lamb to be substituted for the dedicated firstborn (see Exod. 13.13; 34.20).
The implied reader may well expect what actually happens: that God himself provides the substitute.

Powerful in its restraint, the narrative never lets us into Abraham's feel-
ings or intentions. All that the narrator gives us are his actions and a few
words. The actions are more ambiguous than sometimes thought.[61] In verse
3 it is strange that Abraham gets everyone ready to go and only then thinks
to cut the wood. At verse 7 it becomes clear what he has not done: he has
not prepared Isaac for what is to happen. And in verses 9–10 he reverses the
normal order of preparations for a burnt offering, in which the animal was
first killed and then cut up and the pieces placed on the altar (Lev. 1.2–9).

56 Von Rad, *Genesis*, p. 239.
57 Cf. Moberly, *Bible*, pp. 97–8.
58 E.g. Gunn and Fewell, *Narrative*, p. 99.
59 Levenson, *Death*, pp. 129–30.
60 Levenson, *Death*, pp. 3–12.
61 See Wenham, *Genesis 16—50*, pp. 106–9.

(However, this is the only detailed account of a human sacrifice, for which the protocol could have been different.) One might think that in each case he is putting off the fatal moment as long as possible. This is not an account of consistent and single-minded obedience. Yet, it seems to be sufficient to obtain the approval of YHWH, through his messenger, in verse 12: 'you have not withheld your son …'.

As for the words (vv. 5, 8), the initial impression is that Abraham is either concealing what is to happen from his staff and from Isaac himself or has not made up his mind what he is going to do, or perhaps is substituting a groundless hope for realistic expectation. But for the reader who knows the end of the story, these words are heavy with irony. Abraham's seeming embarrassed evasions in fact announce the truth: God *will* provide. Some traditional exegetes have here seen Abraham as a true prophet.[62] The writer to the Hebrews believes that his faith meant that 'he reckoned that God was able to raise even the dead' (Heb. 11.19). If either were true, the test would be much less of a test. Moberly, rather similarly, speaks of Abraham's 'confidence' in his words in verse 8: 'Abraham affirms that God will [provide], when as yet he does not know how.'[63] Rather than expressing Abraham's actual belief, it is better to see this as dramatic irony, addressed by the narrator to the reader. The narrator knows that Isaac will indeed be given back to Abraham as it were from the dead, as Hebrews notes; but there is no reason to suppose that Abraham does. But when he meets with the wholly unexpected provision of God, he picks up his own words to name the place 'YHWH provides' (v. 14). Thus the whole story, seemingly one of God's cruelty in asking of his servant such a monstrous abandonment, is suffused with the knowledge of God's grace.

The climax of the story, and the resolution of the tension, comes with the call of YHWH's 'messenger' (in reality YHWH himself) from heaven in verses 11–12. 'Now I know that you are a God-fearer, since you have not withheld your son, your only (?) son from me.' Moberly details the associations of the idea of the 'fear of God': it depicts 'human integrity, an integrity rooted in responsive recognition of God, in which the potential of human life can be realized'.[64] The approval of Abraham's fear of God is reinforced in the messenger's second speech in verses 16–18. Here YHWH reaffirms his promises and confirms them with an oath, with overwhelming emphasis on Abraham's descendants, who are of course to be derived from the 'only son' who was to have been slain. But whereas previously he has promised these things to Abraham out of his sheer grace, here he makes them the reward for Abraham's obedience: 'Because you have done this …'. The implication is that although YHWH's covenant was of grace, Abraham could only appropriate the promises through his faithfulness. This is what

---

62 Levenson, *Death*, p. 130.

63 Moberly, *Bible*, p. 107.

64 Moberly, *Bible*, pp. 80–97 (quotation from p. 96).

makes the episode important in the Pentateuch as a whole; and with that comes the immense body of later interpretation in which Isaac stands as a symbol or type of the *actually* slain Jewish martyr or atoning Christ.[65]

If the narrator has been successful, readers will at this point be persuaded that Abraham's willingness, with understandable reluctance, to give up him who is most dear to him, is the appropriate and supreme expression of his 'fear' of the God whom he honours and loves more than his gifts. If not, they may doubt whether it was fair dealing in God to manipulate his servant in this way (see below, p. 193). Does such behaviour accord with the mature and responsive relationship between God and believer that Moberly maintains is the intention of the test? Even more problematic in such a relationship, though perhaps not for the implied reader, who would be used to children being at the absolute disposal of their father, is the way in which Isaac, apparently without his consent and even without his knowledge up to the last minute, is used as a passive victim. Jewish tradition has maintained that he was an adult at the time of this event, and therefore must have implied his consent; but most modern exegetes deduce from verse 7 that he is still a child, though old enough to carry enough wood to cremate his own body. Moberly argues that although this is problematic today, it need not prevent our learning from the story.[66] The exclusion of Sarah from the story is also deeply problematic, as feminist writers have commented.[67]

Study one of these three passages (all relatively short): Genesis 21.9–19; Leviticus 10.1–7, 16–20; Numbers 20.2–13. How does the narrator attempt to persuade you that what happened was right? Use commentaries to try to come closer to the point of view of the implied reader. Are you persuaded, and if not, why not?

Overall theme

To identify a consistent theme in the Pentateuch as a whole is not a simple matter, although there are clear unifying threads. As no writer appears to have approached the question of the overall theme of the Pentateuch so directly as Clines, it is inevitable that we should begin with his work.

---

65 I have no space to deal with the view that Genesis 22 and especially verse 14 refer to the Jerusalem Temple (Levenson, *Death*, pp. 111–24; Moberly, *Bible*, pp. 108–18). At any rate, this is not obvious enough to dissuade Samaritans from referring it to their own holy place.

66 Moberly, *Theology of Genesis*, pp. 193–6.

67 Delaney, 'Abraham'. See again Moberly, *Theology of Genesis*, p. 191 and n. 21.

Clines

Clines does not use any one simple definition of 'theme' in his discussion,[68] but it is clear that he understands it as conceptual in character; in other words it is not simply a statement of the subject of the work in question or a summary of the plot. For example, the theme of *Macbeth* might be stated as 'the destructive nature of ambition', but not 'how Macbeth was encouraged to murder Duncan and seize the throne, etc.'. But on the other hand, theme is closely related to the plot of the work: it 'may be regarded as plot with the emphasis on conceptual meaning'.[69] It will be related to both narrative levels, both story and narrative discourse. A statement of overall theme may be a conceptualization of the plot, but it also embraces the values and the-ology which the text seeks to persuade us of.

Clines's own proposal for the theme of the Pentateuch, which he supports by an extensive array of quotations, is as follows:

> The theme of the Pentateuch is the partial fulfilment – which implies also the partial non-fulfilment – of the promise to or the blessing of the patri-archs. The promise or blessing is both the divine initiative in a world where human initiatives always lead to disaster, and a re-affirmation of the primal divine intentions for humanity.[70]

The second sentence here is intended to bring Genesis 1—11 into the ma-terial covered by the statement, though the first half of it is also certainly true of much in what follows. The strikingly paradoxical expression of the first sentence is noted by Clines in the 'afterword' of his second edition.[71] But it draws attention to a significant feature of the plot of the Pentateuch, that it lacks closure in two ways: it points towards the movement of Israel into the promised land, but leaves them on the wrong side of the Jordan; and it offers Israel a choice between obedience and apostasy, which remains open at the end of Deuteronomy.

Clines treats the promises to the patriarchs as embracing three main elements: posterity, a relationship with God, and land; shows that they are constantly alluded to in the text of the Pentateuch; and argues that the action of the work can largely be considered as narrating movement to-wards the fulfilment of these three groups of promises, mostly the first in Genesis, the second in Exodus and Leviticus, and the third in Numbers and Deuteronomy.[72]

Clines's argument is persuasive, and most would agree that his under-standing of the theme of the Pentateuch goes a long way to explaining its

68 Clines, *Theme*, pp. 19–26.
69 Clines, *Theme*, p. 20.
70 Clines, *Theme*, p. 30. Italicized in the original.
71 Clines, *Theme*, p. 128.
72 Clines, *Theme*, pp. 29, 31–47, 48–65.

narrative. But I am not convinced that it altogether succeeds in explaining its shape as we have noted it, a narrative that contains as part of its structure long discourses of law and instruction. Clines emphasizes the character of the Pentateuch as story. Is the reference to such promises as 'they shall be my people, and I shall be their God' sufficient to support this non-story-like feature of the text? To YHWH, Israel is already 'my people' at Exodus 3.7. What follows up to the end of Deuteronomy deepens and structures the relationship, but it is already a fact.

Mann

For this reason it is worth bringing into the argument two other attempts at reading the Pentateuch as a narrative whole. Neither of them specifically aims at stating a theme, but it is not too difficult to derive themes from what they say. The first is that of Mann.[73] Clines begins with a statement of the theme of the Pentateuch, and then expounds it. Mann follows the narrative through, and concludes with the following reflection:

> From the moment God drove Adam and Eve from the garden, the Pentateuch has portrayed Yahweh as a deity in search of community, a God whose primary purpose is the restoration of the order among creator, creature and world that existed before the first human beings broke the first commandment. The Pentateuch is a narrative description of that process of restoration – or better, re-creation – as it took shape in the sacral community known as Israel. At the end of the Pentateuch, that community – *as a possibility* – is now complete ... With this description of the new community of God, the Pentateuch has reached its true end – its *telos* – its goal and purpose.[74]

More briefly, Mann's proposal for the theme of the Pentateuch is that it is the restoration of the order of creation through the establishment of the sacral community of Israel. Though Clines's and Mann's proposals do not contradict each other unless one insists that the theme of a work can only be described in one way (which Clines does not now believe[75]), they emphasize different things. By 'this description of the new community of God', Mann means the establishment of the tabernacle cult (Exod. 25—31; 35—40; Lev. 1—16) and the giving of the constitutive laws of Deuteronomy: the development rather than the initiation of Israel's relationship with God. On the other hand, Mann's formulation subordinates the promises. The promise of land he especially downgrades, by insisting that the Pentateuch *has* in one way attained closure. But there is an ambiguity here, in that Mann

73 Mann, *Torah.*
74 Mann, *Torah*, pp. 160–1. Italics as in the original.
75 Clines, *Theme*, p. 132.

himself admits that the new community is only 'a possibility': 'a reality in terms of what God has done ... [but] only ... a possibility in terms of what Israel will do'.[76] But they will only be able to do it once they have crossed the Jordan, since the laws of Deuteronomy are given to be implemented 'in the land which YHWH your God is giving you'. The promise of the land, like the other promises, is therefore indispensable to the actualization of the new community. But Mann's formulation does have the advantage of explicitly allowing for the cultic instructions and civil laws which constitute such a large part of the Pentateuch, without detracting from its character as narrative. However, it is not clear to me that the community of Israel is intended to be a restoration of cosmic order as it existed 'before the first human beings broke the first commandment'. The order that is established after the Flood in Genesis 9.1–7 is in significant respects inferior to the order of Genesis 1,[77] and Israel takes its place within that order.

Sailhamer

Sailhamer describes what he terms 'the central concern of the Pentateuch' like this:

> First, the most prominent event and the most far-reaching theme in the Pentateuch ... is the covenant between God and Israel established at Mount Sinai. The meaning of this event as it is described in the Pentateuch can be summarized in the following cluster of themes: (a) God comes to dwell with Israel; (b) Israel is a chosen people; (c) God gives Israel the land; (d) Israel must obey God's will; and (e) salvation or judgment is contingent on Israel's obedience.[78]

The word 'theme' in this paragraph is clearly used in the more usual sense, as above (p. 28). This is not quite a statement of overall theme in Clines's sense, let alone one that covers the Pentateuch as a whole. But Sailhamer goes on to say that what 'the author of the Pentateuch ... is telling his readers about the covenant of Sinai' can be summarized in three points:

1 God's original plan of blessing for humanity is linked with his establishment of the covenant with Israel at Sinai. He refers here to Genesis 12.1–3 and Exodus 2.24.

2 This divine plan to restore blessing through the covenant failed because of Israel's failure to trust and obey.

3 Nevertheless, 'God's promise to restore the blessing would ultimately succeed because God himself would one day give to Israel a heart to trust

---

76 Mann, *Torah*, p. 161.
77 See Rogerson, *Genesis 1—11*, pp. 18–25; Houston, 'Justice and Violence'.
78 Sailhamer, *Narrative*, p. 27.

and obey him (Dt 30.1–10).' The Pentateuch has an eschatological outlook, 'in that it looks to the future as the time when God's faithful promise (blessing) would be fulfilled'.[79]

This enables us to state the overall theme of the Pentateuch implied by Sailhamer. The theme of the Pentateuch is God's repeated attempts to restore his original blessing to humanity, through his blessing of Abraham, his covenant with Abraham's descendants, and his enabling of them in the future to trust and obey him.

There is a large measure of agreement between these three writers, for all their differences. (Since they are reading the same text, it would be odd if there were not!) They all agree that the Pentateuch is concerned with God's purpose of blessing for humanity as God intended to achieve it through Abraham and his descendants. They all agree that the purpose remains at least partially unfulfilled at the end of the Pentateuch; Mann lays the least emphasis on this and Sailhamer the most, but they all agree that in important ways the Pentateuch lacks closure. They differ most widely in the emphases that they select among the means which God takes to achieve this end. Clines selects the promises to the patriarchs, including those of posterity and land; this leads naturally to his 'partial fulfilment' formulation and necessitates less emphasis on the covenant and laws. Sailhamer selects the covenant, including the land and the presence of God, but with most emphasis on the necessity for Israel's trust and obedience: hence his gloomy view of what has been achieved by the end of the story. Mann lays the emphasis rather on what *has* been achieved, that is, the establishment of potential community, and plays down the need for the land: hence his more positive estimate of fulfilment.

Assessment and conclusion

For my own part, I am struck *both* by the wealth of references to the promises throughout the Pentateuch listed by Clines, *and* by the sheer bulk of the 'law' within it, as well as by the way in which the covenants with Israel function as climaxes within the story (Exod. 24; 34; Deut. 29—30). I am also struck by how difficult it is to state a 'theme' that takes thorough account of all these aspects. Against Clines, it is difficult to make all the legal material fulfilments of God's *promises*. Conversely, the strength of Clines's view is that the narrative is primarily driven by God's promises.[80] Whenever Israel is in danger, it is above all the promises that rescue them: see Exodus 2.24; 32.13–14; Numbers 14.11–24.

Is there a way to span all these aspects of the Pentateuchal narrative to derive a coherent theme? Consider this. At the beginning of this chapter, in

---

79 Sailhamer, *Narrative*, p. 27.
80 Clines, *Theme*, p. 29, with a reference to Zimmerli, *Man and his Hope*, p. 50.

asking after the genre of the Pentateuch, we decided that it was a work of history, giving an account of a nation's past in order to define and govern them in the present. And the promises *and* the covenant and laws can all be seen as relating to aspects of nationhood, as understood in the ancient world. A nation requires a population, a territory and a god. These are what YHWH promises Abraham to give to his descendants, and in the covenants they are bound to their God YHWH. But a nation is also defined by its culture and customs, and if it is to be a nation *state* requires a government and laws. The moral and civil laws provide for all these things (the government in Deut. 16.18—17.20), and the ritual law defines the service of their God with a degree of detail only necessary in the religious establishment of a state.

Consider also that the promises and blessings given by God to Abraham, Isaac and Jacob must be the outcome of a prior decision by God, that is, that God *chose* Israel (in the persons of their ancestors) to be God's people, out of all the possible choices that could have been made.[81] We can add that this implication may extend to Genesis 1—11. God's choice is made out of all the nations in Genesis 10, and in it the purpose of God for humanity expressed in Genesis 1.28 is fulfilled, though in a changed world.[82] It is an intensive and exclusive fulfilment. There may be a hint that all humanity will in due course benefit from it (Gen. 12.3), but the point is made more clearly later in the Old Testament (for example, Isa. 55.5).[83]

Taking these observations together, I would suggest that the theme of the Pentateuch as narrative could be defined as 'how YHWH chose Israel as his people and prepared them for nationhood'. 'Prepared' allows for the open-ended nature of the Pentateuch that we have already noted. I recognize that this formulation contains two concepts (election and nationhood) rather than one, but as the discussion has shown, it is difficult to bring everything in such a rich and varied work as the Pentateuch within the grasp of a single concept.[84] Election results in blessing, is sustained by promise and comes to fulfilment in covenant; and the covenant, subject to their trust and obedience, grants them the qualifications of nationhood (Exod. 19.5–6).

But however we define the overall theme, it is clear that the Pentateuch's lack of closure, the questions that it leaves open, mean that the theme is not 'wrapped up', as it were, when we reach Deuteronomy 34.12. The comfort and assurance that the reader might expect to receive from the account of God's great project is strikingly denied. Instead, the readers, or hearers, are left with a question that they can only answer themselves, whether they will be faithful to their God and obedient to the divine commands for the good life. Despite God's apparently overwhelming power, God's purposes are

---

81 Kaminsky, *Jacob*, underlines the necessary exclusivity of election.

82 As argued by Lohfink, *Theology*, pp. 16–17, 166–7 (but in relation to P only, not the Pentateuch as a whole).

83 See the commentaries for discussion of the uncertainty of Genesis 12.3b.

84 Cf. Clines's discussion, *Theme*, pp. 22–3.

finally dependent on human beings for fulfilment, and so can be frustrated by human beings.

Further reading

General books on narrative

Abbott, *Introduction* is comprehensive, readable and invaluable. Bal, *Narratology*, gives a different approach, equally readable. The notions of 'implied author' and reliability in narrators and characters were first sketched by Booth, *Rhetoric*. Be warned: all of these refer to works of modern fiction without much introduction.

On narrative in the Old Testament

Walsh, *OT Narrative*, is a good introduction with exercise material. Gunn and Fewell, *Narrative*, is an introduction with a more individual approach. Further illumination may be had from Alter, *Art*; Bar-Efrat, *Narrative Art*; Berlin, *Poetics*. The one work which the serious student of biblical narrative must come to terms with is the opinionated, often wrong-headed, but brilliant Sternberg, *Poetics*. It is hard going, and most readers will find much to disagree with, but the exercise is worthwhile. Fewell and Gunn, *Gender*, exemplify the opposite approach to Sternberg: the Primary History is read from the point of view of the characters that the narrator marginalizes.

The only works I know of that study the entire Pentateuch from a narrative point of view are the three drawn on in this chapter: Clines, *Theme*, Mann, *Torah*, and Sailhamer, *Narrative*, but there are many studies of parts of it, for example, Fokkelman, *Genesis*, Gunn, 'Hardening', on the plagues story, and Olson, *Death*, on Numbers.

On genre

Most form-critical works (for example, Coats, *Genesis*) deal with the genres of small units rather than the whole Pentateuch. Damrosch, *Covenant*, links genre study with historical criticism. Van Seters, *History*, has a broad survey of ancient historiography and treats the Primary History as a history. Blenkinsopp, *Pentateuch*, pp. 37–42, argues for understanding it as a historical work.

3

The Pentateuch as Torah

Consider what you understand by 'law'. Think of different senses in which the word is used. Now reread Exodus 20—23; Leviticus 1—7; 11—27; Deuteronomy 12—26 (or as much as you have time for), and ask yourself: 'How much of this is what I would call law?'

Torah and law

The Pentateuch is referred to in those communities that take it as their foundation document as 'the Torah'. The Hebrew word *torah* in the first place means 'teaching' or 'instruction', as in Proverbs 13.14: 'The teaching (*torah*) of a wise man is a fountain of life.' But in the Pentateuch English versions often translate it 'law', as at Leviticus 11.46 (NRSV): 'This is the law (*torah*) pertaining to beasts and birds [etc.].' This may be the best word to use, but there is a risk of its misleading the reader. English-speaking people who are not lawyers tend to think of a 'law' as being a statement of citizens' obligations, imposed by public authority, which they are bound to obey on pain of being brought before a court and punished. But Leviticus 11 does not mention any punishments for disobedience, and the authority giving the instruction is God, not human.

One reason why *torah* tends to be translated 'law' is the way in which its meaning developed in Hebrew, as we can trace in the Pentateuch itself. Rather differently from its use in Leviticus, it is used in Deuteronomy on numerous occasions, especially in chapters 27—31, to refer to the whole body of teaching given by Moses in this book, as passed down from God. See, for example, Deuteronomy 27.8, 'You shall write on the stones all the words of this *torah*.'

In this way the word comes to refer to the book of Deuteronomy (as it may do in 2 Kings 22.8, etc.), and is then extended to all the books that make up the Pentateuch. And the role that these books went on to play in the life of the Israelite communities could be seen to be closely analogous to the role played by law in other nations, for example among the Greeks. They include many commandments, instructions and legal precedents which are relevant to daily life. So when the Torah was being translated into Greek, it was natural for the translators to use the Greek word *nomos*, meaning 'law' or 'custom', to render *torah*. Translators in other languages, ancient and modern, have followed them in using words meaning 'law' to render *torah* when referring to the instruction of the Pentateuch, or the Pentateuch as a whole. And in the New Testament and later Christian writings, the Pentateuch, or even the whole Old Testament, is referred to as 'the Law' (*nomos* in Greek).

But is 'law' really the best general description of the Pentateuch as the foundation document of Israel? In the previous chapter we looked at it as narrative, as a story. Can it be seen alternatively, as a whole, as law? Watts's answer is, in effect, 'Yes'.[1] Although he decides that the Pentateuch is the unique example of its own genre of Torah, the purpose of his book is to show how the combination in the Pentateuch of story, list of commandments or instruction, and sanctions serve to create law:

> to persuade hearers and readers to observe the law by describing its extraordinary origins in a story stretching back to creation, by specifying the ideal divine–human relationship that it makes possible, and by promising great blessings and threatening worse curses contingent on the audience's response.[2]

This seems fair enough as a proposal. To test it we shall first of all look at the place of the commandments in the narrative of the Pentateuch, tracing how God's teaching of Israel develops progressively in the course of the narrative and arises out of it, with a brief exegetical study of the Ten Commandments. We shall then study it *analytically*, considering the different genres of teaching that we can find within it, and asking what function each kind of law or instruction might have had in society. Finally we shall look at it *thematically*, pointing to some common or typical subjects of the teaching, and offering a brief but detailed exegesis of three passages that exemplify the treatment of three of these.

The unfolding of the revelation to Israel

What counts as 'law'?

We first need to decide what counts as 'law' or 'instruction'. The Pentateuch is full from beginning to end of commands and directions from God. Many of these are simply part of the story; for example, the words of God to the newly created human being in Genesis 2.16–17. What we are looking for is words which may be taken as governing the lives of the implied readers (see table above, p. 12; and p. 22), and not only the characters in the story.

---

1 Watts, *Reading Law*. See also above, pp. 15, 17.
2 Watts, *Reading Law*, pp. 59–60.

The 'children of Israel' in the story are often the addressees, directly or indirectly through Moses, of God's commands and instructions. But there is an implication that most of these commands are addressed through the Israel who is a collective character in the story to the living Israel who are its hearers, as in Nehemiah 8. In Deuteronomy 29.14–15 Moses says, 'I am making this covenant … not only with you who stand here with us today before the LORD our God, but also with those who are not here with us today', that is, the following generations.

So words addressed directly or indirectly (through Moses) to Israel can be taken as addressed to contemporary Israel as the implied readers. But this still leaves much room for ambiguity. For example, what is the status of the instructions given in Exodus 25—31 for the furniture and construction of the Tabernacle and the ordination of the priests? These are carried out in the story, at Exodus 35—40 and Leviticus 8—9. But do they have a bearing beyond that? Are they intended to provide in some way for the furnishing of the temple in Jerusalem or on Gerizim and the ordination of priests and high priests for ever? Most scholars assume so, but there is a good deal that can only apply to the portable sanctuary of the wilderness, not to any permanent temple. Another example is the instructions for the Passover in Exodus 12.1–13, carried out at verse 28. These are contradicted in several points by the instructions in Deuteronomy 16.1–8. Traditional Jewish exegesis defined the provisions in Exodus as 'the Passover of Egypt' and those in Deuteronomy as 'the Passover of the generations'; in other words it was Deuteronomy that gave the instructions to be followed year by year: the Exodus Passover was a one-off.

However, in what follows, I shall include the problematic passages in Exodus. I wish to demonstrate that the Torah tells the story of a progressive induction of Israel into the service of YHWH and life in community, and it seems to me that these passages are part of this programme.

Beginnings

The programme could be seen as beginning with the instructions given to all humanity in Genesis 1.28–30; 9.1–7, for these naturally apply to Israel except where they are explicitly varied later. The 'dominion' of humanity over the earth is a given for Israel, as is the command to 'fill' it, and indeed it is in the understanding that each nation possesses its own land that the land of Canaan is promised to Israel (see, for example, Deut. 32.8).

Distinctive instruction for Israel may be seen as beginning with God's address to Abraham in Genesis 17 establishing the covenant of promise with him, by which God is permanently committed to Abraham and his descendants. Genesis 17.9–14 imposes the requirement of circumcision on the eighth day for all males in the households of Abraham and his descendants, as a sign of the covenant.

While circumcision is thus made the sign of YHWH's initial covenant of permanent commitment to Israel, YHWH's deliverance of Israel from Egypt occasions the command to commemorate it through no fewer than three ritual observances instituted in Exodus 12—13. The first two are defined as permanent obligations: Passover (Exod. 12.14, 24) and the eating of unleavened bread for seven days (Exod. 12.17). The third is the dedication of firstborn males to YHWH: this is a commemoration of the death of the Egyptian firstborn (Exod. 13.14–16).

With the arrival of Israel before Mount Sinai in Exodus 19.1 a far more systematic programme of teaching begins, and in the covenant ceremony of Exodus 24.3–8 they bind themselves to the observance of all YHWH's commands, binding also all their descendants. The people stay at Sinai for just short of a year (Exod. 19.1 plus Num. 10.11) and in that time receive the teaching in Exodus 20—23, Leviticus 1—7 and 11—27 and some chapters in Numbers and set up the mobile sanctuary Moses is instructed about in Exodus 25—31.

The Ten Commandments

But only the first 16 verses of all this teaching, Exodus 20.2–17, the Ten Commandments or Decalogue, are proclaimed directly to Israel from the mouth of God; the rest is given to Moses to pass on to them, or to the priests. Moses in Deuteronomy 5.2–27 recalls the event, and repeats the commandments, with some slight variations. It is clear in both contexts that there is something distinctive about this text over against all the rest of the teaching. In Deuteronomy it is spelt out what this something is: these words constitute the covenant imposed on Israel by YHWH (Deut. 5.2, 22). (However, according to Exodus 24.3 (probably), it includes the following laws in chapters 20—23 as well.) This is what Israel are fundamentally committed to before their God, and so it consists of the commands most fundamental to life with God and to life in society under God. The tendency in Judaism, nevertheless, has been to regard all 613 commandments in the Torah as of equal importance. But Christians have always attached special significance to the Ten Commandments; quite often they have been seen as the *only* Old Testament commandments Christians are obliged to observe (see below, pp. 180–2).

Although the text is already called 'the ten words' in Deuteronomy 4.13; 10.4, and probably Exodus 34.28, it is not quite clear how it is to be divided into ten. Numbering systems differ in different traditions (see the table below). The most serious disagreement is over whether the command against images is *part* of the command to have the Lord alone as God, or a distinct commandment, giving it independent weight.

Numbering the commandments: four systems

	Jews	Samaritans	Catholics, Lutherans	Orthodox,[3] Anglicans, other Protestants
I am YHWH	I	I	I	I
No other gods	II	I	I	I
No images	II	I	I	II
The Name	III	II	II	III
The Sabbath	IV	III	III	IV
Father and mother	V	IV	IV	V
No murder	VI	V	V	VI
No adultery	VII	VI	VI	VII
No theft	VIII	VII	VII	VIII
No false witness	IX	VIII	VIII	IX
No coveting	X	IX	IX—X	X
Mt Gerizim[4]	—	X	—	—

The basic covenant demand

God speaks personally to his people in verses 2–6, announcing his name YHWH and requiring exclusive loyalty of them: no other gods, and no worship of images. This is the essence of the covenant, and it is marked off from what follows by God's use of the first person. There is much discussion over why images are forbidden, on the assumption that they could be intended as images of YHWH. But it is more than doubtful that this is so. The command against images is closely bound up with the command to have no other gods, even folded into it.[5] Quite simply, YHWH does not have images. An image *is* another god: compare the ridicule of idolatry in, for example, Isaiah 44.9–20: an idol just is a god, and as such an absurdity.

---

3 Taken literally, the commandment against images does not forbid two-dimensional icons.

4 The Samaritans' tenth commandment is extra to the usually accepted text. It is drawn from Deuteronomy 11.29–30 and 27.2–7, and makes it clear that Mount Gerizim (near Shechem) is 'the place that YHWH has chosen' for sacrifice, rather than Jerusalem.

5 See Childs, *Exodus*, pp. 404–9.

Honouring what is sacred to YHWH

In verses 7–12 YHWH is referred to in the third person. Here YHWH's people are warned against violating what is sacred to YHWH: notably not any holy place or holy things, but God's name and God's day. The institution of the Sabbath harks back to Genesis 2.1–3 in the first creation account. In observing it, the Israelites will be following the pattern that the creator has stamped upon the universe. The largest difference between the versions of the commandments in Exodus and Deuteronomy is at this point: Deuteronomy (5.12–15) does not refer to creation, but to the exodus from Egypt as deliverance from the incessant labour of slaves, and commends the weekly rest from labour as a blessing to one's slaves. This is in accord with one of the major emphases of Deuteronomy.

Responsibility to the neighbour

Verses 12–17 deal with the individual's conduct in society, and can be seen as protecting major aspects of life within a community of patriarchal extended families: the authority of parents over grown children, and the security of a man's expectation of passing his inheritance to his own sons – 'adultery' in the Bible means illicit intercourse where the *woman* is married; life (protected by v. 16 as well as v. 13, if taken with Deuteronomy 19.15–20) and property. Note that 'steal' (v. 15), the Hebrew *ganab*, only applies to movable chattels, and also to kidnapping human beings (as in Exod. 21.16). Verse 17 has a broader coverage. The dominant interpretation is that it refers exclusively to covetous thoughts. But there is a strand of opinion that it also includes action to attempt to gain what belongs to another; potentially it would embrace the kind of machinations to gain possession of others' property condemned by Micah in Micah 2.1–2, where the same word is used.[6] The word 'house' means 'household', covering all that belongs to the neighbour, which is then specified. The version in Deuteronomy (5.21), by putting the wife first, emphasizes her difference from mere property.

Conclusion

The Decalogue does not mention any sanctions for disobedience, but it soon becomes clear that disobedience of its leading requirement puts Israel in peril of destruction (Exod. 32.7–10). It is not law in the normal sense, but a covenant text containing basic religious and moral teaching. It is not policed by the state, but by God, although later provisions prescribe penalties for breaking prohibitions similar to most of the ten commandments. It is not a positive guide for life, but, in the words of Gerhard von Rad, 'it confines

---

6 Childs, *Exodus*, pp. 425–8.

itself to a few basic negations; that is, it is content with, as it were, signposts on the margins of a wide sphere of life'.[7]

However, later interpretation, especially in the Reformed tradition,[8] has drawn the whole of our religious and moral responsibility under the headings of the commandments, especially by making each negative commandment imply the contrary as a positive duty: for example, instead of worshipping idols, we are to 'worship God in Spirit and in truth' (see further below, p. 182).

The laws that follow are far more detailed. Frequently they fence off smaller spheres within areas already prohibited by the Decalogue, but some offer the basis of a positive ethic. Some would consider that they are based on the Decalogue, drawing out its implications for daily life and religion. But it is hard to make this idea out in detail, and it will not be used here as a key to their interpretation.

> Class discussion (in a Christian environment): Are the Ten Commandments enough? If not, can you find later commandments that are worth putting alongside them, other than the obvious Deuteronomy 6.5 and Leviticus 19.18?

The 'Book of the Covenant'

The body of teaching given to Moses by YHWH in Exodus 20.22—23.33 has been given this name (hereafter 'C') by modern scholars on the assumption that it represents the document read by Moses to the people according to Exodus 24.7, and presumably written in verse 4, although 'all the words of YHWH' in that verse should include the Decalogue also. The conclusion in Exodus 23.20–33 can be regarded as an appendix: it is specific exhortation for the generations of the exodus and conquest.

The short introduction in Exodus 20.22–26 is concerned with the proper sacrificial cult of YHWH, and corresponding to this towards the end we find a section on YHWH's festivals (Exod. 23.14–19; see below). These sections frame the main body of the text, which is concerned for a social order marked by justice.[9]

This can be divided into two contrasting sections. The first section (21.2—22.20) is headed 'These are the ordinances (*mishpatim*) that you shall set before them' (21.1). It is concerned with measures to be taken either to resolve disputes in society or to punish serious offences, and it

7 Von Rad, OT Theology, i, pp. 194–5.
8 Burgess, 'Reformed Explication', and Calvin, 'On the Law and Commandments', in Brown, Ten Commandments, pp. 78–105.
9 Houtman, Exodus, vol. 3, p. 83.

is expressed almost entirely in an impersonal legal style. The section from 22.21 to 23.13 is quite different in character. Here YHWH addresses the individual personally with exhortation and warning to exercise compassion and justice towards the neighbour, and honour and respect towards God. The first section offers ways of managing conflict and avoiding violence in the relationships between relative equals (and also tries to ensure that people treat slaves reasonably). The second addresses differences of power and wealth in society. The powerful can brush legal rules aside if they wish. They need to be taught to act with justice and compassion.[10]

In Exodus the covenant is made on the terms of the Decalogue *and* C. The people twice commit themselves to observe them (Exod. 24.3, 7). Commitment to YHWH is not merely a matter of religion in the narrow sense of the word, but involves the whole of the nation's life. 'It is Yahweh alone who watches over all aspects of life in the world.'[11] This is the essence of the covenantal law typical of the Pentateuch.

The dwelling for YHWH

Quite different is the next major section of teaching, the instructions received by Moses in Exodus 25—31 for the construction of a sanctuary and for the ordination of priests and the establishment of a sacrificial cult in the wilderness – the instructions so far have only provided for a cult to be set up once the promised land is reached. The details have some significance also for the cult in the land. But far more important is the stated purpose of these provisions. YHWH says to Moses (Exod. 25.8), 'They shall make me a sanctuary *that I may dwell among them*'; and the name of the sanctuary is 'The Dwelling', *ha-mishkan* (usually translated 'the tabernacle'). The climax of the instructions comes in Exodus 29.45, 'I shall dwell among the Israelites and be their God', which announces the fulfilment of the promise made to Abraham in Genesis 17.7. The fulfilment actually occurs after the setting up of the Dwelling in Exodus 40.34: 'the glory of YHWH filled the Dwelling'. Only the provision of a royal dwelling suitable for the reception of the Creator God, and rigorously guarded against encroachment, makes this possible.[12] But the sanctuary is also called the 'Tent of Meeting' (as in both the contexts just referred to: Exodus 29.42, 44; 40.34a), for it is the place where YHWH promises to meet with Moses to speak with him.

Covenant renewal

But before the Dwelling can be built, the crisis of the golden calf occurs. Moses eventually gets YHWH to make a new covenant (34.10, 27). YHWH

---

10 Houtman, *Exodus*, vol. 3, p. 83.
11 Nicholson, *God and His People*, p. 214.
12 See Haran, *Temples*, and Jenson, *Graded Holiness*.

announces the terms of the covenant in 34.11–26. There is nothing new here: it is a selection of mainly ritual commands repeated from earlier addresses, mostly from C. The clear implication is that YHWH has the same requirements in the new covenant as in the old one. They are often called the 'Ritual Decalogue' in scholarship, as distinct from the better-known 'Ethical Decalogue' – wrongly, for there are more than ten. Scholars have been confused by the reference to the 'ten commandments' in 34.28, which surely means the original Ten Commandments: these also are reaffirmed by being inscribed on the new tablets (see below, p. 81).

Sacrifice and purity

As soon as the Tent of Meeting is set up, YHWH speaks to Moses out of it (Lev. 1.1). The establishment of a sanctuary gives the opportunity for individuals to offer sacrifice, but also creates the danger that individuals or the community may pollute the sacred space (Lev. 15.31). The ritual of sacrifice and its variations for different purposes are set out in Leviticus 1—7. This is not an instruction manual. One could not learn how to sacrifice animals using only the information in these chapters. They set out not so much how to do it as *what* to do: which elements of procedure are indispensable, what are the essential differences between the different types of sacrifices, and on what occasions they are required or permitted.[13]

Using the instructions given by God in these chapters, Moses is able to carry out the ordination of Aaron and his sons as priests (Leviticus 8—9), and so the sacrificial cult can be inaugurated, and it receives YHWH's personal confirmation (Lev. 9.23–24).

The teaching in Leviticus 10—15 is consequent on the establishment of the Dwelling and the sacrificial cult. These create the danger of disaster (Lev. 15.30) through false steps in ritual (Lev. 10.1–2) or not being careful about forbidden food (Lev. 11.1–23, 40–45) or purifying oneself from ritual uncleanness. The climax of this section comes in Leviticus 16, the prescription for the ritual of the great Day of Atonement, which serves both to cleanse the sanctuary of all its accumulated impurities, and to deliver the community from the dangers inherent in their sins (the individuals who had committed deliberate sins, however, had to 'bear their guilt' – Num. 15.30–31). YHWH speaks personally to the people to tell them to make this a fast day (Lev. 16.29–31). The ritual has to be backed up by personal and communal penitence.

The ritual practices set out in Leviticus 1—16 and the underlying concepts may seem alien to modern western people, yet ones like them are very widespread in the world in similar societies, and in different ways are part of traditional Christianity as well as Judaism.[14] They are of a piece with the

13 Knierim, *Text and Concept*, pp. 98–106, esp. p. 105.
14 See Douglas, *Purity* and *Natural Symbols*, and below, pp. 226–7.

image of the divine Dwelling projected in Exodus 25—29. God is holy, and therefore dangerous to mortal beings, who are prone to sin, and also full of 'uncleanness' arising from the natural functions of men and especially women. Yet, God has condescended to dwell in the centre of the Israelites' camp. This enables them to approach God with presents, which will be graciously received if they are taken up into the sphere of God's holiness by the appropriate ritual. But the divine presence must be carefully guarded against contamination, not for God's sake, but for Israel's; hence the holy presence lies at the centre of a system of concentric barriers and can be approached only by properly consecrated persons and on proper occasions. Even so, the dangers that emanate from imperfect humanity constantly threaten them. The instructions for expiatory sacrifices (Lev. 4.1—6.7) and the rules for purification in Leviticus 11—15 give the Israelites the tools for protecting themselves against these dangers.

'You shall be holy, as I YHWH your God am holy'

Yet something startlingly different is said about holiness in the course of these instructions. In Leviticus 11, YHWH addresses the Israelites personally (whereas most of 1—7 and 12—17 is in an impersonal style) and in verse 44 commands: 'You shall make yourselves holy and be holy, for I am holy' – it is the motivation for observing the distinction between clean and unclean animals. In a sense clearly different from that in which the priests and the Dwelling and the altar are holy (and other people and things are not) the whole of the Israelite people are called to be holy. This takes up a theme already stated in Exodus 19.6, where they are said to be 'a kingdom of priests'.

What this means is worked out particularly in the course of the laws in Leviticus 17—26, known to scholarship as the 'Holiness Code' ('H'), which are most easily understood as a collection of short codes on particular themes, loosely linked by a few common theological motifs, and addressed personally to Israel by YHWH. Variations on the command in Leviticus 11.44 occur several times in Leviticus 19—22. More widely scattered, in Leviticus 18—26, are the admonition 'I am YHWH your God', and references to YHWH's action in bringing Israel out of Egypt as their motivation for obeying his commands. From chapter 18 onwards it is made clear that these commands are a rule for Israel's life in the land. The subjects of the separate discourses include animal slaughter (17), sexual offences (18; 20) community life (19), including ritual in daily life (19.19; 23–28), the holiness of priests and offerings (21—22) and the calendar of religious festivals (23). In all these fields Israel are to consecrate themselves to the God who has delivered them from slavery in Egypt.

The climax comes with a long discourse stated to be made by YHWH to Moses not out of the Tent but once more on Mount Sinai (25.1; 26.46). It considers first the way in which Israel is to deal with agricultural land in the country to which they are coming, both in relation to God and to each other; the fundamental principle is stated in 25.23: 'The land shall not be sold in perpetuity, for the land is mine.' Chapter 26 then sums up by warning the people of what awaits them in case of obedience or disobedience, clearly assuming that the latter option is the one that will be taken up. Yet, they are assured that if they repent and turn back to YHWH, YHWH will be faithful to his covenant with them (Lev. 26.40–45).

Instructions in Numbers

Despite the apparent finality of this chapter, further instructions follow, at Sinai (Lev. 27; Num. 3—6; 8—9; 10.1–10); on the wilderness way (Num. 15; 18—19) and in the plains of Moab on the verge of the promised land (Num. 27.1–11; 28—30; 35—36). These are very various, and I make no attempt to summarize them here: we shall look in detail at one chapter later. In part they clarify instructions already given in Leviticus, in part they deal with miscellaneous minor matters, but one especially important object is to detail the division of labour and honour between the priesthood and the minor clergy, the 'Levites'. It is probably true to say that they all presuppose teaching that has been given previously, mostly in Leviticus.

Deuteronomy

Introducing the laws

The final stage in the education of Israel comes with the series of speeches delivered to them by Moses in the plains of Moab as a farewell address in preparation for his own death and their crossing of the Jordan to settle in the land, which take up most of the book of Deuteronomy. We have already seen that they are described in the book itself as a *torah* or teaching. More specifically, the instructions which Moses gives are introduced in legal terms: they are 'decrees (*huqqim*) and judgements (*mishpatim*)' (NRSV, 'statutes and ordinances': Deut. 4.1, 45; 5.1; 12.1; cf. 6.1).

However, the actual laws are some time coming. Moses reminds them of YHWH's covenant with them at Horeb on the basis of the Ten Commandments, which he repeats (Deut. 5), and urges them to 'love' YHWH their God (6.5), by being faithful only to him, 'fearing' him, trusting him, being obedient to his commands, and teaching this trust and obedience to their children (6.20–25). He reminds them of their unfaithfulness in the past (9.8—10.5), but assures them that if they are faithful, they will enter the land and receive YHWH's blessing there. Again, after the laws, in chapters 28—30, there are blessings and promises for obedience (28.1–14) and, at enormous length, curses and warnings for disobedience (28.15–68); and Moses' final appeal to choose between life and death (30.11–20). Here it is also made clear that the laws are to form the basis of a covenant, distinct from that already made at Horeb (29.1, 10–15).

The laws of Deuteronomy

The laws proper occupy Deuteronomy 12—26. In 5.22–31 Moses had told the story of his reception of these commands from YHWH, as the people's appointed mediator, after the giving of the Decalogue. This is paralleled by the narrative in Exodus 20.18–21; but this goes on to relate the giving of the 'Book of the Covenant'. Many of the laws in Deuteronomy do indeed recall those in C, but normally in a revised form (for example Deut. 15.12–18, on the release of slaves, as compared with Exod. 21.2–11).[15] We shall glance at the historical connection between the two later. Narratively, it appears that after Moses has been told that he will not be able to lead the people into the promised land (Deut. 1.37), he leaves with them an extended body of teaching setting out the conditions on which they may occupy and retain it, and in this developed teaching the laws he has already been given appear with revisions to allow for their new setting.

In distinction from previous laws, these laws address Israel as a fully fledged nation rather than simply a religious and social community. They endow this new nation in its new territory with national institutions: a central place of worship to be chosen by YHWH, at which alone sacrificial worship will be allowed (ch. 12); a national religion consisting of the exclusive worship of YHWH and based on the chosen place (12—14; 15.19—17.7); a national judiciary (17.8–13), and, with reservations, a monarchy (17.14–20); a national clergy (18.1–8); and a national militia (ch. 20). Deuteronomy's Israel, it is clear, is no tribal society. This aspect of the text appears particularly in chapters 12—20. The laws in Deuteronomy 21—25 tend to be more local or individual in focus, like those in C. The national focus returns in the closing chapter, 26. It is on the basis of these laws that Moses announces the making of the covenant of Moab (29.1, 10–15), though curiously he does not elicit from the people any spoken agreement to these terms as in Exodus.

The laws in Deuteronomy 12—26 are not simply stated. They are preached. To a very large extent they are expressed in the second person: Israel as a whole and the individual are personally addressed. Moses urges the laws with passion, supports them with motivations and reasons, some theological, relying on the themes already set out in the parenetic material in chapters 4—11, others moral and legal and practical. He stretches every nerve to convince his hearers (Israel in every age, as I have shown) that the commands he gives are right and good and to be obeyed, not just because

---

15 Cf. Levinson, *Deuteronomy*.

they come ultimately from God but because they are the right thing to do and will bring blessing.

The commandments and instructions of the Torah are given by the authority of YHWH and of Moses, who simply represents the will and commands of YHWH (Deut. 5.31–33). Given that in the narrative YHWH and Moses have each commended themselves as worthy of trust, this means that the hearers of the Torah may take these words as commands to be obeyed and as law for the life of Israel.

Law, moral exhortation and ritual instruction: the teaching viewed analytically

Obviously, there are several different kinds of text included in God's 'teaching'. Even the widest definition of 'law' could not include them all, which is one reason why I have avoided that word in speaking about the teaching as a whole. There is a traditional Christian distinction between moral, civil and ceremonial laws (see below, pp. 179–82). Any community needs civil laws to keep society in order, and any religious community needs rules for its worship; but these do not have to be the same in all communities. (There has to be a rule of the road, but it does not matter whether it is to drive on the right or the left, provided that everyone in the same country does the same.) But the same moral law, it has traditionally been supposed, binds all human beings. So this distinction supposedly enabled Christians to identify which laws they were required to observe, with the Ten Commandments in first place. Unfortunately it often encouraged them to ignore all the others, despite the valuable moral and theological teaching in many of them.

Modern scholarship tends to classify genres of law on the basis of their linguistic form, so that this discipline is known as form criticism. This results in a rather different breakdown. Supposedly, the classification enables us to identify a specific social situation in which a genre originated, the so-called *Sitz im Leben*.[16] Pioneering and still influential work of this kind was done on law in the Pentateuch by Albrecht Alt.[17]

In modern legal systems there is a distinction between civil and criminal law. In civil law someone who has been wronged sues the person responsible to obtain damages. In criminal law the prosecution and the punishment are undertaken by the state. But in ancient societies there were no police and no state prosecutors. It was up to the victim to take the perpetrator to justice, and civil law covers criminal law as well.

---

16 For a general introduction to the form-criticism of the Old Testament, see Tucker, *Form-criticism*.

17 Alt, 'Origins'.

Civil law

Alt made distinctions within the body of civil laws, starting from the first part of C, and these were based on the linguistic form of the laws. One type, which is dominant in that section, is introduced by a 'when', or 'if', clause setting out the circumstances which require a legal remedy, and the main clause then says what should be done in that case. An example is Exodus 22.7: 'When a person gives another (lit. 'a man ... his neighbour') money or chattels for safe keeping and they are stolen from that person's house, if the thief is caught he must pay double.' Often variations on the case are dealt with by further sentences of similar structure, as here (v. 8): 'If the thief is not caught ...'. The expression is normally impersonal: not 'you' but 'a man'. Alt entitled this form '*casuistic* law', from the Latin *casus*, a case, and this term continues in common use.

The other type of law that Alt identified in Exodus 21.2—22.20 is not expressed conditionally, but simply states that anyone who does such-and-such shall be put to death, for example Exodus 21.12: 'Anyone who strikes another (lit. a man) so that he dies shall be put to death.' There are no conditions and no exceptions. Alt compared this with the series of curses in Deuteronomy 27.15–26 and the Decalogue. He believed that legal sentences of these types were unique to Israel, and he lumped them all together under the heading of '*apodictic* law', from a Greek word meaning to show or announce. It was his theory that at regular renewals of the covenant an official speaker would announce the law in such a form, absolute and unconditional.

What these series share is their absolute quality and their simple form. But they are quite different from each other. The death penalty statements are impersonal, and so are the curses, but their effect is quite different: one prescribes a penalty to be carried out by human hands, the other delivers the offender to the judgement of God. The Ten Commandments, on the other hand, as we have seen, are personal in their expression: they say 'you shall not' do so-and-so; and this form is much more widespread in the Torah. For this reason, we do not use this category of 'apodictic law' any more in the way in which Alt conceived it, though you will still see the word used.

Casuistic laws

When the laws from ancient Mesopotamia began to be discovered, including the famous laws of Hammurabi, it was seen that they used an identical construction to the casuistic laws in C, and more consistently. Alt argued that laws expressed in this form would have become widespread through scribal culture in the ancient Near East as a vehicle for the guidance of local courts, and that the Israelites took over their form of expression from the Canaanites and intended them for the same end.

However, it is now generally believed that such legal formulations, whether in Mesopotamia or in Israel, cannot have been intended as laws to be enforced by the courts. For among the ample trove of court documents recovered from Mesopotamia there is not a single reference to Hammurabi's code or any other body of written law. The judges would have used their own ideas of justice, probably usually following custom, to settle cases rather than following a set code. And the same was true in Israel. In three places in the Torah (Exod. 23.1–3, 6–9; Lev. 19.15–16; Deut. 16.19–20) there are instructions for judges warning them to judge fairly and impartially and avoid corruption, but making no mention of any laws or commandments that they should enforce – not even in Deuteronomy. Patrick goes through six accounts in the Old Testament of judicial deliberation and shows that in none of them is reference made to any written law.[18] It is generally assumed that courts would decide according to traditional custom, seeking divine guidance in difficult cases.[19] In Exodus 18.13–27 Jethro urges Moses only to judge difficult cases, consulting God over them. (The process is shown in action in two or three cases in the Torah, for example Num. 15.32–36.) Moses is then to teach the people God's laws. Here the law arises from cases rather than being used to settle them, and it is taught to the people, not to judges.[20]

What then was the function of the casuistic laws? That question may have different answers at different stages of the tradition. For Bernard Jackson, who has published a major study of the *mishpatim* in C,[21] the reason why these rules were not referred to by courts is because originally people were expected to apply them to settle disputes on their own without referring to a court: they were 'self-executing' laws. They are expressed in a way typical of oral folk wisdom. They do not express general principles, but 'customary, narrative images of what is right'.[22] Take, for example, Exodus 21.35: 'When someone's ox gores the ox of another so that it dies, they shall sell the live ox and divide its price between them, and also divide the dead ox.' This would produce a fair result if the oxen were of equal value, but not if they were not. Jackson argues that the words evoke the typical situation of oxen of roughly equal value, and they are not intended to determine cases that are not typical.

Jackson may be right that *some* of the rules may have once been 'self-executing'.[23] But the casuistic form they now have, and some of the typical cases selected, are characteristic of the Mesopotamian codes, and some of the examples that sound practical, like the case of the goring ox, may be en-

---

18 Patrick, *Law*, pp. 191–8.

19 Knight, *Law*, discusses how legal systems in ancient Israel may have worked in practice.

20 See LeFebvre, *Collections*, pp. 40–7.

21 Jackson, *Wisdom-Laws*.

22 Jackson, *Wisdom-Laws*, p. 49.

23 He is criticized by Tomes, 'Home-grown', and Jackson replies, 'Response'.

tirely hypothetical. Various functions have been suggested for the so-called law codes of Mesopotamia: as education for judges in principles of justice, or for consultation as examples of good practice, or, when displayed publicly, as propaganda, showing the justice of the king. The casuistic form they take is the mark of professional scribes, and it seems likely that the setting of casuistic law is not legal practice in the courts, but the culture of scribes.[24] The rules express the scribes' idea of what the law *ought* to be. In some cases they may reflect traditional or revealed judgements in the courts. But Alt was partly right. Israelite scribes either shared a form used throughout the ancient Near East, or borrowed it from Babylon or Assyria.[25] But the *content* of the rules is often very different from those in the Mesopotamian codes. In particular, property offences are treated less seriously than offences against the person, whereas in the code of Hammurabi and elsewhere theft is often punished with death. This may be held to reflect popular sentiment in Israel about the relative weighting of the two types of crime, in a culture still close to its village roots.[26]

Casuistic laws in other contexts

Moving beyond C, we can find many casuistic laws in Deuteronomy. But here they tend to show a different style, as they share in the strongly sermonic style of the book as a whole. The impersonal style is exchanged for personal address, and the simple rule is backed up with appeals and reasons. A characteristic example is the law for the release of debt slaves after six years in Deuteronomy 15.12–18, a revised version of Exodus 21.2–6.

Casuistic style is also used in the ritual law, for example in the regulations for sacrifice in Leviticus 1.2—6.7. Just as in C, the style is impersonal and each main case is introduced with 'When ...', and subsections with 'If', for example Leviticus 1.3: 'If the offering is a whole offering from the cattle ...'. As these rules have nothing to do with courts of law, this is a strong indication that this is a scribal style which might be applied to any subject.

Personal commands

The style of the Ten Commandments, 'You shall/shall not ...', is widespread in the Torah, especially for moral teaching. The commands in Exodus 20.13–16, 'Do not commit murder. Do not commit adultery. Do not steal' (two words each in the Hebrew), are the simplest possible examples. But more usually they are extended with motivations, like most of the laws

---

24 Fitzpatrick-McKinley, *Transformation*.

25 D. P. Wright, *Inventing*, argues that C is directly derived from the laws of Hammurabi.

26 See Baker, *Tight Fists*, pp. 27–8.

in Deuteronomy. 'An alien you shall not exploit or oppress, *for you were aliens in Egypt*' (Exod. 22.21): this sets the style of most of the commands in the second half of C, down to Exodus 23.19, whether they are concerned with social justice, with integrity in the courts, or with YHWH's festivals. They do not set penalties for failure to observe the rule, although some of them warn of divine punishment, as in Exodus 22.23–24, 27: twice comes the warning, 'he will cry out to me, and I shall hear him'. They are not concerned with law and order or ways of settling disputes, but with teaching moral and religious duties. Clearly, if the writer speaks of God's judgement rather than human punishment, his subject is not law, in the ordinary sense of that word, but morality. (Frank Crüsemann, however, disagrees, arguing that such 'meta-norms' influence the way in which the law is applied.)[27] Typically, the command is expressed in the second person singular, because the responsibility lies on the individual. However, in parts of Deuteronomy and to a large extent in Leviticus commands are in the plural, addressing the many individuals of which Israel is made up.

Modern English versions do not help you, if you do not know Hebrew, to distinguish between the second person singular and plural (unless 'yourself' or 'yourselves' occurs). If you wish to do this, use the King James Version: it will always translate the singular with 'thou' or 'thee', and the plural with 'ye' or 'you'.

It has been suggested that such prohibitions could have originally been the way in which tribal patriarchs taught morality to their family. They are common in the wisdom literature, where the situation conjured up is one of a father teaching his children: see, for example, Proverbs 3.25–31. Whereas casuistic style originates as a written genre in the culture of scribes, in the case of personal commands and prohibitions we may be nearer to an oral context; but this does not mean that all or even any of the commandments in the Torah originated orally. But some may well have done.

A similar style is used for other subjects as well as moral instruction. Often the second person singular in Deuteronomy means not the individual, but Israel viewed as a single collective actor, for example in Deuteronomy 16.18: 'You shall appoint judges for *yourself* in all your cities ...' This may be called constitutional law. The style is also sometimes used for ritual law, for example in Leviticus 11 (plural), or Exodus 23.14–19 (singular); frequently in Leviticus 23 (plural), Deuteronomy 16.1–17 (singular).

---

27 Crüsemann, *Torah*, pp. 192–5.

Priestly pronouncements

One further type of utterance is distinctive of certain parts of the Torah. The priests are told in Leviticus 10.10–11 that they must 'distinguish between what is holy and what is common, and between what is unclean and what is clean'. And frequently we find expressed in a simple short sentence the judgement that so-and-so is (ritually) clean or unclean, as in Leviticus 11, where the pronouncement is repeated, 'it is/they are unclean for you' (Lev. 11.4, 5, 6, 7, etc.). Such concise declarations are also applied to other aspects of ritual, especially sacrifice, for example 'it is not acceptable' (Lev. 19.7).[28] This style is extended to the moral sphere in parts of H, for example Leviticus 18.17 'it is depravity', 18.22 'it is an abomination', 18.23 'it is perversion', in each case following a prohibition in the second person singular. Unlike the ritual terms 'unclean' and so forth, these terms do not have a precise meaning, but are general terms of moral condemnation.

Note the difference between these terse, unexplained pronouncements and the motivations in Deuteronomy, which appeal to the hearers' reason: 'so that it may go well with you and with your children after you for ever' (Deut. 12.28); 'all Israel shall hear and be afraid, and never again do any such wickedness' (Deut. 13.11); 'remember that you were a slave in Egypt' (Deut. 15.13, etc.). The contrast is that between the rhetoric of the lawyer or politician, who must argue for assent, as against the terse, authoritative pronouncement of the priest who relies on rules or revelation mysterious to the lay person.

Conclusion: what was the 'Law' for?

Although great importance has been attached to the form-criticism of 'law', its enduring results may seem to be somewhat limited, amounting to no more than the suggestion of priestly, scribal or oral origins. One point has emerged, however, that is quite significant. There is no indication that any type of *torah* was originally law in the sense that we understand it, legislation intended to be applied according to the letter by the courts.[29] The teaching of the Torah is morally clear, but it is not adapted for legal use. It is far from comprehensive, it is rarely precise enough, it condemns offences that are beyond the reach of human sanctions (like the commandment against coveting), and it often warns of the judgement of God rather than mortals.

It might be thought that those laws where the death penalty is ordained for serious offences are clear enough and easily applied. See below for

---

28 See von Rad, *OT Theology*, p. 261.

29 See Fitzpatrick-McKinley, *Transformation*, and LeFebvre, *Collections*. There are still those who hold out for a legislative view of the Torah, or parts of it, for example Fishbane, *Biblical Interpretation*, p. 96, or Tomes, 'Home-grown'. But LeFebvre effectively refutes Fishbane's arguments: LeFebvre, *Collections*, pp. 48–50.

murder. But family vengeance was custom: the laws only offer to regulate the practice. There are other places where the death penalty is probably theoretical. One suspects that no parents would ever have exposed themselves to the shame involved in handing over their son to the stoning ordained for a rebellious son in Deuteronomy 21.18–21. There is no known case of anyone ever being executed for adultery according to Leviticus 20.10 and Deuteronomy 22.22 (compare Prov. 6.32–35).[30]

However, by the late second century BCE at latest the Torah *was* being treated as legislation demanding strict adherence, even if it had to be supplemented and even if many provisions could not be enforced.[31] But is this understanding of it presented by any texts in the Torah itself? The issue is argued out by Patrick and LeFebvre.[32]

Even though there are many passages, particularly in Deuteronomy, which appear to legislate for the conduct of legal cases, at least some laws have to be regarded as idealistic, and they are all best regarded as giving an ideal model of justice rather than as legislation in the modern sense.

We have so far discussed the way in which the Torah may relate to the practice of civil law. But are matters any different with the ritual law, which forms such a large part of the Torah? James Watts points out that it is common for an ancient text to be appealed to for the direction of ritual, and suggests that the authority of the Torah as a whole may have flowed from its initial authority over the conduct of ritual.[33] If that is so, it might mean in turn that the ritual texts were intended to prescribe the conduct of ritual from the start. Certainly this is more likely than with the legal texts. However, LeFebvre casts doubt on this also.[34]

If texts of torah were not intended to lay down rules for the courts or daily life or possibly even the temple, what was their function?[35] In Deuteronomy 31.12 we see that the purpose of the public reading of the Torah is 'that they may learn to fear YHWH your God and be careful to do all the words of this Torah'. In other words, the purpose of the written torah text is to teach the people what God requires of them. It is a covenant document, not a law code. Its function is to teach them how they should behave, to develop a moral conscience, to teach them the essentials of their religion, and to create a sense of community. Slavish adherence to the letter of the law was not required. Rather, they should 'be careful' to take the text as a guide and a model for their conduct and the running of their state or community.[36] This conclusion will be amplified in the final section of the chapter, in which we shall look at examples of torah concerned with three different areas of life.

---

30 McKeating, 'Adultery'.
31 LeFebvre, *Collections*; Kratz, 'Temple'. See below, pp. 135–6.
32 Patrick, *Law*, pp. 200–2; LeFebvre, *Collections*, pp. 55–95.
33 Watts, *Ritual*, pp. 193–217.
34 LeFebvre, *Collections*, pp. 103–22; see below, pp. 126–7.
35 Jackson, 'Ideas of law', pp. 189–96.
36 Fitzpatrick-McKinley argues in a similar way (*Transformation*, pp. 113–45).

Torah and life: the teaching viewed thematically

The Torah covers a very wide range of subjects. Some are confined to certain contexts and types of tradition. For example, the ritual implications of childbirth are dealt with only in Leviticus 12. For the study of these it is best to use the commentaries on individual books. But there are certain subjects that are widespread in different parts of the Torah and different streams of tradition, and it is a few of these that I intend to examine in this section. They include, among others:[37] honour due to parents; release of slaves and permanent slavery; reparation for damage or loss of property; appointments and duties of judges; duty of witnesses in court; perversion of justice; idolatry; sorcery and divination; blasphemy; desecration of sacred things; sacred dues, including firstborn animals, firstfruits and tithes; sacred times (see below); honouring the Sabbath day; adultery and illicit intercourse; murder and manslaughter (see below); treatment of the poor and defenceless (see below); remission of debts and prohibition of interest (see below); food laws, concerning clean and unclean animals, blood, fat and animals dying of disease or attack by wild beasts.

Our exegetical samples cover subjects from three different areas: civil law, social morality and religious practice.

Homicide

The age-old custom, which still exists in many parts of the world, and is referred to on several occasions in the Hebrew Bible (for example 2 Sam. 3.27), was that when someone was responsible for another person's death, a member of the victim's family had to take the life of the person seen as the killer, or even some other member of the family if the culprit was not available, as in 2 Samuel 21.1–9. This applied regardless of whether the killing was deliberate murder or some form of manslaughter or accident (in 2 Sam. 3 the original killing had been in battle). However, in most places where this custom exists the victim's family may accept monetary compensation instead of demanding a death. All the legal texts on the subject of homicide in the Torah accept the custom of family vengeance as valid, but it was clearly felt by the Torah teachers that it would be unjust if no distinction were made between deliberate murder and unintentional homicide: there should be refuge for the killer from the avenger if the killing had been unintentional. The old custom was that asylum was at God's altar (see 1 Kings 2.28; Exod. 21.14). The removal of altars up and down the country called for by Deuteronomy involved setting aside specific places for asylum (Deut. 19.1–3). All the texts also imply that only the killer should die, and Deuteronomy 24.16 makes this explicit.

---

37 I follow here the outlines of the useful classification in the long unobtainable book by Charles Foster Kent, *Israel's Laws*, pp. vii–xxvii.

The most comprehensive text on the subject is Numbers 35.9–34. The Decalogue commandment at Exodus 20.13/Deuteronomy 5.17 simply forbids murder, without defining it, but Exodus 21.12–14 and Deuteronomy 19.1–13 address the issue of intention and asylum. Numbers, however, also raises other issues. Compare also Joshua 20, which is close to the law in Numbers, but not quite the same.

Numbers 35.9-34

This text begins (vv. 9–15), like Deuteronomy 19.1–13, by mandating, in the plural imperative form, the setting aside of 'cities of refuge' for unintentional homicides.

A series of casuistic clauses then explains how homicide should be dealt with. Verses 16–21 deal with the deliberate murderer, and verses 22–28 with the unintentional killer. In each case, as with legal texts generally in the Torah, they are defined not in an abstract way, but through a small selection of what Jackson calls 'narrative images' that give common examples of what is intended, all in sets of three (see above, p. 56).

In verses 16–18 it is striking with a lethal weapon that defines murder, but even this is not defined generally, but with three specific examples. These are narrative images of murder, of what is naturally understood as deliberate killing. The second set of three examples in verses 20–21 are cases where a weapon held in the hand is not used: pushing, throwing something or striking with the bare hands. But in these cases it appears that it has to be shown that there was intent to kill: the terms 'hatred' and 'enmity' point to motive, and 'lying in wait' is a simple pointer to intent.[38] The 'avenger of blood', that is, the responsible family member, may kill the murderer whenever he comes across him (v. 19). The Numbers text, alone among the three texts on the subject, provides for a formal trial (vv. 12, 24–25), but only where the homicide claims asylum and only if he does not venture outside the city of asylum (vv. 26–28): otherwise the avenger has free rein.

Verses 22–23 define unintentional manslaughter mainly by cases similar to those in verses 20–21, but with repeated negatives: no hatred, no previous enmity, no lying in wait; motive and intent are absent, and this is what distinguishes them. No account is taken of degrees of negligence in cases of accident.

The issues are to be settled by a trial (v. 24) before 'the assembly' (*'edah*); normally in Numbers this means the assembly for the worship of YHWH. The unique feature of this law is that it provides for an amnesty on the death of the high priest (vv. 25, 28), on which the manslayer may return home. This appears to be quite as arbitrary as any features of old customary law, and is the most obviously idealistic feature. It may be related to the priestly concern for the pollution of the land by bloodshed in verses 33–34,

---

38 The translation is not certain.

though this is in what appears to be an appendix to the law, which is at first rounded off by verse 29, recommending its eternal validity. This is a very common sentence in the priestly ritual instructions, and this is the only place where it is applied to a civil law. We may here detect a concern to give the civil law the same authority as the ritual law.

Two matters are raised in the appendix. First, the concern that no one should be put to death on the evidence of a single witness (v. 30); see also Deuteronomy 17.6; 19.15. Ancient courts were unable to handle circumstantial evidence. Everything had to be established on the word of witnesses, and clearly there was a great danger that a single witness might give false evidence because of hatred of the accused, or by being suborned.

Second, verses 31–34 rule out the acceptance of financial compensation in place of either death for the murderer or, for the unintentional manslayer, residence in the city of refuge until the death of the high priest. It could obviously be unjust, in that it was at the discretion of the victim's family, and a culprit from a wealthy family might be able to escape death more easily than a poor one (and the power of the wealthy may have made this rule another that was more ideal than practical). But the reason given here is quite different: that bloodshed pollutes the land, and can only be atoned by blood. This reflects a similar idea to that in Genesis 9.6. It may be that the death of the high priest is thought of as an appropriate atoning death.

Behaviour towards the poor and marginalized

Ancient Israel was an unequal society in which poverty was commonplace, and in which class divisions became more severe as time went on.[39] A substantial part of the non-ritual teaching in the Torah addresses this problem. This includes the proposal of national systems to alleviate indebtedness and relieve inequality: see Leviticus 25.8–17, for a restoration of traditional property relations every 50 years, and Deuteronomy 15.1–3, for a cancellation[40] of debts every seven years. These are inconsistent with each other, and would probably have been ineffective if they were ever implemented.[41] Much more widespread, and with a better chance of making a difference, is the teaching of generosity towards poor people and fair and equal treatment of those on the margins of society: traditionally widows, fatherless children (not 'orphans', which in English normally means children who have lost both parents), and resident aliens.

It is significant that both the passages just referred to go on to urge generous treatment of those who have become impoverished or indebted and cannot be immediately helped by the systems proposed (Lev. 25.35–43;

39 See Houston, *Contending*, pp. 18–51.

40 Houston, *Contending*, pp. 181–2 and literature cited there.

41 The Deuteronomic release of debts was in force in Judah around the turn of the eras, but a legal device was invented to nullify its effect.

Deut. 15.7–11). No legal system can ensure justice unless individuals and the community as a whole are sincerely committed to act justly. To encourage a commitment to justice is one function of the kind of moral education that the Torah offers. The Torah, it should be said, does not envisage a radical change in social relationships. 'The poor will never cease out of the land' (Deut. 15.11). The jubilee law assumes a classless society exists, but does not offer a practical way of achieving it.[42] At the same time, the Torah does imply that in principle Israelites are equal: they are all 'brothers', to use the gendered language of the text.[43] Neither they nor resident aliens are to be used as mere sources of profit, and they should be treated with dignity.

Deuteronomy 24.6, 10–15, 17–22

These ideas, with all their tensions and contradictions, can be illustrated from the series of exhortations in Deuteronomy 24. These deal with lending on security (vv. 6, 10–13), the payment of wages (vv. 14–15), the treatment of marginal persons (v. 17), and harvest leavings (vv. 18–22). The teaching given here is similar to that in other collections. It is a good sample of the Torah's teaching on the subject.

Handling pledges: Deuteronomy 24.6, 10–13

There would have been no significant demand for commercial loans in the quite undeveloped agrarian economy of ancient Israel and Judah. Lending is usually treated in the Torah as a charitable act for the relief of poverty. But some lenders may have had less altruistic motives. It is clear from Nehemiah's account of the complaints of Jewish peasants in Nehemiah 5.1–5[44] that a common result of borrowing was to find one's children or one's land in the hands of the creditor. This happened because they were taken as security, or seized when the debtor could not pay. It is quite likely that some creditors lent precisely in order to gain servants or property when this happened, or more generally to gain dependants or to increase their power over dependants they already had.

Now, the teaching in Deuteronomy 24.6, 10–13 does not appear to refer to lending on the security of persons or land, and neither does that in Exodus 22.25–27, nor Leviticus 25.35–38.[45] Baker argues that this is because taking productive assets in pledge, which the creditor could use for gain, was equivalent to charging interest, which all these bodies of teaching forbid

42 Houston, *Contending*, pp. 190–203, esp. p. 199.
43 See Houston, *Biblical Challenge*, pp. 74–91.
44 Compare also, for example, 2 Kings 4.1; Proverbs 22.7.
45 But see Houston, *Contending*, p. 111.

(Exod. 22.25; Lev. 25.36; Deut. 23.19–20).[46] But in that case it is surprising that none of them directly forbid the practice; also it would not apply to the raising of a mortgage, in which the pledge remains with the debtor unless he or she defaults. The presence of teaching on 'Hebrew slaves' (Exod. 21.2–11; Deut. 15.12–18) suggests, on the contrary, that they accepted that lending on security of the person was a fact of life; while the scheme of Leviticus 25.8–17 may be understood as a transformation of the use of land as security. No other item that a poor person was likely to possess could cover a substantial loan; yet this teaching refers to millstones and garments. But a small item, if it was important to the borrower, might serve to guarantee the debt, as with Judah's staff and seal in Genesis 38.[47]

What is urged by the teaching here, in that case? First, to do nothing which might endanger life: do not take a millstone in pledge, 'because it means taking a life [in fact, many lives] in pledge' (v. 6). Second, to respect the dignity of the debtor: rather than marching into the house to seize a pledge, and taking their pick of what they could find, they must wait outside for the debtor to bring something to them (vv. 10–11). And finally, to have regard for the debtor's comfort: a poor person may have a single wrap used as a cloak during the day and a blanket at night; return it at night. This is a version of a text in C (Exod. 22.26–27). But it transforms the motivation from the negative, the poor person's cry to God, to the positive, blessing. To respect the life, comfort and dignity of debtors is to treat them as fellow human beings with the same needs as oneself, fellow members of the community. Although the word 'brother' is not used here as it is in other places, the meaning is the same: treat the person who is temporarily in your power as you would a member of your own family.

Wages: Deuteronomy 24.14–15; see also Leviticus 19.13

It is essentially the same message here. Wage labourers are to be paid promptly, since they have only their wages to depend on for their lives. We do not know the extent of wage labour in the ancient Israelite economy: most work would have been done either by family members or by temporary or permanent slaves. Wage labour will have developed along with the economy, and payment would, to begin with, have been in kind, such as grain.

This time the reference to the divine guardian is negative. A complaint will lead to your being marked as an offender against God. Again, although modern societies have laws about these matters, this is not a law in our sense. The only enforcement is at the hands of heaven.

---

46 Baker, *Tight Fists*, p. 274.
47 Houston, *Contending*, pp. 111–12.

Justice for marginal persons: Deuteronomy 24.17–18; see also Exodus 22.21–24; 23.9; Leviticus 19.33–34; 24.22

The Torah refers repeatedly to a trio of groups of vulnerable persons without a secure stake in society: widows and fatherless children, who were without a man to protect them in a society where in general only men took part in public affairs, and resident aliens who had no land or family in the country. The wives and children of men who had died were particularly vulnerable where the old extended family structure was breaking down, as was the case in the cities under the monarchy and in the Second Temple period.[48] At one time it may be that the term *ger*, 'resident stranger', referred to anyone living in an area where they did not have their roots; but in Deuteronomy (and the rest of the Torah) the word is understood as meaning a non-Israelite permanently settled in Israel's land (see Deut. 14.21).

The text warns against taking advantage of the vulnerability of such people, either in the courts or (again) by the seizure of security. The motivation added is to 'remember that you were a slave in Egypt': this occurs five times in Deuteronomy, at 5.15 and 15.15, where slavery is the topic; and in 16.12, as well as in 24.18, 22, where it is not. However, in all these cases the reader is being urged to be generous to slaves or to marginal persons. It is appropriate for members of a nation that acknowledges the generosity of God in their deliverance from oppression as an ethnic minority subject to forced labour to be generous in their turn to those whom they could so easily oppress. The teaching in C warning against the oppression of resident aliens (Exod. 22.21; 23.9) says, appropriately, 'remember you were an *alien* in Egypt'; but in Deuteronomy 'remember that you were a slave in Egypt' has become a standard expression.

Gleaning: Deuteronomy 24.19–22; see also Leviticus 19.9–10; 23.22

Like the others, these are not enforceable laws, but moral advice. They are reminders to the fortunate beneficiaries of YHWH's blessing that there are others who are in need of that blessing, a position they were once in themselves, and they have no right to keep it to themselves. Gleaning was probably an old custom: the book of Ruth suggests this. The Torah writers see it as a custom which is good and right to maintain, rather than making an innovation.

Conclusion

This teaching as a whole is addressed to those who have land, wealth and authority. It commands them in the name of YHWH to use those advan-

---

48 Houston, *Contending*, pp. 23–4.

tages with generosity and compassion and attempts to generate a sense of community with those who lack them. The need for such commands is in itself an admission that 'the poor will not cease out of the land', and they do not set forth any radical or permanent change in the distribution of wealth and power, rather urging those who listen to them to use them to benefit those who lack them. But at the same time they are told to treat the beneficiaries not as a lower class of beings who may be graciously allowed the crumbs that fall from the table of the well-to-do, but as fellow members of YHWH's people who have as much right to the divine bounty as oneself. This is the point that distinguishes biblical ethics from otherwise very similar exhortations to charity in other bodies of literature and other cultures, and has shaped the ethos of all three religions that stem from the Hebrew Bible (but see below, p. 199).

The feasts of YHWH

Several passages in the Torah deal with the three main seasons of the year at which pilgrimage feasts are to be held, that is, occasions on which people from a wide area attend a temple to hold a celebration in honour of God. The most elaborate presentation is in Leviticus 23, which, when it comes to the autumn season, sets out the three separate observances in the seventh month now known as Rosh Hashanah (Jewish New Year), the Day of Atonement and the feast of Tabernacles or Booths. Parallel with this is the schedule of sacrificial offerings in Numbers 28—29. A simpler calendar is offered in Deuteronomy 16, with the combined observance of Passover and Unleavened Bread in the spring, Weeks (Pentecost or Shavuot) in the early summer, and Booths or Tabernacles (Sukkot) in the early autumn. Deuteronomy, as always, requires that all three festivals should take place at the single place chosen by YHWH. The simplest of all, which we shall look at here, is that found in C at Exodus 23.14–19; its contents are substantially repeated in Exodus 34.18–23.

Exodus 23.14–19

The text is mainly in the second-person commandment form, with two sentences, verses 17 and 18b, in the third person. The list of festivals in verses 15–16 is bracketed by the provision, repeated, that a pilgrimage festival is to take place three times a year (vv. 14 and 17). Verses 18–19 then give as a kind of appendix four specific instructions which are probably connected with the practice of festival pilgrimage, and may each be connected with a specific festival. Only the first festival is given a date. The others are connected with points in the agricultural year. But the festival of Unleavened Bread is not a harvest festival of any kind. You may still read that it is a festival of the barley harvest, but this was exploded long ago. It is too early in the year for that. The calendar in Leviticus 23 is much more specific about dates, though even here there is none for Weeks. This calendar does not specify, unlike Deuteronomy, that the celebration must take place at a specific sanctuary. During most of the monarchic period, there were sanctuaries of YHWH up and down the land.

Unleavened Bread

It is a surprise that in verse 15 Passover is not mentioned, but only the feast of Unleavened Bread. The date of the month Abib is given (March/April), and it is mentioned that it was in this month that 'you came out of Egypt'. The same information in Deuteronomy 16.1 supports the festival of Passover, with which Unleavened Bread is there combined; in Leviticus 23.4–8 the one immediately follows the other. It is widely accepted that originally the Passover was not celebrated at the sanctuary as required in Leviticus and Deuteronomy, but at home, as described in Exodus 12, and hence would not count as a pilgrimage feast.[49] It is difficult to account for the omission of Passover on the basis of the present text of Exodus. The clause 'as I have commanded you' would refer back to Exodus 12.17 and 13.6. But Passover is commanded as a pilgrimage feast too (Exod. 12.14). However, Exodus 12.24 gives the impression of commanding the home observance, with the blood smeared on the doorposts, as a permanent statute.

But is Passover actually omitted? Verse 18 gives two instructions that appear to be general, but while the first has particular relevance, at least symbolically, to the feast of Unleavened Bread, the second may possibly be rooted in the Passover, for there are instructions that none of the Passover lamb may be left till morning (Exod. 12.10; Deut. 16.4). There are deadlines for the consumption of other sacrifices, though mostly not so strict; see Leviticus 7.15, 16–18; 19.5–8. As the eating of fat was forbidden (Lev. 7.22–25), the fat would be burnt on the altar.

See Leviticus 3 for sacrifices eaten by the worshippers. This was normal: 'burnt offerings' entirely burnt on the altar (Lev. 1) were less frequent.

Why does this festival alone carry the warning, 'you shall not appear before me empty-handed'? Probably because it was too early in the year for the harvest. At the other festivals, it was natural to offer a sample of the good things with which God had blessed one. But in Abib, those good things were still in the making: the worshipper must be specifically told to bring an offering, however hard that might be.

---

49 See Propp, *Exodus 1—18*, pp. 428–61.

Harvest and Ingathering

The two agricultural festivals in verse 16 are quite straightforward, but they are given different names from those given in Leviticus and Deuteronomy and still current today. 'Harvest' (Weeks or Shavuot), as its name suggests, celebrates the completion of the wheat harvest, following the barley harvest. The implication is that the feast will be observed whenever this occurs in any particular place according to local conditions (roughly May to June).

As it scarcely ever rains in summer in the land of Israel, the harvest could be left out of doors while the threshing was completed (cf. Ruth 3), and brought in at much the same time in early autumn as the vintage and the olive harvest. 'Ingathering', corresponding to Tabernacles or Booths (Sukkot), then celebrates the blessings of the entire agricultural cycle. 'At the outgoing of the year' implies that the year begins in autumn in this calendar, as the Jewish year does today. The priestly calendar used in Exodus 12 and Leviticus 23, however, begins in spring.

In verse 17, when the theme of the three occasions is repeated, the point is added that it is the males who are required to attend. Yet it was normal for whole families to do so, as in 1 Samuel 1, where Elkanah and his family all attend the feast once a year at Shiloh; and Deuteronomy emphasizes that 'you, your son, your daughter, your male and female slave, and the Levite, the alien and the fatherless child and widow who are in your gates shall rejoice in your festival' (Deut. 16.14; cf. v. 11). But Deuteronomy itself repeats the instruction of Exodus 23.17 in identical wording (Deut. 16.16). Attendance is a duty for adult males, while others, perhaps, are invited and encouraged to come. However, Deuteronomy 31.12–13 makes attendance a requirement for the whole community every seven years at Tabernacles.

Appendices

If verse 18 recalls especially Unleavened Bread and Passover, can verse 19 be connected with Harvest and Ingathering? The connection of the offering of firstfruits with Harvest is obvious. Less so, and a classic teaser, is the final clause 'you shall not boil a kid in its mother's milk'. It was made the basis quite early in Judaism of the total separation of meat and milk in the kosher kitchen. In Deuteronomy 14.21 it is part of the dietary code. But here it is a festal prohibition. The offering of the firstborn (Exod. 13.11–16) would naturally have taken place at a festival (cf. Deut. 15.20), if the eighth-day rule in Exodus 22.30 was not rigidly observed; Leviticus 22.27 seems to be permissive rather than mandatory. The temptation would have been to cook the sacrificed kid in milk from the same flock and so possibly from its own mother. The objection is perhaps a humanitarian one, against using what should have sustained the animal in life to enjoy it in death.[50]

---

50 See discussions in Propp, *Exodus 19—40*, pp. 284–86; and Houston, 'Foods, Clean and Unclean', pp. 333–4.

Further reading

There are relatively few accessible works on Pentateuchal 'law' in general. The best introduction is still Patrick, *Old Testament Law*. See also Blenkinsopp, *Wisdom and Law*, and Crüsemann, *The Torah*. Unfortunately the translation of this important work (published in German in 1992) is very poor and makes some parts difficult to understand. Knight, *Law*, treats the actual practice of law in different contexts.

On law as an integral part of the Pentateuch: Watts, *Reading Law* and *Ritual and Rhetoric*.

For the individual blocks, the best resource is usually the commentaries, especially:

* for the Decalogue: Childs, *Exodus*
* for C: Childs, *Exodus*; Houtman, *Exodus*
* for P: above all Milgrom, *Leviticus 1—16*; Propp, *Exodus 19—40*; Levine, *Numbers*
* for H: Milgrom, *Leviticus 17—22* and *Leviticus 23—27*
* for Deuteronomy: Driver, *Deuteronomy*; McConville: *Deuteronomy*; Nelson: *Deuteronomy*.

On the Decalogue, see among a vast literature von Rad, *Old Testament Theology*, vol. 1, pp. 190–219; Miller, *The Ten Commandments*; Brown (ed.), *The Ten Commandments*, on the history of interpretation, and contemporary interpretations.

For interpretations of the symbolism of the Dwelling, its structure and its materials, see Haran, *Temples*, pp. 149–88, 246–59; Jenson, *Graded Holiness*, pp. 89–114.

On Deuteronomy: Clements, *Deuteronomy*; Weinfeld, *Deuteronomy*.

On the literary forms: Alt, 'The Origins of Israelite Law'. For a critique, see Patrick, pp. 19–24.

On the nature and function of law in ancient Israel and its neighbours and in the Pentateuch: LeFebvre, *Collections*; Fitzpatrick-McKinley, *Transformation*; McKeating, 'Adultery'; Jackson, 'Ideas of law'.

On the ethics of rich–poor relations, Baker in *Tight Fists* gives a comprehensive exegesis of all the Torah teaching in any way related to this subject, while Houston, *Contending for Justice*, pp. 105–18, 169–203, has a more selective treatment with reflections on ideology and theology.

4

Covenant-making in the Pentateuch

The covenants in the Pentateuch

In Chapter 2 we defined covenant-making as a motif that carries the theme of commitment: of God to God's creatures, and more specifically to Israel, and of Israel to God (above, p. 30). Because the making of a covenant is an action, it can be a part of a story; and because it expresses obligation, it can appropriately draw into the ambit of the story both the promises made by Israel's God, which he proceeds to fulfil, and the obligations which he imposes on Israel. I propose that the series of covenants between God and human beings which occur throughout the narrative is not simply one more motif, but the key feature of the Pentateuchal text which brings narrative and law, and the promises of God and their fulfilment, into active relation.

One of the functions of a story is to draw its hearers into its world and thus to make its world a reality in the lives of the hearers. Still more is this so when the story is understood as the hearers' own story. In the Torah it is the world of the covenant, of God's commitment to Israel drawing forth Israel's answering commitment to God. The commitment of the people of Israel to YHWH binds their descendants for ever. Deuteronomy emphasizes this: 'It is not with you only that I am making this covenant.'

To pick out only the most significant of the episodes, we have:

- the covenant given by God to Noah as the representative of all creatures on earth in Genesis 9, promising never to destroy the earth in a flood again;
- two covenants given by God to Abraham as the ancestor of Israel, in Genesis 15 and 17 – these enshrine the promises to Israel, above all 'to be God to you and to your offspring after you' (Gen. 17.7);
- the covenant made by Israel with YHWH at Sinai in Exodus 24, in which they in turn accept what it means to have YHWH as their God;
- the covenant made by YHWH with Israel in Exodus 34 after they have broken the previous one by setting up the golden calf (Moses reminds the people of these covenants in Deuteronomy 5 and 10);
- the covenant made between Israel and YHWH through Moses in Moab according to Deuteronomy. In Deuteronomy 26.17–19, though the word covenant is not used, what Moses describes as happening may be viewed

as the making of a covenant; 29.1 sums up the commandments for Israel's life in the promised land, which Moses has given in chapters 12—26 as 'the words of the covenant ...'; and in a renewed address in chapter 29 Moses makes repeated reference to 'this covenant' to which the Israelites have committed themselves.

The meaning of the word[1]

What was a covenant? Sometimes modern theologians use it in the sense of a committed relationship. But in the Old Testament the word (*berit* in Hebrew) invariably refers to a particular solemn undertaking made, or obligation imposed, at a point in time. But because it affects all subsequent relations between the parties to it, and it may be fulfilled or broken by an action at any time, it can appear to refer to the relationship as well as to the obligation.

The word is used quite often in describing transactions between human beings, including especially international treaties.

Look at the narratives in the three passages, Genesis 21.25–33, Joshua 9.3–15 and Ezekiel 17.11–21, and decide what the common features are that result in the word 'covenant' being used in each case. (Depending on the translation you are using, the Joshua and Ezekiel passages may have 'treaty' rather than 'covenant', but it is the same word in the Hebrew.)

I would suggest that the following points are essential to any definition:

- There are always at least *two parties* involved. In some cases only one party makes an explicit commitment, but normally they do so in the presence of the other, and the phrase 'make a covenant' is usually followed by 'with'. On the other hand, it covers a wider range of actions than would be covered by words such as 'agreement' or 'pact'.
- Making a covenant implies the taking on of a *commitment* by one side or the other, or both. It is not necessarily done voluntarily. This is clear from Ezekiel 17, where Nebuchadrezzar imposes the treaty on Zedekiah; and also in Deuteronomy 5.2, 6, where Moses says 'YHWH made a covenant with us at Horeb ... saying, "I am YHWH your God" ...', etc. Here, the covenant simply consists of the imposition of the ten commandments on Israel: it is in no way an 'agreement'. Covenants can be classified according to whether

---

1 See Nicholson, *God and His People*, pp. 87–109.

(a) The parties are equal and each accepts obligations to the other: for example Genesis 21.25–33; 2 Kings 5.12.

(b) The superior party accepts an obligation to the inferior, probably normally assuming good conduct on the part of the inferior: for example Joshua 9.3–15; Genesis 17.2–8 (see below).

(c) The superior party imposes obligations on the inferior: for example Ezekiel 17.11–21; Exodus 24.3–8; Deuteronomy 5.2–22 (see below). In the context in Exodus there is an implication that the superior party, YHWH, also has or takes on a commitment to the inferior, Israel. Thus types (b) and (c) may be combined in the form of a conditional promise.

(d) A third party imposes obligations on one or both of the parties, defining their relationship: for example 2 Kings 11.17; Hosea 2.18; Deuteronomy 29.10–15 – here Moses is the third party, who 'makes the covenant' (v. 14) between YHWH and Israel.

- It is always a *solemn* commitment, that is, one made with formality and sometimes with ritual. Often the taking of an oath is mentioned, and the records of international treaties (see below) show that this was the normal way in which they were effected. Whether an oath was of the essence of a covenant in all cases is not clear. In Exodus 6.8 YHWH says, 'I shall bring you into the land which *I raised my hand* to give to Abraham, Isaac and Jacob.' Here the picture of a person swearing an oath is used to express a reference to Genesis 17, etc. In Genesis 15 and Exodus 24, and again in Jeremiah 34, rituals are described. The ritual in Jeremiah 34 is essentially the same as that in Genesis 15. This ritual is really an acted oath, implying 'if I do not keep my word, may I be cut in half like this animal'.

- No mention is ever made of a limitation of time on the covenant, neither in the Bible nor in the treaties. Indeed, the phrase 'an eternal (or 'indefinite') covenant' often appears (for example Gen. 17.7; Exod. 31.16). It would seem that the commitment taken on in a covenant was normally for the indefinite future.

The commonest phrase in Hebrew in which the word *berit* appears is usually translated 'made a covenant'. Literally it is 'cut a covenant', *karat berit*. This is often thought to refer to the ritual described in Genesis 15 and Jeremiah 34. Writers in the Pentateuch in the priestly tradition avoid the phrase and speak instead of 'establishing' or 'giving' a covenant.[2]

Putting these points together, we arrive at the following definition: 'covenant' is a word for *an act of commitment made by solemn acts or words on the part of one or both of two parties in the presence of them both, defining their future rights and duties towards one another.*

The motif of covenant-making in the Pentateuchal text does not normally stand on its own, but is the highest and usually the most significant point

---

2 For a discussion of the reasons, see Day, 'Why does God'.

of a range of expressions of commitment. God makes a covenant in Genesis 15.18 to give Abram's descendants the land where he is now living; and in 17.1–8 he makes another, including this promise and that of many descendants, that Abraham will be 'the father of many nations'. But these repeat promises already made and to be repeated. In Genesis 22.16–18 the promise is confirmed by oath. This may not imply much practical difference, since a covenant was normally effected by oath.

On the other hand, places such as Exodus 4.31 and 14.31, where the Israelites express faith in YHWH, lead naturally towards their acceptance of the obligations of the covenant of Sinai.

Cultural models

Every culture has some such institution of solemn commitment: we have, for example, the vows of marriage, or oaths sworn before a notary. In the world of the Bible it is clear that while making a covenant was not an everyday affair, it was a regular custom in particular circumstances, so that everyone would be familiar with it. Two examples are useful in throwing light on our subject, one from family affairs and one from the field of international relations.

Two passages in the Old Testament refer to marriage as a covenant: Malachi 2.14 and probably Proverbs 2.17. Malachi says, 'YHWH is witness between you and the wife of your youth, whom you have been unfaithful to, though she is your companion and *your wife by covenant*.' Proverbs refers to 'a woman who has abandoned the companion of her youth, and *forgotten the covenant of her God*' (or 'her covenant with God').[3] Both these verses appear to refer to a covenant of marriage, to which both wife and husband were parties.[4] However, the written Jewish marriage contracts that we have from ancient times show that the bride was not even herself a party to the contract, which was mainly concerned with financial issues, and was not sworn.[5] It may well be that Malachi and the Proverbs writer call marriage a covenant simply because of its solemn nature.

Far more important in the discussion of covenants in the Pentateuch are the international treaties whose texts we have from the ancient Near East. Most of these are vassal treaties: that is, they are treaties whereby a powerful king binds to his subjection a king whom he has conquered, or installed in a conquered country. It would have been a treaty of this kind between Nebuchadrezzar and Zedekiah that is referred to by Ezekiel. The terms are invariably confirmed by oath, backed up by blessings on the vassal for observing them and curses for breaking them. It is quite clear that the vassal

---

3 Waltke, *Proverbs 1—15*, p. 215.

4 Fox, *Proverbs 1—9*, pp. 120–21. Waltke, *Proverbs 1—15*, pp. 215, 231, gives a different interpretation.

5 Collins, 'Marriage', pp. 107–15.

had to take an oath to observe the terms imposed on him, and in some cases it may be that his lord also regarded himself as bound by oath. The Assyrian treaty texts suggest some acted curses: 'As this chariot is spattered with blood ... just so in the midst of battle with your enemies may they spatter your chariot with your own blood.'[6]

Loyalty oaths exacted by a monarch from his own subjects had similar forms to vassal treaties between kings. The imposition of a loyalty oath would be expected after a coup or irregular succession, in Israel and Judah as well as elsewhere. Such an oath is very likely referred to in 2 Kings 11.17, after Jehoiada's coup in Judah against Athaliah in favour of Joash – the Deuteronomistic editor has added words to make it conform to the pattern of a covenant with YHWH.

Many scholars believe that the treaty texts, or the very similar loyalty oaths, are the key to understanding the covenant texts in the Pentateuch, and we shall return to this later. However, they give us access to just one kind of covenant from that age that may have been well known in ruling and educated circles. We should be cautious in assuming that they must have been the model which is followed in our texts.[7]

Covenant promises by God in the Pentateuch[8]

The 'Covenant with Noah'

The very first reference to a covenant in the Pentateuch is in Genesis 6.18, where God, in telling Noah of the coming Flood, adds, 'But I will establish my covenant with you.' Some would translate 'I will *confirm* my covenant with you', and argue that this refers to an existing covenant, which of course has not been mentioned. It is supposed to be implicit in creation.[9] But the same phrase is used in Exodus 6.4, where it is difficult to interpret in any other way than 'I established my covenant with them'. Moreover, the idea of an implicit covenant is nonsense. Commitment may be implicit, but the whole point of a covenant is to make commitment explicit and guaranteed.

Along with the vast majority of scholars, therefore, I take it that this verse looks forward to the passage in Genesis 9.8–17, where God announces the establishment (clearly) of a covenant with every living creature. The terms of the covenant are that 'never again will all creatures be cut off by the waters of the flood, and never again will there be a flood to destroy the earth' (v. 11). This is an unconditional commitment: nothing is demanded in return of Noah and the future human race whom he represents. God

---

6 D. J. Wiseman, 'The Vassal Treaties of Esarhaddon, *Iraq* 20 (1958), lines *c.* 612–15 (McCarthy, *Treaty and Covenant*, p. 204).

7 Cf. Nicholson, *God and His People*, pp. 78–81.

8 See McKenzie, *Covenant*, pp. 46–51.

9 Dumbrell, *Creation*, pp. 11–43; see esp. pp. 26, 41–3.

has given Noah and his sons commands already (Gen. 9.1–7), but they are not conditions of the covenant. The bow in the clouds will remind God of the covenant. There is no oath or ritual: God simply announces that he is making a covenant. This seems appropriate in the case of God, whose word alone can be trusted.

The implication of the Flood story, in which creation is to a large extent reversed, is that creation is not permanent: the order and fertility of the universe stand in danger of being destroyed. But the point of the celebration of creation in ancient religion is to assure people of the stability and security of the order in which they live. Can creation be destroyed at the mere whim of the creator? God's covenant with creation in Genesis 9 emphasizes that on the one hand the order of creation cannot be relied on as something simply natural; it depends on the will of God. But on the other hand, it does not depend on the *whim* of an arbitrary God. Creation continues because God has promised that it shall – not because it has to, but not just because God feels like it. In other words, the use of the covenant motif here puts what concerns creatures in the province of the grace of God, that is, within God's deliberate and merciful, but not arbitrary, choice.

Covenants with Abraham

Genesis offers us two accounts of God/YHWH making a covenant with Abraham, in Genesis 15 and 17.[10] The covenant in chapter 15 is limited to the subject of the land, although earlier in the chapter Abram accepts an uncovenanted assurance from YHWH that he will have innumerable descendants. That in chapter 17 is much more comprehensive, embracing not only these two matters, but more broadly 'to be God to you and to your descendants after you' (Gen. 17.7). The covenant of chapter 17 is simply announced in the manner of that in chapter 9; but in chapter 15 YHWH subjects himself to a covenant ritual, 'passing between the parts' of the animals that Abram cuts in half.

Genesis 15

The covenanted promise of Genesis 15.18 is a response to Abram's expression of doubt, 'How I am to know that I shall possess [the land]?'. Obviously, the 'smoking pot' and the 'flaming torch' which pass between the animal parts are symbols of the presence of God. And they pass between the sundered halves in exactly the same way as the people of Jerusalem pass between the halves of a calf in Jeremiah 34.18, and for the same reason: in solemn confirmation of YHWH's word. But here there is no question of a

---

10 For source criticism, Genesis 17 is unquestionably a central text of the priestly strand. Genesis 15 is definitely not P, but beyond that there is considerable dispute.

literal acted self-curse or oath. An oath is an appeal to a higher power, and God has no higher power to appeal to. Here is God graciously undergoing the form of a human ritual in order to offer a visual assurance of the promise. The promise already given three times is here established on as firm a foundation as can be found.

As for the content of the promise, we may make a similar point to that about the covenant with Noah. It was (and is) customary for peoples to believe that there was a natural connection between themselves and the land they lived in, that they had a right to it, either because they had supposedly always lived there, or because they had conquered it. In this narrative, however, Israel's relationship to their land is summed up in the figure of Abraham, who was a resident alien in it and owned not as much as a single square foot of it. The footing of his descendants in the land depends solely on this promise of God, on God's gracious but not arbitrary will, dramatized in this powerful acted parable of promise. Readers in a later time, in exile or uncertain of their hold on the land, would take the covenanted word of God here as the assurance of their ultimate possession. This passage and others with a similar message have often been used to justify violent conquest, a problem we shall need to confront later (below, pp. 198–9). It is an unanswerable argument for taking something to say 'God gave it to me'!

Genesis 17

The address of YHWH to Abraham in Genesis 17 is of even greater significance in the Pentateuch as a whole. It points forward to a series of further passages developing the relationship between YHWH and the Israelites, most obviously the address to Moses in Exodus 6.2–8;[11] and it lays stress on the formula 'I will be your/their God', which frames the promise of the land in verse 8. Genesis 17.1–8 brings together the promises of descendants (vv. 2–6), of land (v. 8) and 'to be your God' (vv. 7–8).

Although a covenant of promise, it is clearly not without conditions. There is in the first place the general admonition to Abraham, 'walk before me and be perfect' (v. 2). Then there is the paragraph, verses 9–14, imposing the obligation of circumcision on him and all his male descendants, as a 'sign of the covenant'. But this is not a term of the covenant in the same way as the Ten Commandments are terms of the covenant of Sinai. The flagrant breach of these leads to the annulment of the covenant as such. This is probably the significance of Moses' breaking of the tablets in Exodus 32.19. But if a male is not circumcised, '*that person* shall be cut off from his kindred; he has broken my covenant' (Gen. 17.14). The covenant itself still stands; it depends solely on YHWH's promise, not on human conduct.

---

11 In the diachronic study of the Pentateuch these are all broadly identifiable as part of the priestly strand, P or H.

What does the last and most all-embracing promise, 'to be your God', involve? Its significance can be unfolded by looking at the passages where it is repeated, often along with its correlative 'and you shall be my people'.[12] We may take three key ones from the Pentateuch: Exodus 6.7, Exodus 29.45–46, and Leviticus 26.12.

In Exodus 6.2–8 God speaks to Moses, announcing his name YHWH, which he does not use in Genesis 17, and telling him that he has remembered his covenant – evidently this one. He is to tell the Israelites that he will deliver them 'from under the burdens of the Egyptians ...' (v. 6), 'and I shall take you to be my people, and I shall be your God; and you shall know that I am YHWH your God, who delivers you from under the burdens of the Egyptians' (v. 7). Exodus 29.45–46 occur at the climax of the instructions to Moses for the building of the Dwelling: 'And I shall dwell in the midst of the Israelites, and I shall be their God; and they shall know that I am YHWH their God, who brought them out of the land of Egypt that I might dwell among them.' Leviticus 26.12 is at the climax of the blessings for obedience: 'And I shall walk among you, and I shall be your God, and you shall be my people. I am YHWH your God, who brought you out of the land of Egypt ...'

Thus we see what it means for YHWH to be Israel's God. First, that he delivers them from slavery in Egypt. This is not only the main point of the first passage, it is also referred to as the root of the relationship in all three. Second, that he dwells among them in a formal or cultic sense, in the Dwelling, where he is available to meet with them (Exod. 29.42–43). Third, that he blesses them and dwells among them in their everyday lives – 'I shall walk among you.' The promise of the land in the setting of this formula in Genesis 17.7–8 is repeated in Exodus 6.8, and its fulfilment is implied in Leviticus 26.

We can say of this promise what we said of the promise of the land. That YHWH is Israel's God is not because of any natural relationship between the two: as an example, the god of the Assyrians was Asshur, which is the same name as that of the country, the people and their first capital city: Asshur simply personifies or embodies Assyria in a mythological way. Quite differently, YHWH does not represent or embody Israel: rather, YHWH has chosen Israel. He could have chosen another nation. It was his sovereign and gracious, but not arbitrary, will to choose Israel.

Covenants of obedience to YHWH by Israel

Viewed in their contexts, the various accounts of covenant-making between YHWH and the Israelite people by the mediation of Moses offer a full picture of the mutual obligations between them.

---

12 See Rendtorff, *Covenant Formula*.

The covenant of Horeb: Deuteronomy 5

The simplest view of what is often referred to simply as 'the covenant' is that YHWH imposes the obligation on Israel of obedience to his commandments. This is undoubtedly the impression given by Deuteronomy 5.2, 22: 'YHWH our God made a covenant with us at Horeb ... YHWH spoke all these words [the Decalogue] to your assembly ... and added no more; and wrote them on two stone tablets and gave them to me.' The covenant consists of nothing else but the Decalogue.

The covenant of Sinai: Exodus 19—24

However, long before reaching that point, the consecutive reader of the Pentateuch has been given a somewhat different impression. The motif is foreshadowed in Exodus 19.3–8, when the people arrive before the mountain in the wilderness of Sinai, and Moses goes up to meet YHWH. The kernel of this passage is the conditional promise in verses 5–6a: 'If you seriously obey me and keep *my covenant*, then you shall be my possession among all peoples (for all the earth is mine), and you shall be a priestly kingdom and a holy nation.' The mutuality of the transaction is here concisely expressed.

But what is meant by 'my covenant', since at this point no covenant has been proposed? There is no content to it. All that can be said is that it is an imposed obligation in return for the promise. It seems natural in the context to take it as pointing forward to the conclusion of the covenant in Exodus 24.[13] Yet, YHWH requires and gains an answer even now, an assurance of the people's intent: 'All that YHWH has spoken we shall do' (Exod. 19.8). They repeat these words (very nearly) at 24.3 and 24.7. The difference in chapter 24 is that they have now heard what YHWH requires. Are they signing a blank cheque in chapter 19? Houtman makes the point that although they have not heard the detailed covenant terms, they are not unacquainted with the *kind* of thing that YHWH will ask for, and can be assured, because of his care for their welfare up to now, that whatever the conditions they will be for their good.[14]

YHWH's corresponding assurance is in two parts: 'you shall be my possession (or treasure) among all peoples'; 'you shall be a kingdom of priests and a holy nation'. The parallelism of the second phrase shows it should be understood as 'a priestly kingdom and a holy nation'. Both the nouns look forward to Israel's emergence as a state. The adjectives underline that this nation will be YHWH's special possession. It does not mean a nation that consists of priests or is ruled by priests, but one that is close to God as priests are close to God within a nation. The implication is that although in

13 Childs, *Exodus*, pp. 502–3.
14 Houtman, *Exodus*, vol. 2, p. 436.

chapter 24 (as in Deuteronomy 5) it is only the Israelites that seem to accept any obligations, the covenant is in fact two-sided. The two passages belong together. YHWH takes on himself the obligation to make Israel his possession and holy nation, in return for their obedience to his 'covenant', that is, his commandments.

This is the first context in which the idea of a covenant between YHWH and Israel appears, and reciprocity is of its essence – not, of course, equality.

The renewed covenant: Exodus 34

The same essential features, YHWH's commitment to the honour and well-being of Israel on the condition of their faithfulness to YHWH and observance of his commands, can also be traced in the other contexts where this motif is used. The announcement in Exodus 34.10, 'Behold, I make a covenant', is the response to Moses' humble plea for the people to be forgiven their gross apostasy and introduces YHWH's promise to 'work wonders before your people's eyes'. YHWH has already proclaimed himself a God of mercy and faithfulness as much as of vengeance. In the first place, then, this covenant is a promise.[15] But it is followed by warnings to avoid the idolatry of the peoples in whose land they are going to settle (vv. 11–16), and then by a selection of laws from earlier chapters. These are the conditions. At verse 27 YHWH tells Moses to write down 'these words', because they are the conditions of the covenant he is making.

The covenant of the plains of Moab

Again, the 'covenant of the plains of Moab' on the basis of the Deuteronomic law appears to be put into effect through the elaborately structured statement of Moses in Deuteronomy 26.17–19, which consists throughout of mutually corresponding commitments. The word *berit* is not used here, but declarations in the presence of the other party are of the essence of a covenant. Both parties make declarations which include commitments both by themselves and by the other party, and they are similar to those in Exodus 19. This appears to be a description, by Moses, of a ceremony of mutual declaration.

Commitment to commandments by covenant

The four main accounts of covenant-making between YHWH and Israel, different as they are, all have the effect of committing Israel to the observance of a body of divine commands.

---

15 See Nicholson, *God and His People*, p. 142.

Deuteronomy

The two accounts are perfectly clear in this regard. The Horeb covenant of Deuteronomy 5 consists of the Decalogue, and the Moab covenant of Deuteronomy 29 puts the Deuteronomic law of chapters 12—26 into effect.

Exodus 24.3-8

The examples in Exodus are more puzzling. Brief as it is, the account in chapter 24 is quite complicated. It includes the people's consent to 'the words of YHWH and the judgements (or statutes)', and a sacrificial ritual, in which the blood is splashed over the altar and the people, with the words, 'This is the blood of the covenant which YHWH has made with you in accordance with these words.' The symbolism of the blood here should be interpreted in line with its similar use in such ceremonies as the ordination of priests (Exod. 29.20; Lev. 8.23–24).[16] It marks the transition of Israel to become what YHWH had promised they would become in Exodus 19.5–6, YHWH's 'special possession' and 'holy nation'.[17] But only on condition that they obey 'these words'; therefore the blood marks a covenant 'in accordance with these words'. But what are 'these words'? What words exactly had Moses written and read? In the whole context of Exodus 19—24, the phrase 'the words of YHWH and the legal rules' must refer back both to the Decalogue in Exodus 20.1–17 (see v. 1: 'God spoke, and these were his words') and to the Book of the Covenant, Exodus 20.22—23.33 (see Exod. 21.1: 'These are the legal rules which you shall put before them').

Such expressions of mutual commitment as Exodus 19.5–6 and Deuteronomy 26.17–19 would suggest that it is the opening sentences of the Decalogue, demanding Israel's commitment to YHWH alone and forbidding the use of images, that flow naturally from the idea of a covenant with God (or vice versa). Placing all the national laws and customs, as in the Book of the Covenant or Deuteronomy, under the aegis of a covenant is rather different.

Exodus 34

We have no space here to discuss all the complexities of this passage. Briefly, the covenant mentioned in verses 10 and 27 embraces both promise and commandment, and the commandments include both the Ten Commandments of Exodus 20 (see 34.1, 28 and Deut. 10.4), written out again on the new tablets, and those spoken in Exodus 34.11–26 (see v. 27), 'a second covenant freshly declaring Yahweh's commitment to Israel and what this

---

16 Nicholson, *God and His People*, pp. 171–3.
17 Nicholson, *God and His People*, p. 173.

requires of Israel in the wake of the apostasy which threatened its continued existence as Yahweh's people'.[18]

The rest of the Pentateuch

It remains to ask whether all the laws of the Pentateuch are covenantal, for the four acts of covenant-making only cover the laws of Exodus (not including the instructions in chapters 25—31) and Deuteronomy. What of those in Leviticus and Numbers? Those in Numbers, mostly given after Israel has departed from Sinai, have to be treated as appendices to the main legislation. But Leviticus 26, the conclusion to the Holiness Code, and argu-ably to all the legislation in Exodus and Leviticus, makes significant use of the covenant motif. What happens here is that the covenant of promise in Genesis and the covenant of law in Exodus are merged into a single con-ception.[19] This can be seen already in verse 9, where the language is that of, for example, Genesis 17.6–7, and therefore most commentators have seen a reference to the covenant with Abraham; yet the context implies that this blessing is conditional *in the same way* as Exodus 19.5–6; verses 15 and 25, which speak of the breaking of the covenant, confirm this. Then at the end of the chapter, with its assurance of forgiveness after punishment, YHWH says he will 'remember my covenant with Jacob, my covenant with Isaac, and my covenant with Abraham' (Lev. 26.42), but concludes, 'I will remem-ber in their favour the covenant of the previous generation, whom I brought out of Egypt …' (v. 45). This has to mean the covenant of Sinai.

This completes the covenantal structure of the Pentateuch. All the prom-ises and all the commandments are presented as terms of one covenant with its reciprocal obligations. The importance of this covenantal conception of religion can hardly be exaggerated. Nicholson well brings out the unique character of a relationship between 'God and his people', expressed through the conditional covenant, in the context of the customary religious concep-tions of the ancient world.[20] We have seen how the covenant of promise subverted standard ancient ideas of the natural connection between a people, its land and its God, and rooted Israel's possession of their land and their existence as the people of YHWH in YHWH's free choice and gracious promise. In a world where social and political institutions were conceived to be an earthly reflection of the divine order, and the function of the worship of the gods was to sustain the order of the world which had existed since time immemorial, the covenantal conception based religion

---

18 Nicholson, *God and His People*, p. 148. See Nicholson's whole discussion of the chapter, pp. 133–50; and Moberly, *Mountain*, pp. 101–6.

19 Nihan, 'Priestly Covenant', pp. 104–15.

20 Nicholson, *God and His People*, pp. 191–217.

COVENANT-MAKING IN THE PENTATEUCH

not on a natural or ontological equivalence between the divine realm and the human, but on *choice*: God's choice of his people and their 'choice' of him, that is, their free decision to be obedient and faithful to him ... 'covenant' is the central expression of the distinctive faith of Israel as the 'people of Yahweh', the children of God by adoption and free decision rather than by nature or necessity.[21]

YHWH's relation with his people depends not on institutions but on 'a moral commitment on both sides.' The making of covenants is the one motif in the Pentateuch that draws together the heterogeneous collection of traditional stories, laws and other materials and makes a unity of them, a national history capable of grounding a nation's life.

The treaties and the covenants

I have left to last any consideration of possible ancient sources for the covenant accounts in the Pentateuch, and the one category that is bound to be dealt with here is the vassal treaty texts.[22] The implications for the dating of covenant texts in the Pentateuch will be dealt with in the next chapter (below, p. 100). Here we focus on the theological implications.

The texts of vassal treaties that we have come across are mostly from the archives either of the Hittite kings in Asia Minor between 1500 and 1200 BCE or of the Assyrians in 800–600 BCE.[23] Each treaty consists of words spoken by the Great King, who introduces himself at the beginning of the document. The document expresses his will: the vassal must submit, though it is clear he is expected to give positive assent to the treaty. He must be faithful to his lord, pay tribute, supply troops when required, give up political refugees from the Great King's realm, report any conspiracies against him that he hears of, and so forth.

Much weight used to be attached to the precise form of the records of these treaties, which varies little (see McKenzie). However, no one has been able to show that this form as a whole appears anywhere in the Pentateuch. What is significant is the strong reminiscences of certain parts of the form, especially the demand for loyalty and the curses for disobedience, in the book of Deuteronomy.[24] The main object of the vassal treaty is to secure the vassal's loyalty, and the leading idea in the theological framework of Deuteronomy, which it expresses over and over again in a variety of ways, is that Israel should be utterly loyal to YHWH. Therefore the treaty form is an appropriate expression of its main theological point.

---

21 Nicholson, *God and His People*, p. 216.
22 For details, see McKenzie, *Covenant*.
23 See McKenzie, *Covenant*, p. 32.
24 McCarthy, *Treaty*, pp. 157–87; Weinfeld, *Deuteronomy*, pp. 59–157.

Although the idea that the covenant between YHWH and Israel in the Pentateuch was developed under the influence of the vassal treaties has been widely influential and is still accepted by many, it has not gone unchallenged. The way in which the covenant is ratified in Exodus 24, with a sacrificial blood ritual, is quite different from the emphasis in the treaties on the sworn word of the vassal (or of both parties).[25] The people make a promise, but they do not take an oath.

Coming to Deuteronomy, Nicholson argues that 'it is not a legal document in the sense that the treaties are'.[26] The style is the style of a sermon, not of a legal document, and that is true even of the laws. Even the curses do not prove that Deuteronomy is a treaty document. Other kinds of documents were protected by curses, not only treaties: boundary stones, tombs and, significantly, law codes. There are so many differences between Deuteronomy and a treaty that Nicholson concludes that to maintain the theory you have to start by assuming the relationship with the treaties and argue in a circle.

Nicholson raises a different kind of point, and one with more theological implications, when he questions whether Israelites would have been likely to feel that the suzerain–vassal relation was an appropriate analogy for the relation between God and themselves, especially after Assyrian kings had ravaged their land, extorted huge sums in tribute and oppressed their people. Does Deuteronomy really say that Israelites should 'love' God in the same way that Hezekiah was required to 'love' Sennacherib?[27] The same objection does not apply to the model of the internal loyalty oath, which could not be taken into account at the time Nicholson was writing, but in any case he firmly maintains that to explain expressions like 'love YHWH your God' you do not need a political model. Everyday domestic life is sufficient. And there is no problem about love being commanded: that is common in the Old Testament. Think only of the command to love one's neighbour in Leviticus 19.18.[28]

Nicholson concludes that the treaty analogy does not explain much about the use of covenant language in the Old Testament. I believe he is largely right, but has perhaps overstated the case. The close correspondence in subject and order demonstrated by Weinfeld between the curses in Deuteronomy 28.26–35 and lines in the vassal treaties of the Assyrian king Esarhaddon is, to say the least, interesting.[29]

---

25 McCarthy, *Treaty*, p. 254.
26 Nicholson, *God and His People*, pp. 70–1.
27 Nicholson, *God and His People*, pp. 78–9. See Moran, 'Love of God'.
28 Nicholson, *God and His People*, pp. 79–80.
29 Weinfeld, *Deuteronomy*, pp. 117–22.

Further reading

All aspects of the covenant between YHWH and Israel are dealt with in Nicholson's *God and His People*, but he does not deal with the P texts. There is a good deal on the history of scholarship, and on the dating of the covenant texts; but this is still the best treatment of the treaty parallel, the meaning of the word *berit*, covenant as a theological idea, and the exegesis of the main texts in Exodus. The last chapter, 'The Covenant and the Distinctiveness of Israel's Faith', is an important essay that should be read by all.

McKenzie's *Covenant* is written at a simpler level, and does deal with the priestly texts; but only the first 50 pages are relevant to the Pentateuch, and many issues are not covered.

The commentaries will always be found valuable, especially Westermann and Brueggemann on Genesis, Childs and Houtman on Exodus, and Nelson and McConville on Deuteronomy.

Part B

5

The Composition of the Pentateuch

The problem

We have already noticed disruptions, gaps and contradictions in the narrative of the Pentateuch and inconsistencies in its laws. The effect in narrative study, as we have seen, is to make the narrator appear unreliable; more strongly put, they make the text unreadable. Let us take a look at a few examples.

The revelation of the Name

Exodus 6.2–3 is a key text for the development of the historical criticism of the Pentateuch. God says to Moses, 'I am YHWH. I appeared to Abraham, Isaac and Jacob as El Shaddai, but by my name YHWH I was not known to them.' Yet, there are a number of occasions in Genesis on which God uses that name to Israel's ancestors (for example Gen. 15.7; 22.16; 28.13), or on which they use it themselves, either to him (15.2;[1] 32.9) or to each other (16.2; 24.50). This appears to be a clear contradiction. Exodus 3.13–15 has often been taken to reinforce this case, but there is no clear contradiction there. The frequent use of YHWH by the *narrator* in Genesis is not a contradiction either. But the alternation between YHWH and *elohim* has classically been used as one of the key indicators of different sources, even outside Genesis. This kind of long-range narrative contradiction is easily paralleled, for example in the different reasons given for Moses' death without entering the promised land (Num. 20.12 and Deut. 1.37).

The two creation narratives

There are contradictions between the two accounts in Genesis 1 and 2. But why are there two stories of creation at all? Traditionally, it has been said that while the first account gives an overview of the whole work of creation, the second one focuses on a particular segment of that action. This will do

---

1 Wherever English versions use small capitals, the word represents YHWH: here 'GOD' instead of repeating 'LORD' after 'Lord' in lower case, which stands for the Hebrew word *Adonai*, not the Name.

for a 'synchronic' reading of the whole, but it does not explain the contradictions. An obvious handle for explaining it in terms of diverse authorship is the extreme difference in style and genre between the two accounts. Similar parallel but divergent accounts exist of God's covenant with Abraham (Gen. 15 and 17), God's commissioning of Moses (Exod. 3.1—4.17 and 6.2–8), God's covenant with Israel (Exod. 19—24 and Deut. 5), the spies episode (Num. 13—14 and Deut. 1.19–45), and others.

The Flood story

A different kind of problem is presented by this story. There are not two parallel accounts of it, but there are tensions within the one account. The most obvious is the divergence over the number of 'clean' animals (that is, ones permissible for eating and sacrifice: see Leviticus 11) to be brought into the ark. In Genesis 6.19–20 God's instruction is for two of every kind of animal, but in 7.2–3 it is for seven (pairs?) of each kind of clean animals and of (all?) birds, and one pair of each kind that is not clean. Again, this is a situation that can be paralleled elsewhere. Why did Jacob's parents send him away? To escape from Esau (Gen. 27.42–45), or to prevent him marrying a local girl (27.46—28.2)? Was the Red Sea split in two (Exod. 14.21b–22) or driven back by the wind (most of v. 21)? Did the spies tour the whole land (Num. 13.21) or only go as far as Hebron (v. 22)?

There are also inconsistencies in the laws.

The place of sacrifice

In Deuteronomy 12, Moses insists (three times over) that once settled in the land Israelites may only sacrifice at one place, which YHWH will choose. The following chapters in the law code presuppose this restriction. Yet, earlier, in Exodus 20.24–26, YHWH had given permission for the building of an altar for sacrifice at any place. A contradiction is also often seen between Deuteronomy 12.15–16, which permits the slaughter of domestic animals for food without sacrifice, seeing that sacrifice must now be less frequent, and Leviticus 17.3–9, which directs that slaughter can only be carried out if the animal is first offered to YHWH at the sanctuary – the 'Tent of Meeting' in the setting of the giving of this law. Each of the three divergent instructions belongs to a different one of the three main collections of laws. Similar differences exist between them on many other ritual matters, for example on who may act as a priest: Deuteronomy identifies all Levites as priests (18.1–9 and elsewhere), but in Leviticus 8—9 it is Aaron and his sons who are ordained as priests, and it is taken for granted elsewhere in Leviticus and Numbers (for example Lev. 1.5; 21.1) that priests are 'sons of Aaron'.

> Find other examples of apparent inconsistencies, gaps or contradictions anywhere in the Pentateuch.

The emergence of historical criticism

Traditional readers, Jewish and Christian, were either not worried by these discrepancies, or sought to harmonize them. Such harmonization is still active today. For example, the NIV translation of Genesis 2.19a is 'Now the LORD God had formed out of the ground all the beasts of the field and all the birds of air.' But the Hebrew verb form used in this verse does not normally refer back to a previous action in this way. The translation has been adopted in order to eliminate the contradiction between this verse, which sets the initial creation of the beasts ('out of the ground') after the creation of the first human being, and Genesis 1.20–25, which sets it before. This kind of explanation satisfied most people.

It is nevertheless evidence of this kind that has led scholars of the last 250 years, since the 'Enlightenment', to take a different approach, and use the contradictions as ways into a historical understanding of the biblical writings. This movement has led to great gains in understanding, but at a cost; for a text that is explained historically as the work of people in a number of different historical and social situations is more difficult to accept as inspired and authoritative Scripture.[2]

Moreover, despite all the work that has been done, scholars are further than ever from agreeing about the solutions.[3] In this chapter, we shall look at some of the more important theories about the composition of the Pentateuch. In the following chapter, we look at accounts that have been given of the completion of the Pentateuch and how it became the canonical Torah.

The production of texts in ancient Israel

How convincing any theory appears depends to a large extent on how one envisages the way in which literary work, the creation of books, was done in ancient Israel and Judah. A good deal of work has now been done on this, but since the evidence is limited, parallels from neighbouring ancient cultures have to be used. The model offered by David Carr is what he calls

---

2 For a defence of the necessity of historical criticism (for him simply 'biblical criticism'), see Barton, *Nature*.

3 For accounts of the history of scholarship, see (for the period up to 2000) the account by G. I. Davies, 'Pentateuch', and the extended account and assessment by Nicholson, *Pentateuch*.

'oral-written education and enculturation'.[4] Education in the ancient world was only for a minority, principally for those who would be professional scribes, earlier in the royal establishment, later increasingly in temples. It consisted, beyond the inculcation of basic literacy, of the teaching of standard texts to be memorized, 'written on the tablet of the heart', which were expected to train the student not only in knowledge of the literary culture, but in piety and behaviour. Written copies were made, but the educated person could recite them without referring to them.[5] If one wished to write something new, to develop the tradition that one had received, one could write out the received tradition from memory and revise or expand it as one went along. A new text might be created, but the scribe would use received phrases and formulae to construct it. Deuteronomic writers envisage extending this oral education based on memory of a text that exists in writing to the whole population by the public reading of the Torah: Deuteronomy 31.9–13. In Nehemiah 8 this programme is shown being implemented.

One considerable advantage of this model over the common idea of an oral culture *superseded* by a written one is that it explains how texts might have been preserved through the disruptions of the Assyrian and Babylonian invasions with the destruction of the palaces and temples where written texts would have been stored. The texts were also stored in the memories of those who had been educated in them. Inevitably, however, when they came to write them out, they would have wished to make changes to reflect the changed times.[6]

A review of theories

In the light of this understanding we may now look briefly at the various accounts of the constitution and growth of the Pentateuch.

Different kinds of hypotheses

The very first efforts to explain the discrepancies from a historical point of view used various clues in the text, especially the way in which God is referred to, whether by the name YHWH or the title *elohim*, 'God', to divide the text into two groups of passages or 'sources', which could be seen as having been the work of two different authors, brought together by Moses or another. In various forms this remains the most popular kind of solution. It is usually known as a *documentary* hypothesis, in that the text is supposed to result from the combination of a small number of original

---

4 Carr, *Writing; Formation*.

5 A very similar process is used today in traditional madrasas to inculcate knowledge of the Qur'an.

6 Carr, *Writing*, pp. 167–8.

documents by an editor or *redactor*. What is generally known today as *the* Documentary Hypothesis, which we shall come to shortly, is one particular species of this genus.

But although this was the first kind of theory to be put forward, and for much of the time since it has dominated the field, two other possibilities were also tested in the early nineteenth century and are now being revived. One was the *fragmentary* hypothesis, which held that rather than resulting from the combination of a small number of relatively long sources, the text was the outcome of the gradual accumulation of a large number of short pieces: narratives, poems, laws, etc. The other was the *supplementary* hypothesis: an original, relatively long document was developed by one or more editors who successively added material at various points.

It might be thought that the final texts resulting from these three ways of development would be so different that it would be easy to decide between them. But the Pentateuch is so complex that a good case can be made for any of them. In fact, they are not mutually exclusive. Different parts of the Pentateuch could have developed in different ways (this has usually been accepted for Deuteronomy as against the first four books, the so-called Tetrateuch), and different processes could have been going on at different times.

Definitions, characteristics and analysis of the three main types of hypothesis

Hypothesis	The text is:	Role of the redactor	Mode of analysis
Documentary	A combination of a small number of continuous sources running through the text	Stitching together the sources unobtrusively	Source criticism
Supplementary	The result of the addition of successive layers of material to an original shorter text, or group of texts	Includes the creation of original narrative and interpretation	Redaction criticism
Fragmentary	The combination of a large number of short texts	Creation of a linking narrative	Form criticism

The Documentary Hypothesis

The basic theory

The Documentary Hypothesis as known since the early nineteenth century proposes that the Tetrateuch is a combination of a 'Yahwist' document, using YHWH, usually referred to just as 'J',[7] and two using *elohim* in Genesis, before the revelation of the name YHWH to Moses in Exodus 3 or 6. These two are distinguished because their styles are so different. Even in translation, you can tell the difference between texts like Genesis 1; 9.1–17; 17; Exodus 6.2–8 (now referred to as the Priestly work or 'P') and ones like Genesis 20—22 and Exodus 3.9–14 (the 'Elohist' or 'E'): stately, precise and repetitious as against flowing and story-like, not unlike 'J'. In line with J, E and P, the letter 'D' is given to Deuteronomy. The assignment of material to 'P' has not been questioned much since the mid-nineteenth century, and, with its distinctive style, it remains the most secure element of any analysis. Once all the ritual material in Exodus 25 to Numbers is included, together with the Holiness Code, Leviticus 17—26, it forms much the greatest part of the material in the Tetrateuch.[8]

Wellhausen's historical theory

It is one thing to distinguish documents in the Pentateuch, but can one go on from there to see how the Pentateuch developed? This is what Julius Wellhausen achieved. His work of 1878,[9] which is still worth reading, marks an era not only because it established the view of the Pentateuch's development which reigned more or less secure for 100 years, but even more because of his *method*, which can be improved, but never gone back on, even if it is sometimes ignored. His was the first serious attempt to use the religious history of Israel to explain the development of the Pentateuch. Deuteronomy he regarded as a historical fixed point, as the book discovered in the temple in the eighteenth year of Josiah (622 BCE) according to 2 Kings 22, and the authority for that king's religious reform described in 2 Kings 23. He did not have the advantage of any archaeological investigation of the history, but he did carefully compare the ritual authorized in P with

---

7 The German spelling of 'Yahweh' is 'Jahweh'.

8 The most important *narrative* passages normally assigned to P are: Genesis 1.1—2.4; 6.9—9.17*; 17; 23; 27.46—28.9; 35.9–13a, 22b–29; 46.6–27; 50.12–13; Exodus 1.1–7*, 13–14; 2.23–25; 6.2—7.13; 7.14—11.10*; 12.1–20; 14*; 16*; 24.15—31.18; 35—40; Leviticus 8—10; Numbers 1—4; 7; 13—14*; 16—17*; 20.1–13; 25.6–18; 26; 27.12–23; 31; Deuteronomy 34.7–9. An asterisk means that only parts of the passage belong to P. I have counted as narrative instructions to Moses which he carries out in the narrative. For complete lists of texts supposed to belong to the three main Tetrateuchal documents, see Driver, *Introduction*, or Eissfeldt, *Introduction*.

9 Wellhausen, *Prolegomena*.

what the historical books from Judges to Kings tell us of Israel's religion. This evidence shows that P must be the latest, not the earliest, of the four documents. It sets up an elaborate ritual system dominated by the priests, essentially that of Second Temple Judaism, of which there is no trace in the earlier historical books (as against Chronicles). Deuteronomy introduces the first change in the relatively flexible pre-exilic religious customs by centralizing the sacrificial cult and the judicial system in one place, where the Levites are to serve as priests. P accepts the centralized cult, but restricts the priesthood to the 'sons of Aaron', and as against D increases their perquisites and introduces expiatory sacrifices not heard of before. J and E (which for Wellhausen includes the Book of the Covenant) represent the pre-exilic customs, where there is a multiplicity of sanctuaries. E is later than J because it shows some influence of the pre-exilic prophets. Thus the chronological order of the documents is JEDP.

Wellhausen did not suggest precise dates for J and E, but many of his successors did. There has been a tendency to place J as far back as the tenth century, during the 'United Monarchy'.[10] E's concerns are apparently those of northern Israel, and its composition has generally been placed under the kingdom of Israel in perhaps the eighth century.[11] J and E were supposed to have been combined by a redactor (R^{JE}), perhaps in the period after the fall of Samaria. Both Wellhausen and his successors in many places make no attempt to distinguish between J and E, simply referring to the JE narrative. After the composition of P in the post-exilic period, it would have been combined with JE by the final redactor, R^{JEP}.

Wellhausen's system, or variations of it, is what is usually meant today by the Documentary Hypothesis. It soon became dominant in critical scholarship, and it still is. Yet, it has never gone unquestioned. It has the great advantage of eliminating the need for a special explanation for every problem, but its corresponding weakness is that every passage – or verse, or half-verse! – has to be assigned to one or other of the documents whether there is evidence for it or not. Added to this is the fact that it is difficult to distinguish E from J outside Genesis; so, many question whether E ever existed as an independent source. Moreover, there are enough passages in the Tetrateuch written in a style very like Deuteronomy (for example Exod. 13.3–16), for it to be proposed that much of the JE material had been worked over by a Deuteronomistic editor – in fact this was recognized by Wellhausen himself. But as we look at later answers to the problem of the Pentateuch, we shall find that they all acknowledge their debt to Wellhausen by making at least some attempt to prove that they more accurately reflect the social history of Israel and Judah, with the help of the developments in our knowledge since his day.

---

10 Von Rad proposed that J was responding to the establishment of David's kingdom and empire: 'Problem', pp. 68–73.

11 Cf. e.g. Friedman, *Who Wrote?*, pp. 50–88.

Adherents of the Documentary Hypothesis from Wellhausen or before have normally accepted that the so-called documents would not each have been written at one time, but would have developed over a period. In the case of D and P, this idea has been made specific.

The development of Deuteronomy

As regards Deuteronomy, although almost the whole of the book has a consistent theological and stylistic character, it has usually been accepted that it was not all written at one go. There are a number of reasons for this. Most obvious are the multiple introductions in 1.1–5; 4.44–46+5.1; 6.1–3; and 12.1; and there is considerable repetition. Wellhausen himself distinguished between the original law code (chapters 12—26) and later frameworks. It is widely agreed that the present book of Deuteronomy is the result of a process of development, but the layers are identified rather differently by different writers.[12] Most accept that the outer framework in chapters 1—4 and 29—30 is secondary, as well as chapter 27 (an obvious insertion) and the narrative and poems in chapters 31—34. More dispute arises over the inner framework in 5—11 and 28, particularly the 'flashback' parts of Moses' second speech in chapters 5 and parts of 9—10; how are these related to Exodus? There may also be additions within the law code.

The growth of the priestly writings

To turn to the priestly writings, those who accept the Documentary Hypothesis have generally distinguished between the main narrative of P, referred to as Pg (g for the German *Grundschrift*, 'basic text'), usually seen as written in the exilic period, and various supplements (Ps), some of them narrative, for example Exodus 30—31, where YHWH's instructions appear to start again after coming to an obvious climax and conclusion in 29.43–46, and Exodus 35—39, and (in more recent work) all or most of the narratives in Numbers. But most of them are legal: almost the whole of Leviticus, including the Holiness Code (Leviticus 17—26) and the legal and ritual material in Numbers.[13]

The Holiness Code was regarded by Wellhausen, and subsequently, as an older code incorporated by the priestly writers into their own composition. More recently it has been seen as a supplementary layer added to P, not only in Leviticus 17—26 but also elsewhere. It uses the style of direct address for the instruction of the people, and makes certain corrections to P's views.[14]

---

12 See Mayes, *Deuteronomy*, pp. 41–7.

13 See the essays in Shectman and Baden, *Strata*.

14 Wellhausen, *Prolegomena*, p. 376; Knohl, *Sanctuary*; Milgrom, *Leviticus 17—22*, pp. 1349–55.

A quite different division has been suggested recently, taking the priestly narrative in Genesis as completely distinct in origin from the priestly laws in Exodus to Numbers, and originating in northern Israel; they were then joined together by the Holiness redaction.[15]

Tradition history

On the basis of the understanding of the development of the written Penta-teuchal traditions given by the Documentary Hypothesis, Gerhard von Rad and Martin Noth, in the mid-twentieth century, attempted to probe the hypothetical development of oral tradition before the written sources, in reliance on the principles of form criticism that had begun to be applied to the Pentateuch.[16] Others in Scandinavia sought to explain the origins of the narrative more exclusively on the basis of oral tradition.[17]

For von Rad the achievement of J was to bring together separate tradi-tions in a continuous, theologically accented history from creation to the settlement of the land by Israel – he always spoke of a Hexateuch, including Joshua, rather than the Pentateuch. He identified two traditions in particu-lar that he thought would have been preserved in the pre-state period at national sanctuaries. One was the story of Israel's deliverance from Egypt and guidance into the land. The other was the encounter with YHWH at Sinai/Horeb and the giving of the law and covenant.[18] The 'Yahwist' com-bined these traditions, however awkwardly, into one story, integrated them with the various traditions of the ancestors by means of the promise of the land; and before them all placed his new primeval story, now found in Genesis 2—11.[19]

Noth's conception of tradition history was not dissimilar, but he argued from the similarity of the J and E narratives as then understood that the var-ious traditions had been brought together even before J in a basic narrative that he called G, which might have been written or oral.[20] The emergence of this tradition implies that there was already an Israel before the exist-ence of any state, not just individual tribes, a nation with national cultic institutions, because this national entity is what the Pentateuch is concerned with.[21] Thus the 'major themes of the tradition' – 'the guidance out of Egypt, the guidance into the arable land, the promise to the patriarchs, guid-ance in the wilderness, and revelation at Sinai' – even if originally preserved in different tribes or circles, became the property of the whole nation.[22]

15 King, *Realignment*.
16 See especially Gunkel, *Stories of Genesis*.
17 See Knight, *Rediscovering*; Jeppesen and Otzen, *Productions*.
18 Von Rad, 'Problem', pp. 3–48.
19 Von Rad, 'Problem', pp. 48–67.
20 Noth, *Traditions*, p. 39.
21 Noth, *Traditions*, pp. 42–5.
22 Noth, *Traditions*, pp. 46–62.

Nothing remains in current scholarship of these bold syntheses. New views of the history of Israel have made it impossible any longer to consider that there were national institutions in the pre-state period, even if evidence suggests that some of the tribes felt a degree of solidarity. The emergence of a comprehensive 'Pentateuchal' tradition must be brought down to a later period; many today would make it very much later. Further, the modern study of folklore has cast doubt on the idea that oral tradition alone would preserve narratives accurately over periods of centuries.[23] Today, tradition history is concerned more with written texts, placing them against their probable social background in Israel and Judah of the monarchic or even later periods.

Newer views

Today the Documentary Hypothesis, though still the most widespread account, is questioned and abandoned by many, especially in German-language scholarship. There is more than one reason for this.

The shift to redaction criticism

Scepticism over the method of isolating sources that had been used since the eighteenth century, as for example in the work of R. N. Whybray and R. Rendtorff,[24] has led to a strong trend, at least on the European continent, towards fragmentary and supplementary views of the older parts of the Tetrateuch and a marked retreat of any form of documentary hypothesis. In particular, most scholars no longer distinguish a continuous E source, while recognizing the presence of diverse sources, some using different divine names.[25] For many, the Pentateuch as a whole can be accounted for by extending the supplementary theories long entrenched in the understanding of D and P, so that in place of the 'documentary' sources J, E and P, the narrative was built up in layers successively added to a few thin threads of original story.

The most consistent and comprehensive account of the Pentateuch (and more) along these lines is that of R. G. Kratz.[26] He believes the non-P strands of Genesis on the one hand and Exodus to Joshua on the other developed separately at first, before being joined together and then joined with P. The one trace of the Documentary Hypothesis that remains is the understanding of P as an originally distinct document. But some others treat P as a supplementary layer added to the older text, as we shall see.

---

23 See Kirkpatrick, *OT and Folklore*, and below in Chapter 7.

24 Whybray, *Making*; Rendtorff, *Transmission*.

25 Recently Yoreh, *First Book*, defending E, argues that it is the oldest part of the Pentateuch. But his E is not a continuous history.

26 Kratz, *Composition*.

Many scholars now make some layers of non-P material later than P; for these Pg is the first writer to link together the ancestral narratives of Genesis and the story of the Exodus. The case is argued in most detail by K. Schmid.[27] In their original meaning, according to Schmid, the stories of the ancestors and the exodus do not fit together, but are rival rather than consecutive accounts of the origins of the nation.

This account revives tradition history in a new way and in application to a later period than the theories of von Rad and Noth. In Hosea 12, which shows knowledge of most episodes in the story of Jacob, he is presented as a fitting model for his fickle and deceitful descendants: verses 13–14 contrast him with Moses, the prophet and agent of YHWH, 'your God from the land of Egypt' (v. 10).[28] The two cycles of stories originate in different social settings. The ancestors may have been celebrated by the rural people.[29] The religious ideal is inclusive – God is known under several names – and the people conceive of themselves as springing from their own land. But the Exodus–Moses story probably originated as the official founding legend of the (northern) kingdom of Israel and on being adopted in Judah was invested with an aggressive nationalist exclusivity: YHWH as the one god of Israel and Israel as the people of YHWH.[30]

New views of Israel's history

The biblical account of the united monarchy of David and Solomon is now widely doubted, and with it von Rad's dating of J in the tenth century. It is not only the *early* history of Israel that is questioned. We have seen how the account in 2 Kings 22 of the discovery of a book of the law in the eighteenth year of Josiah is the pivot of the Pentateuchal history accepted by Wellhausen. However, more recently the reliability of the account in Kings has been questioned. While there is no reasonable doubt that Josiah carried out some kind of religious reform, the account in chapter 22 is written in order to show that he was acting in accordance with the Torah and may depend, it is argued, on a 'literary convention of book discovery' rather than an actual event.[31] If this is so, the secure pivot has vanished, and some would now date Deuteronomy as a whole later than 587.[32] But this view in turn has been strongly contested.[33]

---

27 Schmid, *Genesis*. See also Dozeman and Schmid, *Farewell*, and Dozeman's *Exodus*. There are also English-language essays in Gertz, Schmid and Witte, *Abschied*.
28 See de Pury, 'Jacob Story', and cf. G. I. Davies, *Hosea*, pp. 272–84.
29 Schmid, *Genesis*, p. 108.
30 Schmid, *Genesis*, pp. 144–7. Kratz gives a similar account: *Composition*, pp. 304–5.
31 See Römer, *Deuteronomistic History*, pp. 49–56.
32 E.g. Kratz, *Composition*, p. 132.
33 See Levinson, *Deuteronomy*, pp. 9–10, and the works cited there.

The treaties and the covenants

A related issue is this. We saw in the previous chapter that many scholars believe that the forms of international vassal treaties and Assyrian loyalty oaths influenced the formulation of covenant texts in the Pentateuch. But which treaties one sees as influential and on what texts, makes a considerable difference to how one understands the dating and development of the Pentateuch. At one time, when the Hittite treaties of the second millennium were the only ones known, it was argued that key covenant texts such as the Decalogue must date from the very beginning of Israel's history.[34] However, it is now realized that the adoption of political and diplomatic formulae like the loyalty oaths and treaties points to the work of an administrative bureaucracy that did not exist before the rise of the monarchy, and once it did, the obvious source would be Assyria. Close work on the texts has shown that it is in Deuteronomy that one finds the really close parallels, especially in chapters 13, 28 and 29.[35] It seems likely that although an actual treaty pattern is not discernible in Deuteronomy, it has been heavily influenced by the language used in this tradition. The authors found the language appropriate in that their main concern was to warn Israel to cleave in single-minded loyalty to YHWH. It may also be that the writers supported a revolt by Judah under the leadership of king Josiah against the overlordship of Assyria, to which the call to be loyal to YHWH alone was central, and deliberately turned the imagery of the treaties to which they had been subjected in a new direction.[36]

This does not necessarily mean that references to covenants can only go back as far as the time of Assyrian domination, though this is now widely held (see below). If Nicholson is right that the treaties (or loyalty oaths) are not required to explain most of the covenant texts, their date may not be directly affected.

Deuteronomistic influence

However, many studies now detect Deuteronomistic influence in the key theological themes of supposed J and E material, implying a much later dating for it. This began with Lothar Perlitt's influential study of covenant theology in 1969.[37] Perlitt saw the theme of the covenant as one unknown to the pre-exilic prophets or the core of Deuteronomy, but coming into the

---

34 Mendenhall, 'Covenant Forms'; also Baltzer, *Covenant Formulary*. The argument is summarized in McCarthy, *Old Testament Covenant*, pp. 10–34; Nicholson, *God and His People*, pp. 57–9.

35 McCarthy, *Treaty*, pp. 157–87; Weinfeld, *Deuteronomy*, pp. 59–157; pp. 91–129 for the textual comparisons.

36 Nicholson, *God and His People*, p. 154.

37 See Nicholson, *God and His People*, much of which deals with Perlitt's work in detail.

Pentateuch largely in the exilic period in the inner framework of Deuteronomy, particularly in chapters 5, 9—10 and 28, and then in the Sinai pericope in Exodus (chapters 19—24 and 32—34). Unlike the core of Deuteronomy, which is centred on the requirement for centralization of the cult, Deuteronomy as edited, he argued, is a covenant document centred on the demand for the worship of YHWH alone and expressed in the terms of the political treaty and loyalty-oath tradition. This can be seen as a response to the breakdown of traditional society and the destruction of the political nation. The only source of identity for Judaeans, whether in their own land or in exile, now lay in YHWH alone. This is centrally expressed in the Decalogue, which is headed by that fundamental demand, is largely expressed in Deuteronomistic language, and is in Deuteronomy 5 presented as the content of the covenant of Horeb.

The trend continued with H. H. Schmid's work on 'the so-called Yahwist' (1976), which looked at a much wider range of 'J' material, including the promises and the call of Moses as well as the Sinai pericope, and showed how close the themes of promise, covenant, faith, obedience and so on were to either the pre-exilic prophets or Deuteronomy, or both. The conclusion, taken up by many, was that although a variety of early fragmentary material is preserved in the older Pentateuchal sources, the editorial hand or hands that have given it its theological profile were at work around the sixth century, certainly after Deuteronomy and for many later than the Deuteronomistic history (Joshua to Kings, probably mid-sixth century).

Many continental writers, in particular, share this understanding. Erhard Blum argues that the non-P narrative material in the Tetrateuch was formed into a coherent composition ('KD') by a Deuteronomistic writer who intended to write a 'prequel' to the Deuteronomistic history, and contributed all the important theological material, especially the accounts of promises and covenants, and the call of Moses in Exodus 3.1—4.18.[38] Van Seters has a simpler theory, in which all the non-P narrative and legal material in the Tetrateuch is the work of a single historian, whom he calls J (not to be confused with the J of the Documentary Hypothesis!), who writes in the sixth century in order to extend the Deuteronomistic history back to creation.[39] Both these writers see P as supplementing the work of J/KD.

What then of the belief, going back to Wellhausen and before, that J and E must be pre-Deuteronomic because they betray no knowledge of the Deuteronomic restrictions on the cult? The same argument could be applied to Samuel and Kings, where approved prophets and kings sacrifice in different places, even after 'YHWH has given you rest from all your enemies round about' (Deut. 12.10, generally supposed to refer to the reign of David). No one doubts that these books are edited by Deuteronomists, but they are seen

---

38 Blum's principal works are not available in English. For a good account with evaluation, see Nicholson, *Pentateuch*. He deals with Blum's work in several places. See also G. I. Davies, 'Composition'.

39 Van Seters, *Prologue, Moses, Law Book*.

as enshrining earlier traditions. The same could easily be true of the Pentateuchal narratives and laws, such as the pre-Deuteronomic altar law in the
Book of the Covenant (Exod. 20.24–26).

The date of P

A fourth influence on the discussion of the Pentateuch today flows in the
opposite direction to these. It derives from the study of the priestly stream
in the Pentateuch as a comprehensive ritual text. A number of scholars,
particularly the Israeli Yehezkel Kaufmann and those influenced by him,
retaining the documentary analysis of the text and the classical delimitation
of the sources, have argued that P represents the ancient ritual customs of
Israel, and that in several respects Deuteronomy marks a radical break with
ancient custom, above all in the demand for the single place of sacrificial
worship and its secularizing consequences. Kaufmann argues, against Wellhausen, that there is nothing in P (or H, which Kaufmann treats as part
of P) that requires centralization: the tent of meeting is intended as part
of a historical portrayal of wilderness Israel, and its analogue in the settled land is *any* sanctuary of YHWH.[40] According to Weinfeld, P and D
differ not because one is earlier than the other but because of the totally
different sociological settings of the two: P from priestly circles concerned
with ritual and D from court scribes concerned with political and secular
matters; moreover Deuteronomy sometimes quotes priestly laws, but the
reverse is not the case.[41] Therefore the consensus going back to Wellhausen
placing D earlier than P is wrong: P is earlier than D and uninfluenced by
it.[42] Knohl, followed by Milgrom, has modified the position by seeing H
as a supplementary and interpretative redaction, responsible not only for
Leviticus 17—26, but for interpolations and supplements throughout P.[43]
Milgrom takes it as a response from priestly circles to the social crisis of the
late eighth century, with some final, but not extensive, editing down to the
exile.

The school bolsters this position by arguing that the language of P is
classical biblical Hebrew like that of J, E and D, but clearly differentiated
from the 'late biblical Hebrew (LBH)' found in Chronicles, Ezra–Nehemiah
and Daniel and even from the sixth-century Ezekiel.[44] R. Polzin examines
this issue impartially and concludes that the language of Pg is indeed largely classical, but with some later features, while that of Ps is rather closer

---

40 Kaufmann, *Religion of Israel*, pp. 175–8.

41 Weinfeld, *Deuteronomy*, pp. 179–89. But see below, p. 113.

42 See Kaufmann, *Religion of Israel*, pp. 153–211, as well as Weinfeld, *Deuteronomy*;
also Haran, *Temples*, pp. 132–48; Milgrom, *Leviticus 1—16*, pp. 3–35; *Leviticus 17—
22*, pp. 1357–64 (on H). These writers differ in many ways, but they agree on the priority
of P (and H) to D. So does Friedman, *Who Wrote?*

43 Knohl, *Sanctuary*.

44 Hurvitz, 'Evidence of Language'; Milgrom, *Leviticus 1—16*, pp. 3–8.

to LBH; unfortunately he does not examine H.[45] This possibly suggests a sixth-century date for Pg; but the issue is difficult owing to the small quantity of the evidence.[46]

Survival of the Documentary Hypothesis

Although it has been rejected by many, the Documentary Hypothesis still remains, in one form or another, the most commonly accepted explanation of the history of the Pentateuch in the English-speaking world.[47] Variations of it have been strongly defended by, for example, R. E. Friedman, Joel Baden and E. W. Nicholson.[48]

Nicholson offers an extensive critique of many of the newer theories. He argues in broad outline for a return to Wellhausen, but with an important supplementary element in JE: that most of the promises made by God to the ancestors in Genesis, especially Genesis 15 as a whole, together with allusions to the oath to the fathers in Exodus and Numbers, belong to a stage of redaction in the late pre-exilic or exilic period, and the same goes for the accounts of covenant-making at Sinai and possibly the stories of rebellion in the wilderness.[49] This concession is more far-reaching than Nicholson appears to realize. If it is correct, it means that most of the themes that we identified in Chapter 2 as central to the Pentateuchal narrative as a national history are owed to creative authors rather than being rooted in old tradition. The narrative of JE might be formally consecutive, but it would lack thematic unity. In particular, the narratives of the patriarchs and the exodus would have little to connect them, almost as in K. Schmid.

Testing the theories

The interpreter of the Pentateuch today is faced with a wide variety of models for understanding the materials of the Pentateuch, their dates of origin and the way in which they have been brought together. In this section of the chapter, we shall take four key passages as test cases and see how the available theories fare in explaining them.

It must be admitted, however, that the evidence is nearly always insufficient to decide between one theory, or one variation on a theory, and another. If it were sufficient, there would not be such a variety of theories. Even if one takes the most widely agreed result, for example the extent of P, easily identified by its distinctive style, it is possible to argue that such

---

45 Polzin, *Late Biblical Hebrew*.
46 See Blenkinsopp, 'Assessment'; Milgrom, 'Antiquity'; King, *Realignment*, pp. 28–49.
47 This is clear from a glance at many recent commentaries and introductory works.
48 Friedman, *Who Wrote?*; Baden, *Composition*; Nicholson, *Pentateuch*.
49 Nicholson, *Pentateuch*, pp. 142–3, 244–5. See also Emerton, 'Promises'.

styles are easily imitated and that common style or motifs or even theology does not prove that two texts have been written by the same person or at the same period. It might 'be asked once again what the value is of a study whose results are so disputable and uncertain. The answer may well be that the study itself is more valuable than its results. Given that the Pentateuch is the result of a process of growth of some kind, an observation that few dispute, historical–critical study enables us to point to connections between the literary phenomena and what we can determine of the historical and social matrix in which that growth took place, even if we cannot reconstruct the process with any certainty.

The questions that may be asked in relation to our test cases include these:

- Is a documentary or a supplementary approach more helpful in analysing the non-P Tetrateuch?
- Can E and J be distinguished?
- Is P a source or a redaction?
- How is the Holiness Code related to Deuteronomy?
- Are there post-P texts?
- What is the direction of influence between Deuteronomy 5 and Exodus 19—20 (24)?

To understand the arguments here, you need to get a thorough knowledge of each passage. Read it through, go through it again and highlight points where you can see possible contradictions, or variations such as in the divine names (in most English versions, 'God' as against 'the LORD'). Only then read the relevant section here.

Jacob at Bethel: Genesis 28.10–22

At first sight, the Documentary Hypothesis finds easy confirmation here. Verses 16 and 17 are seen as a 'doublet', that is, two verses that go over the same stage of the story. This would be a sign of the combination of parallel narratives. The story is from E, but broken by an insertion from J in verses 13–16. This is argued from the use of the divine names, and backed up by subsidiary arguments. In addition, the introductory sentence in verse 10 is seen as J, and verse 21b ('YHWH shall be my God'); but this was seen as likely to be a later interpolation, as it does not fit with *elohim* in the earlier part of the sentence. John Skinner's commentary provides a clear statement of the consensus.[50]

The approach of form criticism and tradition history led to a change in this assessment. It was seen that the kernel of this story, as of many in Gen-

---

50 Skinner, *Genesis*, p. 376.

esis, was an aetiology. It was the foundation legend of a holy place, in this case the great temple of Bethel, the chief shrine of the kingdom of Israel (1 Kings 12.29–33; 2 Kings 23.15; Amos 7.10–13). Such a story would have been told at the temple as the warrant for its existence. The elements of a foundation legend will normally include the vision of the divine being(s), the recognition of the place as holy, and the setting up of the sanctuary (two of these appear in each of Exod. 3 and 2 Sam. 24). Verses 11–12 and 17–19 are essential to this story.

> *Aetiology.* A story explaining the origin of some object, place, custom or name; for example, the Babel story (Gen. 11.1–9) is an aetiology of the variety of languages.

On the other hand, verses 13–14, in which YHWH gives Jacob a promise closely similar in wording to that to Abram in Genesis 13.14–17, can be seen to belong to a wide-ranging redaction of the stories of the ancestors, tying them together as a single narrative of YHWH's promise. Verse 15 seems to be more closely related to the story of Jacob himself and his particular situation; Genesis 31.3 and 46.2–4 belong with it.[51] Jacob's vow in verses 20–22 also belongs to his own story, but it has often been thought it could not go with verse 15, since 'the same thing cannot simultaneously be a divine promise and the condition of a vow'.[52] To our way of thinking, yes, but maybe not to an ancient writer.

These considerations have led in recent study to supplementary analyses of the text, dropping the documentary paradigm altogether and instead seeing the original unit built up in the process of transmission into successively larger entities.

According to David Carr, the legend as it appeared in the original story of Jacob consisted of verses 11–12, 17–22, while '[t]he promise-focused material in 28.13–16 appears to be an insertion composed in light of the context into which it has been inserted'.[53] In other words, this is not part of a continuous 'J' narrative, and in any case is more recent than the Elohistic context. Carr calls the composition *with* the promises the 'Proto-Genesis' composition. He draws an interesting distinction between the ideologies of this composition and its precursors, including the Jacob story. In the latter, the narrative future is the audience's present: in this case the temple of Bethel, with its tithes, is the 'gate of heaven', where earth and heaven meet. But in the 'Proto-Genesis' composition, the promises are directed, after the

51 Rendtorff, *Problem*, p. 135.
52 Westermann, *Genesis 12—36*, p. 453.
53 Carr, *Fractures*, p. 208.

fall of the kingdoms, to the *future* of the audience, to their regaining their land and sovereignty and security.[54]

In conclusion, we may say that the supplementary understanding of this text is more convincing than the documentary, since Genesis 28.13–16 is not part of a continuous narrative separate from Genesis 28.11–12, 17–22. This may support the model of Genesis as a composition of originally distinct Abraham and Jacob narratives arranged serially rather than in parallel on the lines suggested by Carr; but it may alternatively support Yoreh's idea of an E text supplemented by J. Investigation of the tradition history has also shown that there are traditions in Genesis, and therefore very likely elsewhere, that were in circulation in the monarchic period, and were almost certainly in writing before the end of the eighth century.

The call of Moses: Exodus 3.1—4.18

The comprehensive way in which this passage is linked with the entire Pentateuchal story makes it peculiarly important in any study of the Pentateuch. Israel's 'fathers', Abraham, Isaac and Jacob, are repeatedly referred to (Exod. 3.6, 15, 16; 4.5); in each place the God who has appeared to Moses is identified with their God, thus linking the two main origin stories. The text takes up the suffering of Israel in Egypt and forecasts much of the story of the exodus, the meeting with God at the mountain of revelation and the conquest of the land. This is not some stray piece of tradition (which is not to say that it does not contain old tradition): it was composed as an integral part of a comprehensive narrative of at least (what was to become) the Pentateuch, and perhaps a Hexateuch including Joshua.

These are not the only kind of links the text has with Hebrew traditions. The whole passage is structured as the call of a prophet or deliverer, like Judges 6.11–40 (Gideon) or Jeremiah 1.4–10.[55] It thus prepares for the picture of Moses' activity throughout the Pentateuch. The theme of the revelation of the name YHWH appropriately introduces a story in which YHWH will be the dominant actor and a body of teaching headed by the command to have no other gods. Deuteronomistic motifs are prominent, for example in the name Horeb in Exodus 3.1 (Deut. 5.2, etc.) and the description of the land in Exodus 3.8, 17 (cf. Deut. 6.3, etc., 7.1). The theme of faith which dominates Exodus 4.1–9 is one that recurs at key points in the narrative: Genesis 15.6; Exodus 4.31; 14.31.

However, the piece is related to its immediate context in a rather awkward way. It does link smoothly on to 2.23–25, with the 'cry' of the Israelites apparently picked up in 3.7, 9, and the names of the ancestors as well, as we

---

54 Carr, *Fractures*, pp. 305–7.

55 See Childs, *Exodus*, pp. 53–6; Habel, 'Call Narratives'; Van Seters, *Moses*, pp. 42–6.

have seen. As most of 2.23–25 is regarded as P, and this is not, an interesting question arises, to which we shall return. But looking to the other end of the passage, 4.18 rounds it off neatly, but 4.19 which follows makes little sense in that context. It does, however, make a link with the beginning of 2.23, 'after a long time the king of Egypt died'. Moreover, in our passage the name of Moses' father-in-law is Jethro or Jether (3.1; 4.18; cf. Exod. 18), whereas in the story of Moses' flight to Midian (the country is mentioned in 4.19) it is Reuel (2.18).

Looking now to the internal features of the passage, tensions have been noted in it. Dozeman gives a list of no fewer than ten,[56] among them: the switches between YHWH and *elohim* in 3.1–14; the apparent duplication between 3.7 and 3.9; the word about Moses' staff in 4.17 compared with 4.1–9, where only one of the three signs has been performed with it; and in 3.6 the awkwardness of 'your father' (you singular, father singular) next to the reference to the three ancestral figures.

Unsurprisingly, therefore, adherents of the Documentary Hypothesis have regarded this as another prime site for source division. It is clear that if there is an E at all, it must be present in this passage, which marks the revelation of the name YHWH to Moses (3.13–15) ahead of that in P (6.2–8). Up to 3.15, *elohim* or *ha'elohim* (with 'the') is used several times (3.4b, 6, 11, 12, 13, 14, 15; normally in narration, but in 3.12 in God's speech). After it, only YHWH, which however also appears in 3.2, 4a and 7.[57] All supporters of the Documentary Hypothesis regard 3.9–14 as E (3.9–10 do not contain a divine name, but they link smoothly on to v. 11), and 3.7–8 as J. After that, however, opinions diverge, and it is especially difficult to sort two continuous narrative lines out of 3.1–6, which makes perfect sense as it stands, as indeed the whole story does, setting aside the minor blemishes in 3.6 and 4.17 and the repetition in 3.7–9.[58] Thus Propp, the most recent advocate of the Documentary Hypothesis in Exodus, gives a very different analysis from the consensus reported by Childs, assigning far more of the passage to E.[59] Moreover, if, as generally supposed, 2.11–23a and 4.19–20 are J, and our passage fails to cohere with them, how can *any* of the passage be from J?

Several recent critics, as well as earlier opponents of historical criticism, have therefore argued that both the change of names in 3.1–7 and the repetition in 3.7–9 can perfectly well be accounted for in a unitary text. The repetition is rhetorical. The carefully limited use of YHWH in 3.1–7 may be intended to make it clear to the reader who the god is who is being revealed and so prepare for the revelation of the name to Moses in 3.14–15.

---

56 Dozeman, *Exodus*, pp. 97–8. But not all of them are confined to 3.1—4.18.

57 This does not include the frequent use of a form of *elohim* before a name: 'the God of Abraham', 'the God of Israel', etc. There is the added complication that in several places the textual witnesses diverge.

58 Cf. Childs, *Exodus*, p. 53.

59 Propp, *Exodus 1—18*, pp. 190–7; Childs, *Exodus*, p. 52.

Ha'elohim ('the god') may represent Moses' point of view, and either *elohim* or YHWH is used where the narrator speaks objectively.[60]

In line with the observations that the passage is extensively connected to the rest of the Pentateuch, contains prophetic and Deuteronomic motifs, can be read as a unity[61] and is not quite smoothly related to its context, many of the more recent critics treat it as a key element of a comprehensive Penta-teuchal composition linking previously separated traditions.

For Van Seters it belongs to his 'J', and one of its specific objects is to link the ancestral narrative with that of the exodus.[62] The later 'P', which Van Seters regards as a redaction of J, not an independent source, linked to this passage at 2.23–25. Others argue that the best way of explaining the smoothness of the link is that the passage is post-priestly. K. Schmid argues in detail that this passage was not only composed later than P but in depend-ence on it.[63] Dozeman has mounted a refutation of Schmid's arguments.[64] One might add a few more points against Schmid's view. The different name of Moses' father-in-law suggests that the author is taking up an existing tradition rather than simply supplementing what is there; and the burning bush may well be a distinct tradition of the discovery of a holy place.[65] This seems to exclude a very late origin for the piece. Moreover, the language of the passage is classical biblical Hebrew without any sign of a move towards 'late biblical Hebrew' as profiled by Polzin. Exodus 3.1—4.18 and 6.2–8 are not so similar that mutual independence must be excluded. The link to 2.23–25 is simply explained: this was the obvious place for a redactor to make the link between P and non-P texts.

I would cautiously conclude that the most probable explanation of the evidence is that Exodus 3.1—4.18 and 6.2–13 are key passages in two inde-pendent compositions bringing together the major origin traditions of Israel. The former is likely to be the earlier, dating perhaps from the early sixth cen-tury and representing the first comprehensive effort to provide the defeated, occupied and partially exiled nation with theologically based support for their existence as a nation without a state. There is insufficient evidence for the composition of this passage from separate independent strands of narrative.

The Decalogue: Exodus 20.2–17 and Deuteronomy 5.6–21

The Decalogue in Exodus is one element of the complex Sinai pericope. The part of this that is paralleled in Deuteronomy 5 extends from chapter 19 to

---

60 Schmid, *Genesis*, p. 177.

61 Several scholars regard 3.15 as a later addition, despite the fact that it is the true answer to Moses' question. But Moberly (*OT of OT*, pp. 21–6) shows how verses 13–15 logically cohere.

62 Van Seters, *Moses*, pp. 47–9.

63 Schmid, *Genesis*, pp. 182–93.

64 Dozeman, 'Commission'.

65 See Childs, *Exodus*, p. 55; Houtman, *Exodus*, vol. 1, p. 353.

chapter 24. The problems in this whole passage are too many and complex to be tackled in a book of this nature, so we shall confine ourselves here to the Decalogue, with occasional reference to its context.

The leading position of the Ten Commandments in the accounts of law-giving in both Exodus and Deuteronomy, and their centrality in the moral teaching of Christianity in particular, have meant that readers have clung to the belief that they are truly ancient more tenaciously than with any of the other legal texts. The word often used is 'Mosaic', despite the fact that it is the only group of commandments in the Torah that is *not* transmitted, or to be transmitted, by Moses!

Any such view runs into a series of awkward problems:

1 Most obviously, the two versions of the Decalogue are different; not enormously, but significantly so. This suggests that however old it may be, it has undergone change in transmission.

2 It is a compilation of various commands which differ from each other in form. The series of prohibitions is broken by two positive commands (Sabbath and parents). In verses 2–6 (of Exodus 20) YHWH speaks in the first person; in verses 7–12 he is referred to in the third person; in verses 13–17 he is not referred to. The commandments differ greatly in length, from the elaborate precision and extended motivation of II and IV to the concise-ness of VI, VII and VIII (two words each in Hebrew).[66] Many have tried to obtain a shorter and 'more original' form, with all the commandments of equal length, and with the other irregularities to some extent smoothed out.[67] But the idea that all the commands were originally of equal length and in the same form is unlikely, for what we have in the Decalogue is a combination of commands for the exclusive worship of YHWH with a basic moral code – two different kinds of thing which it is difficult to suppose could have been originally expressed in the same form, any more than they are now.[68]

3 Commandments I, II, IV and V are expressed in thoroughly Deuter-onomistic language in both versions: 'out of the house of slaves', 'other gods', 'bow down and worship', 'the alien who is within your gates', 'the land which YHWH your God gives you', etc. On the other hand, Exodus 20.11 is clearly priestly, with its reference to the P creation story.[69] The prevalence of relatively late language is generally admitted. The attempts at a shorter original form remove much of the Deuteronomistic colouring, but not all.

4 The Decalogue is a poor fit in its context in Exodus: Exodus 20.1 does not follow smoothly on the end of chapter 19, and 20.18–21 would fit

---

66 Protestant numbering, as also under (3); see table, p. 46.

67 See, e.g., Nielsen, *Ten Commandments*, pp. 84–5. Taking equal length as his guid-ing principle, he lengthens the short commandments as well as shortening the long ones.

68 Cf. Houtman, *Exodus*, vol. 3, p. 8.

69 It has been recently identified as H: Knohl, *Sanctuary*, p. 67.

better in that place.[70] There are various theories of how and why the text has been disrupted. One possibility is that the Decalogue is a late addition to it, and a possible corollary is that since it has, in Exodus, been edited by a priestly writer, it is likely to be this editor that has added it.[71] In this case the covenant in chapter 24 would have previously been presented as made on the basis of the Book of the Covenant alone, and the addition conforms the narrative in Exodus to that in Deuteronomy 5. Other possibilities are that it originally followed Exodus 19.19, and 19.20–25 has been added;[72] or that it has been moved from after 20.21.[73] In these cases it is possible, though not certain, that Deuteronomy 5 is arranged to follow the *present* order of events in Exodus 20.

It is not surprising in view of this evidence that many recent scholars have reached the conclusion that the Decalogue is a Deuteronomistic composition, perhaps from the time of the exile, bringing together key religious and moral commands, most of which are found in one form or another in all the Torah collections.[74] Thus in effect it would sum up the religious and moral teaching of the Torah. Some would argue that it is original to its context in Deuteronomy and from there later introduced, awkwardly, to that in Exodus. But if this is so, it does not necessarily mean that its original *form* is that in Deuteronomy.

However, it cannot be ruled out that behind the current obviously Deuteronomistic composition there lies an older commandment series centred on the command for the exclusive worship of YHWH. That there were at least certain circles in pre-exilic Israel in which YHWH's exclusive claim was recognized is suggested by various pieces of evidence: Hosea 2, Jeremiah 2 and Psalm 81, which contains the closest thing to a quotation of the first two verses of the Decalogue outside the Torah, Psalm 81.9–10, associated with other traditions now found in the book of Exodus.[75] The reference to Joseph in verse 5 points to an origin in (northern) Israel, but this does not necessarily mean it goes back to before 722.

Two questions still need to be asked. What was the original context, social *or* literary, in which the Decalogue could have emerged? And is the Exodus or the Deuteronomy version nearer to the original?

Taking the latter question first, the two different motivations for the Sabbath commandment suggest that neither version is likely to be *the* original. While the Exodus version draws on the P creation story, Deuteronomy 5.14 (end) adapts the seventh-day rest commandment in Exodus 23.12, continu-

---

70 See Nicholson, 'Decalogue', pp. 422–3.

71 Nicholson, 'Decalogue', p. 431; Van Seters, *Moses*, p. 276, n. 88.

72 Johnstone, *Exodus*, p. 97; Kratz, *Composition*, p. 140; Dozeman, *Exodus*, pp. 425, 432.

73 Cf. Nicholson, 'Decalogue', p. 423, who says it was generally agreed (in 1977).

74 E.g. Johnstone, 'Decalogue'; Kratz, *Composition*, pp. 142–4.

75 Cook, *Social Roots*, e.g. p. 35.

ing the practice of the Deuteronomic code of updating material from the Book of the Covenant. But there is a widespread view in recent, especially German-language, scholarship that the version in Deuteronomy 5 is more original, along with the whole context.

This is unlikely. The version in Deuteronomy is distinctly longer than that in Exodus, which would usually imply that it is expanded, rather than that the Exodus version is cut down. Twice it includes the clause 'as YHWH your God has commanded you', which most likely refers to the previous giving of these commandments in Exodus. The order of the tenth commandment in Deuteronomy, with the wife first, is more easily explained as a revision in Deuteronomy. 'House' in Exodus 20.17 means 'household', 'family and property' and is followed by the various items within the 'house' that one might covet. The meaning of 'house' is later reduced to the buildings of the homestead, and the man's wife is given more importance than those.

Thus it is most likely that the Exodus version is closer to the original, apart from the motivation of the Sabbath commandment.[76] An original Decalogue in what became Exodus has been copied with revisions in Deuteronomy, and revised in another way by a priestly editor in Exodus.[77]

To turn now to the origins of this text, Alt's theory of 'apodictic law' led to the hypothesis that it was announced at regular assemblies to renew the covenant.[78] This was widely held until the impact of Perlitt's arguments broke up the consensus (see above, pp. 100–1). But the assumption that the Decalogue had something to do with the covenant, in origin as well as in its present contexts, was surely correct and is generally agreed. The clarity and weight of its emphasis on the exclusive claim of YHWH makes it perfectly adapted to that purpose. Even more significant is the fact that unlike all other legal or instructional texts in the Torah it is addressed directly by God to the people, rather than being mediated by Moses.[79]

But if there was no institution of covenant renewal, there is no available institutional or social setting for such a remarkable address. Its setting would have to be in a *text*, one such as Exodus 19—20 or Deuteronomy 5, a narrative of covenant-making in which YHWH personally proclaims his fundamental requirements of his people. The requirements involve both their absolute loyalty and their observance of basic moral standards, which accounts for the awkward yoking of different styles of commandment in one series. If, as most critical scholars today suppose, this narrative originated in the Deuteronomistic movement, it would have been composed around the time of the exile of Jerusalem and offered to a dispossessed and disoriented people as the only possible basis for continuing nationhood. But what we said above suggests that in some form it could go back much

---

76 Most commentaries recognize this, and so does Kratz, *Composition*, p. 127.
77 So Johnstone, 'Decalogue', p. 383 (= *Chronicles*, p. 197).
78 Alt, 'Origins', pp. 124–32, esp. p. 130. See above, p. 55.
79 Nicholson, 'Decalogue'; Crüsemann, *Torah*, pp. 354–7.

further, possibly to the time before or after the fall of Israel in 722, when it could have found the same function.

Clean and unclean animals: Leviticus 11 and Deuteronomy 14.3–21[80]

These instructions may be rather obscure to non-Jewish readers of the Pentateuch, but they are the basis of practices that are essential to Jewish identity in the modern as well as in the ancient world. For our purposes in this chapter they are a valuable illustration both of the differing theological understandings of the life of the people of YHWH that have been brought together in the Pentateuch and of the complex relationships between the Priestly, Holiness and Deuteronomic bodies of legal texts. The study of these passages brings forward and may help to settle the question of the priority between them raised once more by the Kaufmann school.

It is clear that Deuteronomy 14.4–20, following the general principle in verse 3, gives the same teaching as Leviticus 11.2b–20 and in similar priestly language. We have to ask whether one text has been derived from the other or both from some earlier text different from either. Leviticus 11.21–23 then makes an exception to the rule that no flying insects are to be eaten, which does not appear in Deuteronomy.

It seems certain that Deuteronomy 14.4–20 has *either* been borrowed by the author of Deuteronomy 14.3 from a priestly scroll *or* added by a later editor, again drawing on a priestly source.[81] But is that source Leviticus 11 as it stands? Surely not: why then would the exception allowing locusts to be eaten not be mentioned, nor the prohibition of 'things swarming on the ground' in Leviticus 11.41–42? The obvious conclusion is that the editor of Deuteronomy is using an older form of the priestly teaching that corresponded to Leviticus 11.2b–20 only.[82] Only after Deuteronomy was edited in this way was the teaching of Leviticus 11 expanded.

The additions in Leviticus 11.21–47 are not all of one piece. The language and ideas of Leviticus 11.43–45 are typical of the Holiness Code (compare, for example, Lev. 19.2, 36; 20.24–26); the text is one of the strongest pieces of evidence that H is a redactional layer spread throughout P rather than a separate code. The object is to make theological sense of the rules about animal food: they are a means by which YHWH's people are to dedicate themselves to him, making themselves holy as he is holy.

It is a probable deduction that the editing of Deuteronomy that brought

---

80 In this section I am drawing mainly on my own earlier work: Houston, *Purity*.

81 This is the usual view: see, e.g. Mayes, *Deuteronomy*, p. 238.

82 Milgrom's attempt to argue that the Deuteronomic editor was abridging Leviticus 11 as a whole (*Leviticus 1—16*, pp. 698–704) is unconvincing. According to him, Deuteronomy 14.20 implies the permission of locusts. But in Deuteronomy 14.4b–5 permitted animals *not* listed in Leviticus are listed! He also says Deuteronomy 14.21a includes the prohibitions in Leviticus 11.42–43. It is hard to take this seriously: it implies that it would be an act of charity to give an alien a dead mouse or lizard, let us say.

in 14.4–20, doubtless some time after the original publication of the code in the late seventh century (or whenever it was), was nevertheless earlier than the Holiness redaction which gave Leviticus 11 more or less its present shape, since it knows the priestly teaching only in an older form, without Leviticus 11.21–23, 42–43. This does not tell us how early that older form was composed, but although it is itself the work of learned scribes with interests in nature and its classification, it has a basis in the practice of the Hebrew tribes since their emergence – they neither kept nor ate pigs – and also in cultic practice throughout the area since the Bronze Age – pigs were never normally sacrificed, and donkeys very rarely.[83] Priestly teaching of this kind could easily date from the monarchic period, even in its written form, and could have been attached to the priestly narrative at a later point.[84]

On the other hand, the evidence is that work was being done on Deuteronomy at an earlier time than the Holiness redaction of priestly material. This is against the views of the Kaufmann school, which argues that while Deuteronomy quotes priestly material, as here, there are no references to Deuteronomic laws in P or H. This is hardly accurate in any case. While there may be no laws in Deuteronomic wording, there is certainly usage of Deuteronomistic phraseology: 'a land flowing with milk and honey' occurs in Leviticus 20.24; 'your brother' referring to a fellow Israelite occurs several times in Leviticus 25 as well as scattered over Deuteronomy 15—24; and most significantly, Leviticus 26 refers to *both* the covenant with Abraham *and* the covenant of Sinai/Horeb.[85] In a word, H is the latest of the legal strands, and all the previous ones are available to the author. According to Eckart Otto its legal hermeneutic brings together Deuteronomy and P, and thus creates the Torah.[86]

The most interesting aspect of the law of animal kinds is the theology which undergirds it, understood slightly differently in D and H; in the context of this chapter this is important in suggesting possible dates. I have suggested, with some evidence from ancient parallels, that the original law was primarily intended for the teaching of the people at festival time to ensure that the holy *place* and its cult were not defiled.[87] In both its current versions it is concerned with the daily life of the people and their own holiness. In Deuteronomy, the law is brought in as a detailed illustration of the command to eat no 'abomination' (Deut. 14.3), which itself is an expression of the understanding of Israel as a people holy to YHWH (14.2, taking up the theme of 7.6). 'Abomination' (*to'ebah*) I take as indicating 'that category of things that the delicate find odious or abhorrent':[88] that category of things which are demeaning to the dignity and self-respect of God's holy

---

83 Houston, *Purity*, pp. 124–80.
84 Cf. Carr, *Writing*, pp. 169–70.
85 Nihan, 'Priestly Covenant'. See above, pp. 96, 102.
86 Otto, 'Holiness Code'.
87 Houston, *Purity*, p. 232.
88 Weinfeld, *Deuteronomy*, p. 226, quoted by Houston, *Purity*, p. 60.

people. I do not find here a situation of conquest, exile, humiliation and mixing of peoples, but rather a sense of national pride after the throwing off of the Assyrian yoke. In contrast, the H redaction suggests the danger of assimilation among the peoples (Lev. 20.24–26); in this situation Israel are to cling all the more firmly to their dedication to YHWH, to ensure that they are holy as he is holy. This reflects the setting of exile or the early Persian period.[89]

Conclusion

As a tentative conclusion from this exercise, here is a very brief sketch of how we might conceive the development of the Pentateuch.

The starting point is a number of old traditions in the kingdoms of Israel and Judah. They include tales about tribal heroes, who were supposed to be the ancestors of the tribes inhabiting different parts of the country, and were revered by them. They also include the contrasting story of the escape of Israelites from Egypt by the agency of Moses, the prophet of YHWH, and their immigration into Canaan. Implying the sharp distinction of Israel from other peoples and their special patronage by YHWH, this may have had a more official character as a national founding legend in the kingdom of Israel. It may alternatively, or as well, have been cultivated among circles of Levites.[90] It is possible that it included an address by YHWH to the newly liberated people imposing exclusive loyalty upon them. Collections of these stories began to be made by literate persons, royal or temple scribes, and they formed part of the oral-written curriculum of their educational work. There is a strong possibility that in the more culturally diverse northern kingdom the ancestral tales (but not that of the exodus) were told referring to the divine by the non-committal *elohim*, whereas in Judah YHWH was used throughout. This would account for the evidence of 'E' and 'J' material in Genesis, but does not imply the existence of continuous 'E' and 'J' narratives.

Triggers for the development of these collections into continuous narratives appeared in the collapse of the kingdom of Israel in 722 BCE and of that of Judah in 587 BCE. Whatever the previous relationship of the populations of the two kingdoms, they had much in common, above all the veneration of YHWH as the national god, and this enabled them, after 722, to develop a common tradition expressing an identity which did not depend on statehood. It was the literate elite that expressed this in oral-written form. The name of Israel was adopted as the name of the (at least in aspiration) united people. The old northern traditions were brought together with southern ones and frequently overwritten, using the divine name YHWH. Isaac (from the Negeb) was made the father of Jacob (from Bethel and Shechem) and

---

89 Houston, *Purity*, pp. 241–4; 248–53.
90 Cook, *Social Roots*.

Abraham (from Hebron) the father of Isaac. But it was probably not until the fall of Judah was threatened or accomplished that all the stories, those of the ancestors of the tribes, and that of the exodus and conquest, were formed into a continuum, with the device of making the tribes (in the persons of their ancestors) go down into Egypt and return and bound together by the theme of YHWH's promise. (I see no need to date this process as late as the time of the Second Temple.)

Oral-written material of non-narrative kinds was also being passed on in monarchic Israel and Judah: a collection of model civil laws and ritual instructions of the priests – and of course other types which did not eventually form part of the Pentateuch. What is remarkable is that legal material began to be worked into the narrative, perhaps as early as the late monarchy. The most obvious reason for this is the need to give authority to the laws. Now in the ancient Near East generally it was kings who authorized law, as in the famous laws of Hammurabi. But the Hebrew monarchies were becoming weak and discredited, and soon disappeared altogether. What better, especially for a now stateless people, than to put the laws in the mouth of God, or of Moses, the first and greatest of the prophets of God? As we know, both these were done. It is possible that groups in the former state of Israel maintaining the tradition of the worship of YHWH alone first attached a covenant narrative, with an early form of the Decalogue, to the exodus story, which may already have included a 'mountain of God' narrative. This would have highlighted the command of exclusive loyalty to YHWH. The civil laws, and further teaching on social morality and the honour of God, then became an address of YHWH to Moses (the 'Book of the Covenant'). If the older traditions included a demand by YHWH for exclusive worship, that would have provided a natural point of attachment. A revised version of these laws became Moses' own farewell speech before his death in Deuteronomy.

This development reflects two things: the teaching of certain prophets, which had influenced the literate elite, that YHWH's protection of his people might be revoked by their disloyalty or injustice, implying that the divine connection was not natural but a matter of choice and commitment,[91] and the end of the state and destruction of Jerusalem, which could be and was interpreted as the judgement of YHWH. The continued existence of Israel could no longer be guaranteed by state or temple, but only by their embracing an identity rooted in their commitment to YHWH.

At some time probably not very far removed from this, an alternative version of the story was written, placing the emphasis on the gracious promise ('covenant') of YHWH to the ancestors, and culminating in the glory of YHWH's descent into the Dwelling built at his command. It was prefaced with a prologue placing this national story in a worldwide and even a cosmic context, and it lacked the aggressively nationalistic tone of the now

---

91 Nicholson, *God and His People*, pp. 191–217.

heavily Deuteronomistic older account. The focus of this account on the Dwelling, a frequent description of a temple in its aspect as 'house of God', and its tendency to attract ritual instruction as supplementary material, confirms the classical critical understanding of this account as of priestly origin.

Even in an enlarged form, this narrative probably did not extend to the conquest. It expresses a priestly understanding of Israel as a people (including *gerim*) gathered at the sanctuary of God. This understanding, as against the more nationalistic one, had advantages as Israel faced an indefinitely extended future as a subordinate colonial people. But many groups in the Persian provinces of Yehud (Judah) and Samaria valued the older account. Priestly circles probably initiated the composition of a Torah for the people re-establishing itself in their land. First they rounded out P with a final parenetic redaction emphasizing the holiness of the people (there is no sign of H in non-P passages). Then they combined this with the older account as far as the death of Moses. But this will be the subject of the next chapter.

Suggested exercises

There are unavoidable difficulties in working on the history of Pentateuchal texts. The texts that I am offering here as examples for students to work on are on the whole less complex than those dealt with above, but all the same I would suggest that they are more suited for collective work by a class, under the guidance of the teacher, than for individual students. I am suggesting a few secondary texts in each case, which will give examples of the kinds of solutions to the critical problems that have been offered; but other commentaries and general works of historical criticism (such as Kratz, *Composition*, and Van Seters, *Prologue* or *Moses*) should also be consulted. The teacher may be able to offer contributions from foreign-language works.

1 Genesis 6.5—9.17
   Skinner, *Genesis*; Wenham, *Genesis*; Blenkinsopp, *Pentateuch*, pp. 54–97.

2 Genesis 22.1–19
   Westermann, *Genesis*; Carr, *Fractures*; Yoreh, *First Book*.

3 Exodus 12.1–28
   Propp, *Exodus 1—18*; Dozeman, *Exodus*.

4 Exodus 14
   Propp, *Exodus 1—18*; Dozeman, *Exodus*.

5 Deuteronomy 15.1–18
   Mayes, *Deuteronomy*; Levinson, *Hermeneutics*; Van Seters, *Law Book*.

6 Deuteronomy 28
   Mayes, *Deuteronomy*; McConville, *Deuteronomy*; Weinfeld, *Deuteronomy*.

Further reading

Expositions of the standard form of the Documentary Hypothesis will be found in introductions such as Driver's or Soggin's, including lists of texts usually assigned to one or other document. The introductions of Eissfeldt and Fohrer include their own subdivisions of J. Eissfeldt's is the most detailed of all these. Within each book of the Pentateuch all the critical commentaries also give this kind of information, and some of the more recent, such as Dozeman's *Exodus*, also present more recent views outside the frame of the Documentary Hypothesis.

Friedman's *Who Wrote the Bible?* is a popular presentation giving a lively, opinionated argument for the Documentary Hypothesis with the modification of a pre-exilic P. His arguments are no worse than other scholars', but he rarely engages with other arguments (except Wellhausen's), depends on a conservative view of the biblical history, and has a rather naive view of individual authors. Unfortunately, his article 'Torah' in *ABD* simply gives his own views.

The best exposition of the reasons for treating P as the last of the four main documents of the Documentary Hypothesis is still Wellhausen's *Prolegomena*. But it should be understood that Wellhausen takes the hypothesis itself for granted. Arguments against Wellhausen's view are easily accessible: in Friedman (as above), Kaufmann's *Religion of Israel*, Milgrom's commentary on *Leviticus*, and King, *Realignment*. They are addressed by Blenkinsopp, 'Assessment', and his argument is in turn countered by Milgrom, 'Antiquity'.

Going away from the Documentary Hypothesis, the most useful discussions of recent work as far as 1997 or 2000 are in Nicholson, *Pentateuch*, and G. I. Davies, 'Introduction to the Pentateuch'. Ska (*Introduction*, pp. 96–164) goes further back for a history since ancient times. Ska's book as a whole deals mainly with the issues discussed in this chapter and the next, though it goes wider in places. David Carr, in *Formation*, and Konrad Schmid, in *Old Testament*, offer their own respective accounts of the history of the composition of the whole Bible, including the Pentateuch. Ska's and Schmid's books are written for students, though some students may find them hard going. Carr is mainly writing for scholars, I think.

Kratz's *Composition* is the most consistent presentation of a redactional analysis, and in principle it deals with every verse. But since he covers Genesis to Nehemiah in about 350 pages, his argumentation in detail is necessarily rather thin. However, the book is perfectly readable provided it is read with the Bible alongside it. A minimum of Hebrew is used, in transliteration.

John Van Seters is a lone wolf, but *Prologue to History* and *The Life of Moses*, besides being readable, are worth reading not just for his distinctive views, but for the wealth of ideas about the background of the text that they contain.

6

The Coming to Be of the Torah

This chapter deals with the completion of the Pentateuch in roughly the forms[1] in which the communities that recognize it as Scripture now know it, and with the process by which it may have become so recognized, its 'promulgation' or 'canonization', to use words that are often used but that may well be misleading. I am dealing with these two things together because some theories see them as being two aspects of the same event: the Pentateuch was fixed in something like the form we know it in order to create an authoritative text, more authoritative in some respects than what had gone before. But these two things did not necessarily coincide in this way, as we shall see.

When was the Torah completed and authoritative?

There can be no reasonable doubt that by the second century BCE at latest a Pentateuch much as we know it was taken as authoritative, in one sense or another, by Jewish and Samaritan communities. The most direct evidence for this comes from Qumran. Here a large number of manuscripts of all five books of the Pentateuch were found.[2] Here also were found scrolls that in different ways acknowledge the authority of the Pentateuch: for example the Temple Scroll, which takes part of the Pentateuch as its base text and elaborates it by adding in related Pentateuchal laws and interpretations and presenting the whole as direct divine revelation; or the Damascus Document, which in a manner more familiar to us offers interpretation of explicitly quoted Pentateuchal laws as authority for its own instruction.[3] Both these books were probably composed in the second century BCE. This reverence for the Pentateuch is certainly not a sectarian peculiarity, for Ben Sira, early in the second century, representing a Judaism very different from that of

---

1 'Forms', because the Masoretic (Hebrew) Text read by Jews, the (Greek) Septuagint, which for centuries was the Old Testament of the Christian Church and still is for the Greek Orthodox, and the Samaritan Pentateuch all vary from each other in a number of places.

2 Details in Tov, *Textual Criticism*, p. 104.

3 See Crawford, 'Use'.

Qumran, places 'the law of the Most High' as the first item in the scribal curriculum (Ecclus. 39.1). Admittedly, this does not tell us precisely what he reckoned as 'the law of the Most High'; but a few chapters later in his 'praise of famous men', he mentions a number of characters from the Pentateuchal narrative: not only Enoch, Noah, Abraham, Moses and Aaron, but the much less prominent Phinehas from Numbers 25 (Ecclus. 45.23–24), in the least read of the books of the Torah. The narrative of the Pentateuch certainly functioned for him as authoritative history. And a little later, in the persecution of Antiochus Epiphanes (167 BCE), 'the scrolls of the law' or 'of the covenant' are targeted for destruction (1 Macc. 1.56–57). Their connection with Jewish customs had been identified and taken seriously.

On the other hand, at the end of the fifth century, the papyri from Elephantine belonging to the Jewish garrison community there on the southern border of Egypt betray no knowledge of the Pentateuch, even though they were in contact with Jerusalem and Samaria.[4] Even when Hananiah, an important Jewish figure who did not belong to the community, probably from Jerusalem, writes to them about the observance of the festival of Unleavened Bread, he does not apparently refer to any Pentateuchal text.

And even in Judah in the fifth century, Nehemiah, according to his own memoir, gives orders which may broadly reflect Pentateuchal norms, for example with regard to the remission of debts (chapter 5) or Sabbath observance (13.15–22), yet without any reference to a specific text.[5] Yet, the book in which his memoir is incorporated, Ezra–Nehemiah, certainly shows knowledge of the Pentateuch and presents it as authoritative for the life of the Jewish community. Texts from both Deuteronomy (for example 7.1–4; 23.3–8: Ezra 9.1) and Leviticus (23.39–43: Neh. 8.13–18) are applied within the narrative, and many points from the narrative of the Pentateuch are referred to in Nehemiah 9. This would seem to show that the Torah read in public in Nehemiah 8.1–12 is meant by the narrator to be the Torah we know in the sense that it includes both narrative and law, both P and D.[6] This does not conclusively prove that the community in general, beyond the writer's circle, at the time of writing (let alone at the time of Ezra, whenever that was) accepted its authority, but it does show at the very least that the Pentateuch, more or less as we know it, existed, and was regarded as an authority by some. The date of this writing is uncertain, but it seems that most are prepared to accept a date round about 300 BCE.[7] A similar date would be given to Chronicles, which also presupposes the authority

4 Porten and Yardeni, *Textbook*; Cowley, *Aramaic Papyri*. See Kratz, 'Temple and Torah', pp. 82–9.

5 Apart from a reminiscence of Deuteronomy 30.1–5 in Nehemiah 1.8–9, the parts of Nehemiah written in the first person (1.1—2.20; 4.1—7.5; 12.31–43; 13.4–31) do not make reference to the Torah text.

6 Grabbe, *History*, p. 337.

7 Williamson, *Ezra, Nehemiah*, p. xxxvi; cf. Grabbe, *History*, p. 343.

of the Pentateuch; and the Pentateuch was translated into Greek about the mid-third century.[8]

It therefore seems safe to conclude that the Pentateuch was roughly complete by the end of the fourth century, if not earlier,[9] and that between 400 and 200 it came to be regarded generally by communities claiming the name of Israel as the leading authority in matters of religious law at least, if not over other areas.

The authority of the Torah

Ritual and civil law

This is a quite remarkable development, since previously, and in other cultures as well as in Israel, authority in religious matters had generally belonged to the oral instruction of priests. James Watts plausibly suggests that the Torah's initial authority was over ritual, as in many cultures old texts are revered as guides to ritual, and it was then gradually extended into other fields.[10] In the Hebrew Bible itself we hear relatively little of the Pentateuch or its precursors, such as Josiah's Torah scroll, being applied to other than ritual matters.

Descriptive and prescriptive law

Michael LeFebvre makes a different distinction, between descriptive and prescriptive law.[11] We have previously seen that Pentateuchal laws, like other ancient Near Eastern codes, did not originally *prescribe* rules to be applied literally by courts and other authorities, but *described* the nature of justice, the application of law, or the proper worship of God, or whatever the subject of the law might be (above, pp. 60–2). When Jeremiah 34.8–16 cites the law on release of debt-slaves in Deuteronomy 15.12–18, LeFebvre shows that the application is loose and confuses the seven-year debt release law in Deuteronomy 15.1 with the slave law.[12]

But this had changed by the Hellenistic period. The evidence is very thin for the early part of that period, but the books of Maccabees, in the late second century, presuppose that Pentateuchal Torah is to be applied literally and prescriptively, even if a particular rule might be considered merely part of a narrative description. For example, the 'seekers' attacked in their caves by the king's troops on the Sabbath day (1 Macc. 2.32–38) refuse to 'come out' (v. 34), which LeFebvre suggests is a literal application of

---

8 These and other points are summarized by Grabbe.
9 Crüsemann, *Torah*, pp. 333–4
10 Watts, *Ritual*, pp. 209–14. See below.
11 LeFebvre, *Collections*.
12 LeFebvre, *Collections*, pp. 83–7.

Exodus 16.29, where Moses tells the Israelites to stay in their tents and not go out to look for manna on the Sabbath day.[13] But when they are slaughtered because they refuse to take up arms, Mattathias and his friends pass a resolution that armed resistance to attack is permissible on the Sabbath (1 Macc. 2.41). The law is considered to remain binding; it can be amended in special circumstances, but this must be formally agreed.[14]

More controversially, LeFebvre argues that this development had not taken place by the Persian period. As we have seen, there are several places where the Pentateuchal Torah is shown as being applied in Ezra–Nehemiah. But the application frequently diverges from the text. For example, in the celebration of the feast of Tabernacles in Nehemiah 8.13–18, Leviticus 23.39–43 is read and applied. But the list of species of trees whose branches are used is not the same, and they are put to a different use: instead of being used to 'rejoice before YHWH' (Lev. 23.40, presumably in the festal procession), they are used to build booths (Neh. 8.15–16), while in Leviticus this is a separate activity. LeFebvre argues that this shows that Ezra does not take the Torah as prescriptively binding, word for word, even though the whole account elevates its general authority.[15]

But most scholars believe that Ezra–Nehemiah does presuppose the prescriptive use of the Torah. But this is assumed rather than specifically argued. The lack of literal fit between the text and the application has not gone unnoticed, and Michael Fishbane has attempted to explain the modes of exegesis which may have been applied by Ezra and others in order to derive the desired conclusion from the text.[16] Thus the divorce of foreign wives depends on a combination of Deuteronomy 7.1–4 and 23.3–8 in Ezra 9.1, showing that as well as the ancient peoples of Canaan, Ammonites, Moabites and Edomites were forbidden marriage partners and prohibited from becoming part of Israel; while the application of Leviticus 23.39–43 is achieved by a midrashic technique: noting the derivation of *sukkot* (booths) from the verb *skk* meaning to cover over (with branches), thus proving that the branches should be used for the booths.[17] But LeFebvre argues that such subtle midrashic argument is only evidenced from much later and it is anachronistic to find it at this period.[18]

More important than any specific authoritative function is the acceptance by communities of Jews and Samaritans everywhere, without any state enforcement, of the Pentateuchal Torah in the function we identified at the beginning of this book: as the foundation document of Israel, giving them their identity and their meaning, and prescribing their way of life and behaviour. It seems likely that this did not happen in one fell swoop, but

13 LeFebvre, *Collections*, p. 225.
14 LeFebvre, *Collections*, pp. 225–8.
15 LeFebvre, *Collections*, pp. 111–12.
16 Fishbane, *Biblical Interpretation*, pp. 107–34.
17 Fishbane, *Biblical Interpretation*, pp. 111, 114–21.
18 LeFebvre, *Collections*, pp. 138–9.

gradually. But the evidence cited above, as well as the slightly later witness of the New Testament and other first-century CE material (for example Philo of Alexandria) shows that it was firmly established by the turn of the eras. It should be understood that this general acceptance of the Torah's authority, even in a prescriptive sense, does not imply agreement on the details of ritual and custom. On the contrary, the evidence of disagreement, for example in the Qumran halakhic document 4QMMT, is precisely the best evidence that it is taken prescriptively: divergences have to be justified on the basis of the text.

Narrative authority

As important as the prescriptive function of the text is its narrative aspect, telling the origin story of Israel. There are a number of texts within the Hebrew Bible that appear to draw on the Pentateuch in a brief retelling of the story. They are usually regarded as late, not necessarily only for this reason; they include Joshua 24, Psalms 78, 105, 106 and Nehemiah 9. All of these refer to elements from a wide range of traditions found in the Pentateuch. John H. Choi has attempted to argue from the discrepancies and omissions that they all show as against the Pentateuch that they are not drawing on the Pentateuch in anything like its present form.[19] This judgement seems to underestimate the degree of freedom that ancient writers could use in employing a source, as well as making assumptions that they may not have shared about the relative importance of elements of the tradition. (Must they have mentioned Sinai if they refer to commandments and were using the Pentateuch?) It seems more reasonable to conclude that these late writers (not easily datable) did in fact know and use the Pentateuch in something like its present form, but that they did not regard themselves as bound to a slavish literalness.

Historical context

In studying the completion of the Torah and its rise to authority there are circumstances that we need to take account of.

Persian rule

If the Pentateuch was substantially complete by the end of the fourth century and already beginning to acquire authority, it is the work of the Persian period. How was Persian rule exercised in the local context?[20] The small

---

19 Choi, *Traditions*, pp. 105–81.
20 For the following, see Grabbe, *History*, pp. 132–66; *Judaism*, pp. 74–5.

provinces of Judah (Yehud was its official name in Aramaic) and Samaria were under the general oversight of the satrap of Beyond the River, but the Nehemiah memoir suggests that their local governors had wide discretion over local affairs. Satraps, at the highest level of regional government, were normally Persians and often members of the royal family, but governors of provinces could often be of local origin. It seems that both Israelite provinces usually had Israelite governors: Nehemiah was Jewish and most other governors of Yehud that we know of have Hebrew names; and Sanballat, governor of Samaria, was able to pass the office on to his son Delaiah, whose name indicates that his father was a YHWH-worshipper. It is usually believed that in Yehud the high priest had considerable power; many writers speak of a theocracy, or, in relation to the governor, of a 'dyarchy', that is, rule by two men.[21] But Lisbeth Fried has shown that the royal bureaucracy had absolute power under the king; priests played no part as such in civil government (though they might be appointed to civil posts).[22] But of course they controlled their own temples and religious institutions. The illusion of a 'dyarchy' arises because our sources are concerned especially with religious matters. Naturally, for example, Haggai addresses the high priest as well as the governor when he urges the rebuilding of the temple (Hag. 1.12). Even so, it is clear that governors felt themselves entitled to interfere in the high priest's domain (for example Neh. 13.4–14). This raises the possibility of civil involvement in the promotion of the Torah, as Ezra 7—10 suggests (see further below).

Diaspora

The communities that came to recognize the Torah were not confined to Palestine. There were major Jewish communities in Babylonia, where they had been since the deportations of 597 and 587 and had flourished; in Egypt the garrison at Elephantine (near Aswan) has already been mentioned, and once the city of Alexandria was founded in the late fourth century, its Jewish community grew rapidly; and there were others elsewhere. There was also a Samaritan diaspora: third-century inscriptions on the Aegean island of Delos mention 'Israelites who pay the temple tax to Mt Gerizim'.[23] All these communities were in regular contact with the homeland. The Elephantine correspondence shows the community there seeking help from Yehud and from Samaria. Pilgrimage to the festivals at the Jerusalem temple became an important part of the piety of diaspora Judaism, though Josephus, in speaking of millions, no doubt exaggerates the numbers.[24]

---

21 So even Grabbe, *Judaism*, pp. 74–5.
22 Fried, *Priest*.
23 Kartveit, *Origin*, pp. 216–25.
24 Josephus, *Jewish War*, 6.420–5; Goodman, *Rome*, pp. 66–7.

Samaria

While it has been usual to refer only to Judah and the Jewish diaspora in considering the rise of the Torah, it should not be forgotten that the same Torah was accepted by Israelites living in Samaria, who had a temple on Mount Gerizim to the south of Shechem, built probably in the middle of the fifth century.[25] Sectarian ('Samaritan') additions to the text (such as the 'Samaritan tenth commandment') (see above, p. 46), making it clear that this was the exclusive place for sacrificial worship, were probably not made until the first century BCE.[26] Before that the text apparently used by the people of Samaria was also widespread in Judah. It had additions harmonizing different parts of the text with each other.[27]

The issues at stake

Gary Knoppers and Bernard Levinson, in their editorial introduction to the valuable collection of essays *The Pentateuch as Torah*, helpfully set out the issues with which the book, like this chapter, is concerned.[28]

1 How was it that such a composite work as the Pentateuch emerged, containing both narrative and law and combining at least two major sources? 'What was the historical, social, religious, or economic impetus to compile and promote one written corpus of law over many?' We have begun to answer the first question in the previous chapter, but the other remains outstanding. In fact most of the following points elaborate on it.

2 Within what social milieu did the composition and 'promulgation' of the Pentateuch originally take place? Was it within a very narrow Judaean scribal elite, or was it foundational educational material that at some point became 'normative law'? And if so, did this transformation in function take place in the Persian period or as 'an act of communal self-definition in resistance to creeping Hellenization' in the Greek period?

3 Did the creation of the Pentateuch involve a negotiated compromise between priestly and lay leaders in the Judaean community, as suggested for example by Crüsemann?[29]

4 Did the creation of the Pentateuch involve the rejection of a Hexateuch, including the account of the promised settlement of Israel in Canaan? If so, was this step related to the character of Judaism as a diaspora from the

---

25 Magen, 'Samaritan Temple'.

26 Pummer, 'Samaritans', pp. 248–9.

27 Tov, *Textual Criticism*, pp. 80–100; more details in Kartveit, *Origin*, pp. 259–312.

28 Knoppers and Levinson, *Pentateuch*, pp. 2–8.

29 Crüsemann, *Torah*, pp. 340–3.

Babylonian period onwards? Or to the evaluation of Moses as pre-eminent prophet over against all subsequent prophets (Deut. 34.10–12)?

5 What part was played by the diaspora communities in the rise of the Pentateuch to its status as foundation document? And was the Pentateuch itself developed in Judah or abroad, presumably in Babylonia?

6 How is the common possession of the Pentateuchal Torah by both Judaeans and Samarians[30] to be explained? Did the Samarians simply accept a Torah composed by Judaeans, in Jerusalem or in Babylonia, or did they play some part in its composition?

7 When and how did the Pentateuch move to a normative legal status in these communities?

8 Was there an external stimulus that facilitated the process by which the Pentateuch came to exist and to achieve authority? What part, if any, did the Persian imperial power play? The 'theory of imperial authorization' developed by Peter Frei offers evidence that local codes were recognized by the Persian authorities (normally locally rather than at the centre) and adopted, for the area, as imperial law. The account in Ezra 7—10 and Nehemiah 8 might suggest this happened with the Torah, and this has led to prolonged discussion.[31]

9 Knoppers and Levinson's final question is: what light does the reception, translation and interpretation of the Pentateuch in the last few centuries BCE shed on the process of its composition and becoming the acknowledged Torah?

In what follows I shall not deal with each of these issues individually, but most of them will be at least touched on. First come questions concerning the social context within which the Pentateuch was developed and came to be recognized as authoritative (compare 2 and 3 above), and second the involvement of diaspora and Samarian communities (5 and 6). Third, I shall discuss the question of 'imperial authorization' (8 above). With the context thus set, I shall look at the main questions concerning how the Pentateuch reached its present form (1 and 4); and the final development of its authority (7 and 9).

What was the Torah needed for?

This subject, despite its importance, has not yet been given a satisfactory treatment.

---

30 It is now usual to confine the expression 'Jews and Samaritans' to the time after the definite break between the communities, whenever that was.

31 See the essays in Watts, *Persia*; Schmid, 'Authorization' and Carr, *Formation*, pp. 217–21.

Social compromise?

Crüsemann makes an interesting start with his idea of a compromise between priestly interests and lay ones, especially those of the peasantry constantly under the threat of indebtedness.[32] He sees this expressed concisely in the covenant of Nehemiah 10, which guarantees the temple its supplies, but at the same time assures debtors of the seventh-year release (Neh. 10.32). But there is a contradiction here. Crüsemann assumes that Pentateuchal law is prescriptive and enforced; but in that case there would be no need for the covenant, which is a voluntary agreement; and if it is a compromise, it is a very one-sided one, with eight items in favour of the temple and part of one in favour of the farmers! – not to mention the discrepancies between the Pentateuch and the covenant.[33] If we drop the assumption that the Torah was prescriptive law in the Persian period, it is easier to explain all this, and it also makes any 'compromise' superfluous.

Temple ritual

There are several relevant contexts which might be taken into account as situations in which the Pentateuch as a composite document originated and gained authority. Carr has underlined the use of the Pentateuch's precursor documents by scribes as educational material for a relatively small elite,[34] and invokes the imperial authorization theory to explain the composite document's status as law.[35] Kratz and Watts point rather to its character as a norm for religious ritual.[36] Kratz notes how between Elephantine and Qumran 'temple and Torah' came together. Temple rituals and customs had gone into the make-up of the Torah, and after editing and reflection the Torah then influenced the practice of the temple. Watts suggests that the authority of the Torah may have at first been recognized only over the ritual of the temple, and was then extended to areas of daily life that could be ritualized, such as diet and purity. Only from the second century BCE is there direct evidence of its authority beginning to be recognized in civil law.[37]

Watts also introduces the idea of theocracy, in the sense of priestly rule, and argues that the Torah implicitly authorizes this, through the fact that the high priesthood, in the figure of Aaron, is made so visually impressive, and is the only institution that is prescribed in any detail, even though explicitly it does not give priests much power – even over their own rituals.[38]

---

32 Crüsemann, *Torah*, pp. 339–43.
33 LeFebvre, *Collections*, pp. 112–22.
34 Carr, *Writing*.
35 Carr, *Formation*, pp. 204–7, 217–21.
36 Kratz, 'Temple and Torah'; Watts, 'Rhetoric'; *Ritual*, pp. 209–14.
37 Watts, *Ritual*, pp. 209–17; LeFebvre (see below, pp. 135–6).
38 Watts, 'Rhetoric'.

But we have noted that there was no such theocracy in the Persian period, and by the beginning of the Hellenistic period the Pentateuch was essentially complete. This theory is superficially attractive, but needs rethinking.

Teaching for the people

It is perhaps the continuing function of the Torah in education which is in reality the most important aspect in rooting it as the document guaranteeing the identity of Israel. Nehemiah 8 is an ideal picture of the process. It is the whole people, at least those in reach of Jerusalem, who hear the Torah read, not just an elite. This conforms (apart from the date) with the instruction in Deuteronomy (31.10–13) for the (Deuteronomic) Torah to be read every seven years at the feast of Sukkot before the entire people.

Both the Deuteronomy text and the narrative in Nehemiah indicate the expected result. They are 'to hear and learn and fear YHWH your God and be careful to observe all the words of this torah' (Deut. 31.12). What this means in practice is illustrated in the story. The people take what they hear so seriously that they weep (Neh. 8.9), although the leaders tell them to rejoice. This seems to imply that they are beginning to 'fear YHWH their God'; and this is followed up by the further study session of the 'heads of the people' with Ezra (Neh. 8.13), which is devoted to the details of the commandments.

What they learn from the Torah goes far beyond any legal or ritual function. They learn a number of stories of the birth of Israel as a nation, all of which make it clear that they have been from the start under the providential care of their God, and the story of the covenant in particular shows that they are called to serve him through the observance of the commandments. They learn this as a nation and as individuals, but they do not learn the commandments or observe them as the result of any legal 'promulgation', but rather through hearing them and taking them to heart. Many other texts could be quoted to the same effect, for example Deuteronomy 6.4–9 and the psalms of the Torah, Psalms 1, 19, 119. All of them speak of the personal appropriation of the commandments through mind and heart and their putting into effect by the will; but even above that of learning to know and love and fear YHWH the God of Israel. To this day this is the context in which the Torah is heard and obeyed. Its recognition as a prescriptive authority for community life and civil law is a further development.

Beyond Jerusalem

There is no difficulty in seeing how the Torah in the long run became the common possession of Israelites in Judah and Samaria, in Babylonia and Egypt and around the world. All these communities were in touch with each other, and all were in situations in which the possession of a body of literature which assured them of their place in God's world and their high calling to be 'a kingdom of priests and a holy nation' would strengthen their sense of identity over against others in their neighbourhood.

The interesting and controversial question is whether and to what extent any communities outside Judah or scribal cadres outside Jerusalem participated in the composition and initial recognition of the Torah. Opinions are highly divergent.

The Babylonian exiles

Carr, following many others, attributes the composition of both the 'post-D' (as he calls it) and 'P' precursor documents to exile groups in Babylonia, and their combination in a proto-Pentateuch to recently returned exiles. He argues that the entire knowledge of the national traditions and expertise in their handling reposed in the *golah*, the exiled community, after 587 (if not 597); whatever of northern traditions was preserved had been taken to Jerusalem at the fall of Samaria, and even in Judah the *golah* was the dominant cultural force.[39] If Ezra–Nehemiah is any guide to the outlook of the *golah*, it was peculiarly narrow. The Holiness Code stresses the separation of Israel from other peoples (Lev. 20.24–26) and is widely seen as part of a late, if not the final, redaction of the Pentateuch. This may tend to confirm that recently returned exiles participated in some of the last moves in the development of the text, but it neither excludes the participation of others nor proves that exiles in Babylonia had been equally dominant at earlier stages. There are features of the Torah that are more eirenic and at variance with this xenophobic approach, for example the presentation of Abraham as the ancestor of neighbouring nations to Judah in the south of Palestine as well as Israel and the favourable view of Egyptians in the Joseph story and in Deuteronomy 23.7–8 [8–9].

Bethel

A number of scholars have argued that, even after the fall of Jerusalem, traditions, and perhaps compositions, were preserved in Judah at the temple of Bethel, which, they argue, continued in existence even after its alleged desecration by King Josiah (2 Kings 23.15).[40] The land of Benjamin, including Bethel, was annexed by Judah some time in the seventh century, was not devastated by the Babylonian army in 589–587, and formed part of Yehud in the Persian period. Thus the *golah* would not be the only source of trad-

---

39 Carr, *Formation*, pp. 225–6, 204–24.
40 Blenkinsopp, 'Judaean Priesthood'; Middlemas, *Troubles*, p. 144; Knauf, 'Bethel'.

itions in Yehud going to make up the Pentateuch. One could expect that northern traditions would have taken pride of place in any compositions from Bethel. They could have included, for example, the story of Joseph, which Redford shows from the Egyptian background is unlikely to have taken shape before about 650 BCE.[41]

Samaria

Finally, to make up for general earlier neglect, a number of scholars in recent years have suggested ways of accounting for the common possession of the Torah by Judah and Samaria, some of which give an active role to the Samarians.[42] We do not know of any other such community that existed in the fifth century, had its own temple and was orthodox by Torah standards; this point would exclude Elephantine.[43] If the Pentateuch did not reach its final agreed state until after the mid-fifth century, the latest developments must have at least received active approval from Mount Gerizim. The Pentateuch is as favourable to Samaria as it is to Judah. Genesis 14 makes 'Salem', that is, Jerusalem, a holy place recognized already by Abraham; and Genesis 22 may also refer to Jerusalem (above, p. 35, n. 65). But Deuteronomy 27 prescribes ritual to be carried out by the Israelites on Mounts Gerizim and Ebal either side of Shechem. Unlike Jerusalem, Mount Gerizim is given its proper name.

Kratz suggests that it may have been the Samarians who first elevated the Pentateuch to Torah because they needed a recognized authority for their new temple, which did not have a local tradition because there had never been a temple on Mount Gerizim before.[44] For the same reason, I have suggested that the combination of P and non-P documents may have taken place with the needs of the Mount Gerizim community in mind. In the fifth century the Jerusalem priesthood had close connections with Samaria (Neh. 13.28!), and the two priesthoods may have accepted the composition jointly.[45]

---

41 Redford, *Joseph*.

42 See Knoppers, 'Parallel Torahs'; Houston, 'Salem and Gerizim'; earlier, several essays in Knoppers and Levinson, *Pentateuch*, esp. Schmid, 'Authorization', pp. 35–6; Kratz, 'Temple and Torah', pp. 98–101; Nihan, 'Torah'; Pummer, 'Samaritans'.

43 To argue that setting up a second temple in the land of Israel was unorthodox is to prejudge the point at issue between Jerusalem and Gerizim.

44 Kratz, 'Temple and Torah', pp. 98–101.

45 Houston, 'Salem and Gerizim'.

The theory of imperial authorization

The relevance of the theory

Why should this idea be considered in relation to the emergence of the Torah? Three reasons in particular may be mentioned.

1 This is what the text of the book of Ezra–Nehemiah appears to imply. We have already seen that in the context of the whole book Nehemiah 8 should be understood as saying that the Torah that the readers of Ezra–Nehemiah knew – and this is apparently not very different from the one that we know – was that read by Ezra to the people of Jerusalem. It is referred to as 'the Torah of Moses' at Ezra 7.6 as well as Nehemiah 8.1. This in turn implies that in the decree of Artaxerxes 'the law of your God that is in your hand' (Ezra 7.14; cf. vv. 12, 21, 25–26) is understood by the narrator to refer to the Torah. However, assuming the decree is authentic, it did not necessarily mean the same thing to Artaxerxes or to Ezra.[46] But if it did, then the imposition of a version of the Torah on Judaeans and Samarians is indeed 'authorized' by a royal decree.

2 It is emphasized by Carr that a particular stimulus was required to trigger the unusual step of combining the P and non-P strands of the Pentateuch.[47] The necessity of presenting a single document to the authorities would have been a stimulus of sufficient strength. Of course, others are possible, as I have suggested, and not all theories of the Pentateuch's development make this combination the decisive step in the emergence of the Torah.

3 The theory in its present form as it applies to the Torah is a corollary of Frei's theory. He quoted a number of cases where it appears that local laws were publicly confirmed by Persian officials, and in his view made part of the law of the empire.[48]

The authenticity of the decree

To what extent can the decree of Ezra 7 be taken as authentic?[49] There are expressions in the decree that would never have been used by a scribe in the Persian chancery, such as 'the king and his seven councillors' (v. 14) or the name 'Israel' (vv. 13, 15), and the quantities of supplies in verse 22 are fantastic. It cannot be fully authentic. The alternatives are: it is a genuine decree which has been elaborated; or it is simply invented, either by the author or by an earlier Judaean source. One cannot really decide the

---

46 Ska, *Introduction*, pp. 222–3.
47 Carr, *Formation*, pp. 215–21.
48 See the summary of his argument in Frei, 'Imperial Authorization'.
49 Besides the commentaries, see, among others, Grabbe, *History*, pp. 76–8; more detail in 'Persian Documents'; also 'Law of Moses', pp. 92–4; Fried, *Priest*, pp. 212–27.

question in isolation from that of the reliability of the account as a whole. Grabbe summarizes well its contradictions and improbabilities, and these surely undermine confidence in the decree itself.[50]

If, nevertheless, the references to 'the law of the God of heaven', or 'the law of your God', are authentic, what might they originally have meant? Most scholars have assumed, like the author of Ezra, that they refer to the Pentateuch, and that Ezra was entrusted with a mission to enforce Pentateuchal law on Jews (and Samarians?) in the province Beyond the River. But we cannot simply argue from the rest of the material about Ezra that the 'law of your God' must be the Pentateuch. Ska argues that it must be a set of ritual laws, related to P+H, but not necessarily identical.[51]

Fried argues that it is not a document at all; 'the law (*data*) of God' for a Persian meant the natural law of justice, truth and right, and it is the same here with the borrowed word *dat* in Aramaic.

There may well be a historical kernel in this account, but it is virtually impossible to say what it is. It does have a historical significance, but it is of a different kind: it sums up in the form of a representative narrative the probably much longer process by which the Judaean community (ignoring the Samarians!) came to accept the Torah as the guidance for their life to which they were committed by covenant. All that happens in Ezra–Nehemiah is under the sponsorship of the Persian king: the rebuilding of the temple, the rebuilding of the walls by Nehemiah – and the acceptance of the Torah. That is obviously what the editor wishes to convey. Is there any other evidence that might suggest that such sponsorship is plausible for the Torah?

Can the theory apply to the Pentateuch?

This is where the modern theory of imperial authorization comes in. Peter Frei summarizes it helpfully in his contribution to the collection of essays *Persia and Torah*.[52] There are a number of cases where Persian authorities approve a set of local regulations, which he lists in some detail.

None of the other contributors to *Persia and Torah* accept the theory unreservedly, and more than one reject it outright. We need not follow the discussion of the theory as such, accepting that there are cases where locally established norms were confirmed by the imperial representative, if not the king himself, where the empire's interests were involved. But is this relevant to the Torah? The main objection must be the length and complexity of the Pentateuch as well as its overall genre of narrative history.

What would have been the empire's interest in the promulgation of the Torah? In the most general way it was in its interest that in every subject community law and justice were maintained and their religious cults

---

50 Grabbe, *History*, pp. 324–31.
51 Ska, *Introduction*, p. 224.
52 Frei, 'Imperial Authorization'.

observed in agreed fashion. But this could hardly be secured by the Pentateuch in itself, with its contradictions and lack of clarity on the points that
might interest a ruler. And it was absolutely essential, if imperial officials
were to sign off on it, that it should be in Aramaic. But not a trace of any
Aramaic translation of the Pentateuch exists from this period, and if it had
done, there are not a few points that might give pause to an imperial official
reading it.

Carr gets round the problem of lack of imperial interests by supposing
that it was the *golah* whose interests would be served by the authorization of
the Torah, enabling them to enforce their interpretation of the community's
traditions, and that they persuaded the authorities to do so. And although
Carr does not refer to Ezra in this connection, it might well be held that it is
just this that is referred to in the story of Ezra.

The case is not proved. We must also remind ourselves that any theory of
this kind must pass the test of explaining the Samarian as well as the Judaean
possession of the Torah. None of the applications of the imperial authorization theory have attempted to do so. The theory would only explain the
effective identity of the two versions if held in a strong form which no one
now defends, where the local norm becomes imperial law and is therefore
enforced by satraps and governors on populations whom they determine to
be appropriately subject to it.[53]

How was the Pentateuch completed?

Theories in modern scholarship of how the composition of the Pentateuch
was completed are many. Most of them have benefited from some of the
reflections on possible political and social contexts that we have looked
at above. Samaria, however, has usually been ignored, to the detriment of
the theories' coherence. In this section we shall not look individually at all
the theories, but pick out the main issues which arise from them. So far as
the structure of the Pentateuch gives hints of how it was composed, the
main points scholars have concentrated on have been the evident diversity
of P and non-P sections, the gaps between Genesis and Exodus and between
Numbers and Deuteronomy, and conversely the smooth connection of
Deuteronomy and Joshua, and the connections of the Holiness Code with
the other legal collections.

---

53 Pummer, 'Samaritans', p. 258. Schmid, 'Imperial Authorization', defends the theory but makes this point very clearly (p. 38). However, his essay is too short to develop
it.

The integration of P and non-P

Wellhausen and his followers saw the final move in the composition of the Pentateuch as the combination of the priestly source with the already composed JED document. This combination (or, for Blum and Van Seters, redaction) is still seen by most as a key move, if not the key move, in the composition of the Pentateuch, even if not chronologically the very last. For Crüsemann, as we have seen, and for Blum, this is the result of a social compromise. Blum expresses it more in terms of rival intellectual circles than conflicted social classes: the compromise is demanded by the necessity to present a single document to the authorities for their 'authorization'. Carr accepts this idea, but suggests that, rather than a broad social consensus, it was a small body from the *golah* that wished to 'enforce their vision of the future' on the inhabitants of Yehud in the form of a single document embodying two streams of redactional work in exile.[54]

The question of the Hexateuch

The textual transmission of the book of Joshua has been quite separate from that of the Pentateuch since the third century BCE at latest. The earliest Greek text of Joshua differs substantially from the standard Hebrew text, whereas in the Pentateuch the two traditions are much closer. Like the rest of the Prophets and Writings, the book of Joshua was not transmitted, or at least not preserved, in Samaria.

Nineteenth- and much of twentieth-century scholarship, however, ignored these facts. In the classical Documentary Hypothesis, the four presumed sources were traced through the Pentateuch into Joshua, and the final redaction created a Hexateuch. The separation of Joshua from the Pentateuch is described as 'artificial'; the 'contents [of Joshua], and, still more, its literary structure, show that it is intimately connected with the Pentateuch'.[55]

Noth's widely influential theory of the Deuteronomistic History, published in 1943, broke with this view. Noth cast out J, E and P from the book of Joshua and D from the Tetrateuch, and made Deuteronomy 1—3, 31*, 34*, the first part of the work of the author of a continuous history of Israel, including Joshua, Judges, Samuel and Kings, incorporating the Deuteronomic law and composed in the mid-sixth century BCE.[56] At a much later point, the Pentateuch was created, after the combination of JE with P, by cutting Deuteronomy off from the rest of the Deuteronomistic History and attaching it to the Tetrateuch. There is indeed a clear break before Deuteronomy, and it is difficult to see Deuteronomy 1—3 as a likely beginning

---

54 Carr, *Formation*, pp. 217–21; for the work in exile, pp. 255–92.

55 Driver, *Introduction*, p. 103.

56 Noth, *Deuteronomistic History*, esp. pp. 12–17; Römer, *Deuteronomistic History*, pp. 21–5. The asterisks indicate that not all of the chapter is included.

for the book if it had been part of the same literary work as Exodus and Numbers from the start. The story of Israel in the wilderness, for the writer of this section, was a well-known but separate work. But that does not show that his own work continued to 2 Kings!

However, recent scholarship, while accepting Deuteronomy as the start of a new composition including at least Joshua, has detected a later redactional history shared by the Pentateuch and Joshua. At one time, it appears, there was indeed a Hexateuch (if not an Enneateuch stretching from Genesis to Kings).[57] Joshua 24 plays an important role in this argument: a chapter that sums up the story of the Hexateuch, and presents a covenant accepted by all Israel, in the land, at the northern centre of Shechem, while the theme of Joseph's bones (v. 32) links it with a series of texts in Genesis and Exodus.[58] But out of this Hexateuch a Pentateuch was created: Joshua did not remain part of the foundation document. How and why did this happen?

Otto's is the most detailed theory.[59] In this, the 'Hexateuch redaction' of the early fifth century, which climaxes in Joshua's assembly at Shechem, is centred on an ideology of the land and maintains an all-Israel outlook in which Samaria is also Israel. It also rejects the imperial ideology of Persia: YHWH's Torah takes precedence over the law of any foreign king. The main interest of the 'Pentateuch redaction', on the other hand, representing the outlook of the Babylonian *golah*, is in the law. It ends with the death of Moses, the mediator of the law.[60]

Conversely, Schmid places more emphasis on the theological significance of omitting the account of the conquest. As a people without its own land, Israel must now live with the promise only and not the fulfilment: an interpretation common enough in synchronic approaches.[61]

The ancestors and the exodus

Everyone accepts that P bridges the gap between Genesis and Exodus. The dispute is over whether non-P material bridging the gap is composed before or after the publication of P. If after, as according to Schmid and several of the contributors to *Farewell to the Yahwist*, then the creation of a continuous story from creation to the exodus, and beyond, is one of the later moves in the composition of the Pentateuch. The setting of the story of Israel in an international and indeed cosmic context is seen by Schmid as a response to the intellectual atmosphere of the early Persian empire with its aspiration to universality; and he links this with a cautious acceptance of the imperial

57 Schmid, *Genesis*, p. 236.
58 Gertz, 'Transition', pp. 81–2.
59 Otto, 'Holiness Code'.
60 Cf. Carr's theory above.
61 Schmid, *Genesis*, p. 273.

authorization theory.[62] But we have found his theory dubious in relation to Exodus 3—4 and therefore doubtful altogether.[63]

The 'final' redaction[64]

The recent recognition of the Holiness Code as part of a wide-ranging late redaction of the priestly writings[65] inevitably raises the question whether this redaction should be seen as (part of) the 'final' redaction of the entire Pentateuch. This is argued by Knohl, who sees H material bridging different sources.[66] Otto and Nihan see the Holiness Code as bringing together the viewpoints of the Book of the Covenant, Deuteronomy and P.[67] Its note of exclusivity (for example Lev. 20.24–26) is absent in P and links it with late *golah* attitudes. But there are no signs of the hand of H in non-P sections, which suggests that this redaction took place before the combination of P with other sources. This would not prevent the editor of H from using other sources. Numbers is now often seen as the location of the latest additions to the text.[68] The last few verses of Deuteronomy, 34.10–12, summing up the career of Moses, were probably added when the Pentateuch was separated from Joshua.

The Pentateuch becomes a prescriptive legal code

How and when did the sense become established that the Torah's laws were prescriptions to be applied literally to every circumstance with which they deal, whether ritual, civil or moral? The evidence is so thin that speculation is unavoidable, but LeFebvre offers a plausible account.[69] It is appropriate to pinpoint the Hellenistic period, for Greek cities had had prescriptive written laws since the sixth century, and their ideal of civilization was the possession of laws and being ruled by law rather than by a despotic king or tyrant, as they saw happening among the 'barbarians' of the East.[70] LeFebvre suggests that in this context there were two pressures on the Jews (and I would add the Samaritans) moving them towards viewing the Torah prescriptively. One was the intellectual climate in the Hellenistic era in favour of law-

---

62 Schmid, *Genesis*, p. 256; 'Imperial Authorization'.
63 Above, p. 108.
64 'Final' in scare quotes because ongoing additions and adjustments make it impossible to say what was the very last editorial intervention.
65 See above, pp. 102, 113–14.
66 Knohl, 'Who Edited?'
67 Nihan, *Priestly Torah*; Otto, 'Holiness Code'; Nihan, 'Priestly Covenant'.
68 E.g., Nihan, 'Festival Calendars'.
69 LeFebvre, *Collections*, pp. 146–240.
70 See also Knoppers and Harvey, 'Mediterranean Context'.

governed societies. The other was the system of law courts established by
Ptolemy II (282–246 BCE). The Ptolemies were the rulers of Egypt, and also,
up to 200 BCE, Palestine. The Ptolemaic legal system established separate
courts for 'Greeks' (a cultural rather than ethnic designation) and (in Egypt)
for Egyptians. Judges in the Greek courts were directed to decide (after the
king's own legislation on certain matters) according to the laws applying to
the parties' citizenship or ethnicity. This meant prescriptive Greek laws for
Greeks. In the Egyptian courts, Egyptian laws were to be used; thus although
Egyptian laws had not been understood in this way previously, they inevitably began to be treated prescriptively. Although there is no direct evidence
for how this legal reform affected Judaea and Samaria, it is at least plausible
that the system of separate courts for natives was also applied in Palestine.
If so, there would be pressure on judges in Israelite areas to judge according
to the Torah and to treat it prescriptively.[71]

Effectively this reinstates a theory of imperial authorization, but shifted
to a more plausible period, one where the imperial power itself, unlike the
Persians, had prescriptive laws and probably expected native peoples to have
their own. On top of this administrative pressure, and in the long run much
more important, there was the cultural pressure in favour of law-based poli-
ties. LeFebvre points to the long line of Jewish writers in Hellenistic and
Roman times who asserted the antiquity of the law of Moses over any Greek
laws. They thus asserted that the Jews were a civilized people rather than a
barbarian one, living by laws rather than by mere custom and the arbitrary
decrees of a ruler. This polemic is most easily accessible in Josephus' work
Against Apion.[72]

Taken together with the character of the Pentateuchal Torah, these contextual pressures led in the end to the Jews becoming a law-governed people
in a sense rather different from the Greeks. The Torah was to govern not
only the sphere of life that we call legal, but also, of course, religious ritual,
and above all daily life. For the rabbis, at least after 70 CE, customs that
were not directly based on prescriptions of the Pentateuch might either be
derived by midrashic means from the text or simply asserted to be 'Torah
given to Moses from Sinai' and orally transmitted. In either case it was felt
to be necessary to assert the Mosaic origin of the prescription. But the use
and interpretation of the Pentateuch will occupy us in a later chapter.

Further reading

The reading list for the previous chapter is also relevant to the aspect of this
chapter dealing with the completion of the Pentateuch.

The relevant historical background is dealt with in many publications:
one of the best is Grabbe's *Judaism from Cyrus to Hadrian*.

71 LeFebvre, *Collections*, pp. 173–82.
72 LeFebvre, *Collections*, pp. 184–203.

The volume of essays *The Pentateuch as Torah* is essential reading on all aspects of this chapter. Many of the essays have been referred to in this chapter, but they are all worth reading, and taken together they give a good rounded impression of most of the problems and some of the answers.

On the theory of imperial authorization, the volume *Persia and Torah* usefully gathers opinions on both sides, and it may be supplemented by Schmid's essay in *The Pentateuch as Torah*. Ska presents a fresh view on the matter: *Introduction*, pp. 217–26.

The possible role of Samaria in the development of the Torah is tentatively broached in several essays in *The Pentateuch as Torah* (see the footnote above), more definitely by Knoppers in *The Pentateuch*, and at more length by me in 'Between Salem and Gerizim'.

The question of the change in the character of the Torah's authority is dealt with most thoroughly in LeFebvre's *Collections, Codes and Torah*. Anne Fitzpatrick-McKinley gives a slightly different view in *The Transformation of Torah from Scribal Advice to Law*.

7

The Historicity of the Pentateuch

Most readers of the Pentateuch, Jewish and Christian, down through history have taken it for granted that everything they are reading about, from creation to the death of Moses, really happened, because the Pentateuch is authoritative, inspired Scripture. If you accept one or other of the critical views of the Pentateuch which have been set out in the previous two chapters, you will not be able to believe that. Over the last 200 years or more there has been a debate over how much, if any, of the Pentateuch is historical, and among critical scholars the results have been largely negative. Standard histories of Israel and Judah today begin their narratives at a point well after the end of the Pentateuch. All the questions we have been discussing of genre, composition, and sources, written or oral, are involved in the debate. In addition, you might expect there to be some evidence from archaeology or from written evidence from the second millennium BCE to back up the historicity of the Pentateuch if it has any.

History as cultural memory

However, we must first remind ourselves of the fact with which we started, that the Pentateuch functions as the foundation document of the community (or communities) of Israel, and that an essential part of that foundation is that it is the story of the origins of Israel. To put it another way, whether or not the Pentateuch is historically true, it is certainly history *as Israel remembers it*. This idea is worth a little exploration, since the theory of *cultural memory* has become important in the study of culture and ancient history in recent years.

Cultural memory

The sociologist Maurice Halbwachs in the 1920s developed a theory of what he called 'collective memory'.[1] He argues that our individual memories depend on the social frameworks which give them form and meaning, family or class, religion or nation. These social groups can be said, meta-

---

1 Halbwachs, *Collective Memory*.

phorically, to have memories themselves, in the sense that they guide and form the memories of individuals. Both as individuals and as social groups we remember what has meaning for us and forget what does not. Putting it more strongly, we reconstruct the past according to its meaning for the present.

Halbwachs's ideas have been taken up and developed by the historians Jan and Aleida Assmann, who use the term 'cultural memory' to refer to those collective memories that are expressed in the cultural artefacts of tribes, states or religions.

Jan Assmann's book on cultural memory in the ancient world has direct relevance to our subject, and his ideas have been taken up by many recent writers on the history of Israel.[2] Primarily these memories are of *foundation stories*, in other words precisely the kind of story that we find in the Pentateuch, a story that has meaning for the society that remembers it, that relates its origins and provides it with its identity: 'foundational history that is narrated in order to illuminate the present from the standpoint of its origin'.[3] Foundation stories are of course set in the past. But there are two different kinds of past that may be remembered. One, which Assmann calls the 'absolute past', is the past of what we usually call 'myth', which can 'be made present in rituals and festivals'. The other, the 'relative past', belongs to historical time, and as time goes on it gets further away from the present; it 'can be brought to life not through ritual reenactment, but only through memory'.[4] This is the kind of past that is remembered in the Pentateuch. The events of Genesis 1—11 appear to be an exception; but these are not stories about the 'world of the gods' such as were told in most nations of the ancient world, and as far as we know they were not enacted in ritual. However, Assmann applies the term 'myth' to foundation stories of both kinds, without necessarily implying anything against the actual historicity of those that are set in historical time. The heroic defence of Masada and the suicide of its defenders in 73 CE is an example of an undoubtedly historical event that has become a myth for modern Israelis. The past enters cultural memory, becomes 'myth', when it has meaning for the present and the future, when it is 'a reality of a higher order, which not only rings true but also sets normative standards and possesses a formative power'.[5]

Foundational and contra-present applications

However, there is an important distinction to be made in the way in which such myths are used, and it will be seen to be relevant in thinking about

---

2 Assmann, *Cultural Memory*; see also P. R. Davies, *Memories*; Hendel, *Remembering Abraham*.

3 Assmann, *Cultural Memory*, p. 38.

4 Assmann, *Cultural Memory*, p. 61.

5 Assmann, *Cultural Memory*, pp. 59–60.

how cultural memory works in the Pentateuch.[6] The story may be used to confirm the institutions of society as they now are as god-ordained and unchangeable, as for example the Osiris myth does for the Egyptian kingship: this is a 'foundational' application. Alternatively, it may be seen as expressing 'contra-present' values that are *contrary* to the reality of present-day society and challenging to it. It may even encourage revolution in the established order or rebellion against alien rule. Assmann quotes the example of the expectation of the Messiah by Jews under foreign rule, rooted in the cultural memory of David.

There are two main ways in which cultural memories may be preserved and expressed: through ritual and through writing. For illiterate societies ritual is the avenue of memory; this may well include the oral performance of epic poetry or other narrative accounts of the founding myths. Israel, on the other hand, at a certain point in its history – Assmann places it in the reign of Josiah – became a society relying on writing, Scripture, for its cultural memory. And it is easier to turn written history from foundational to contra-present application.

Cultural memory and the Pentateuch

On this theory, the past, whether it is real or imagined, historical or legendary, becomes a 'memory figure' or focus of memory when it responds to particular needs of the present and may help to shape the society's future, especially if it counters the reality of the present. The Pentateuch, of course, does not present just one event of the remembered past, but a narrative embracing very many foci of memory, all doubtless serving different needs of the evolving society of Israel. But we may identify as central to the narrative as it now stands the promise to Abraham, the deliverance from Egypt, the making of the covenant of Sinai/Horeb and the setting up of the Dwelling for YHWH. Our study of the history of the composition of the Pentateuch in Chapter 5 would suggest that a complex development stands behind the present form of each of these. This might mean that in the process of development each of them may have been found appropriate to different 'presents' in the life of Israel, or to the present of different groups within Israel.

Exodus and covenant

Thus Assmann, dealing with the story of exodus and covenant – he treats both together as a single story – identifies two groups at different points, each of which may have found 'its self-image, its aims, and its hopes' supported by this story of a people under foreign oppression who are drawn

---

6 Assmann, *Cultural Memory*, pp. 62–6.

into the wilderness, outside any settled territory, to be bound by covenant to their God. The most obvious is the Jews in exile, who find here the basis for confidence that 'upholding the law of God opens up the path to liberation from slavery and persecution'.[7] But the story of the exodus is unlikely to have first taken a central place in cultural memory with the Babylonian exile; Assmann takes it that it was this belief itself, already central, that ensured that the exile did not lead to the deportees being swallowed up among the nations. For its earlier rooting, he looks to Morton Smith's theory of the 'YHWH-alone party', which campaigned for the exclusive monolatry that now structures the Pentateuch and is especially sharply expressed in Deuteronomy.[8] Their struggle against the polytheism and idolatry of their people and rulers is reflected in the presentation of the Pentateuch (and the Former Prophets) of a people committed to their God by covenant who yet continually turn against him, whether in favour of a golden calf or of Baal-Peor, and have not enough faith in him to possess the land he has promised them. Like the meaning of the story for the exiles, this is a 'contra-present' application.

This is a possible, even a likely, setting in which the narrative of covenant-making might in its earliest form be a focus of memory. But it is not clear that the same is true of the exodus. In what context may this memory have resonated with present experience? There is good evidence that the remembrance that 'YHWH brought us up from Egypt' was central to the identity of the kingdom of Israel by the eighth century: see, for example, Hosea 11.1 or Amos 9.7, which ironically neutralizes it. Karel van der Toorn calls it the 'charter myth' of the kingdom, referring to 1 Kings 12.28.[9] If it was the foundation story of the kingdom of Israel, it must have carried meaning in and for the circumstances in which that kingdom arose. Rainer Albertz, accepting the biblical account in 1 Kings 11—12, according to which it emerged from a revolt against the forced labour imposed by the Davidic dynasty in Jerusalem, suggests that 'the battle against Solomon's forced labour by Jeroboam and the northern tribes was fought with an appeal to the liberation of their forefathers from Egyptian forced labour'.[10] The story would have challenged the present reality of oppression, but quickly turned into the *foundational* myth of the established kingdom, and that is why Amos in turn challenges it.

Ronald Hendel regards the experience to which the memory of the exodus appealed as the Egyptian military presence in Canaan, which lasted about 300 years, from the fifteenth to the twelfth century. 'The memory of Egyptian oppression could extend to all who had felt the oppression of Pharaoh at any time in the remembered past.'[11] This implies that such a memory would have endured over the two centuries between the withdrawal of the

---

7 Assmann, *Cultural Memory*, p. 181.
8 Smith, *Palestinian Parties*; see also Lang, 'Yahweh-Alone Movement'.
9 Toorn, 'Exodus as Charter Myth', p. 123.
10 Albertz, *Israelite Religion*, vol. 1, pp. 141–2; quotation from p. 142.
11 Hendel, *Remembering Abraham*, p. 60. See Redford, *Egypt*, pp. 125–237.

Egyptians and the establishment of the kingdom of Israel, a point we shall consider below. Alternatively, Andrew Mayes refers to the invasion by Pharaoh Shishak around the time of the founding of the kingdom. [12]

The promise to Abraham

The other central foundation story in the cultural memory of Israel as preserved in the Pentateuch is the promise to Abraham, Isaac and Jacob. When this story, especially in its priestly form, was united with the Deuteronomistic narrative of the covenant of law, it would have lightened the burden of guilt implied by the latter, and assured the people of Israel that their God would not abandon them, whatever their sins and whatever the punishment that they might have to bear. The covenant with Abraham is an 'eternal covenant' (Gen. 17.7). The obvious context in which this would first become central to the cultural memory is during the Babylonian exile, when events were experienced in the light of previous prophecy as the judgement of God on their apostasy. But God would bring them back to the land promised to Abraham. The way in which beliefs in the two covenants later came to work together is well illustrated in the conclusion to the warning of judgement in Leviticus 26.41–45. [13]

That is not the earliest interpretation of the stories of the ancestors in the cultural memory of Israel. Before being combined with the story of the exodus, they would have implied the continuous possession of the land of Canaan by the tribes of Israel and Judah. That is the way in which the Judaeans left in the land after the fall of Jerusalem interpret it, according to Ezekiel 33.24: 'Abraham was one man when he took possession of the land, and we are many: the land is given to us to possess.' The narrative also refers to the ancestors of other nations. Taken as a whole, it implies that 'the bounds of their habitations', specifically their boundaries with Israel, of all the small peoples or states of Syria–Palestine have been 'determined' by God: Moab and Ammon (19.30–38), the Ishmaelites (25.12–18), Aram (Gen. 31.51–54), Edom (33.16; 36) and even the Philistines (21.22–34). All the nations referred to are spoken of as they existed in the first millennium. [14]

Obvious items of cultural memory are the stories of the ancestors' building of altars or (at Bethel) consecration of a standing stone. These are set at places where there were important sanctuaries in the monarchic period: Shechem, Bethel, Hebron, Beersheba. God appears to the ancestors at the same places. In this way, the sacredness of these sites and the appropriateness of the sanctuaries built there are confirmed. Jerusalem, however, is referred to only obscurely. [15]

12 Mayes, 'Pharaoh Shishak'.
13 Nihan, 'Priestly Covenant', pp. 104–15; above, pp. 82 and 113.
14 Wellhausen, *Prolegomena*, pp. 318–25; Van Seters, *Abraham*, pp. 52–64.
15 See above, p. 129.

The Dwelling for YHWH

What of the account of the setting up of the Dwelling for YHWH? The group to which it is relevant is obvious: it is the Aaronid priests, the clan in charge of both the Jerusalem and Mount Gerizim temples. But compared with other foundation stories of temples it is highly unusual. Whereas they regularly relate the appearance of the deity, or 'theophany', at a particular place, which is thereby marked out as the holy place where the human hero establishes the shrine – the classic example in the Pentateuch is the theophany to Jacob at Bethel in Genesis 28[16] – here the theophany does not sanctify any place on earth, but requires the making of a portable shrine which is to be taken wherever the deity leads (Exod. 40.34–38). It is not, as is frequently assumed, a blueprint for or projection of the second temple in Jerusalem. Not only was that, obviously, not portable, but it did not contain the most important furniture of all: the Ark and the *kapporet*, the 'cover' (NRSV) or 'mercy seat' (KJV), which are listed first in the instructions for the building of the Dwelling (Exod. 25.10–22). Rather, it is a cultural memory, a foundational story. Does it confirm the God-sanctified rightness of the present temple (and which one?), or is it applied contra-presently, portraying the ideal sanctuary for which the present temples, if any, are but poor substitutes? Obviously the latter. If it is an exilic narrative, as is usually held,[17] it assures the sons of Aaron of YHWH's commitment to dwell once more in a sanctuary served by them.

You can try your own hand at this. Consider the possible function in cultural memory of one or more of the following episodes from the Pentateuch:

- Abraham's purchase of the field and cave of Machpelah for the burial of Sarah (Gen. 23), where later he himself, Isaac, Rebekah, Leah and Jacob are also buried (Gen. 49.29–32).
- The instructions to the Israelites in Egypt for the observance of the Passover (Exod. 12.1–13).
- The destruction of Korah and his company when they rebel against the authority of Moses and Aaron (Numbers 16—17).
- Moses' making of the bronze serpent for the cure of those bitten by the poisonous snakes (Num. 21.4–9; see 2 Kings 18.4).

---

16 See above, pp. 104–6.
17 See above, pp. 96, 102–3.

Finding history in the Pentateuchal traditions

The question of oral tradition

If we are to find memories of real historical events or situations in the Penta-teuch, we run up immediately against the problem of oral tradition. Does the Pentateuch contain versions of Israelite oral tradition? And if so, is it possible for factual information about the remote past to be conveyed by it? Discussing the question is not made easier by the bitter dispute of recent years over the historical use of the Bible, in which some extreme positions on both sides have been staked out.

The assumption of oral tradition

It was generally assumed in twentieth-century scholarship that the substance of the historical memories in the Pentateuch was derived from oral tradition. Gunkel's ground-breaking commentary on Genesis envisaged the stories of the ancestors as popular tales, while scholars like von Rad thought the trad-itions of exodus and covenant were preserved at sanctuaries.[18] Recently, however, scholars have become sceptical of this, Van Seters, for example, attributing most of the material to written composition, and allowing a very limited role to oral tradition, in the form of folklore rather than histori-cal tradition.[19] Recent writers on the origins of the Pentateuch have largely ignored the question. However, it was carefully examined by Patricia Kirk-patrick, who concluded, on the basis of work in folklore studies, that there was no way of distinguishing texts that were based on oral tradition from ones that were not, and consequently that there are 'no absolute grounds for assuming an original oral source'.[20]

Scholars have generally assumed a model in which traditions were handed on orally and then at a certain point written down, after which they were simply copied in writing. But this model has been brought into question by the work of Susan Niditch and David Carr. Oral and written techniques con-stantly interacted. Ancient Israel was an 'oral world', and all its members, even ones who could read and write, shared in an oral culture. Even works that may have been composed in writing show traits of orally composed works. Niditch suggests as a model for the composition and transmission of 'the story of Israel' oral performances at festivals, possibly assisted by writ-ten notes, that gradually attained a fixed form, and might then have been recorded in writing, which would then be again read aloud, or memorized.[21]

---

18 See Gunkel, *Stories*; von Rad, 'Problem of the Hexateuch'; above, p. 97.
19 Van Seters, *Abraham*, Part II; *Prologue*; *Moses*.
20 Kirkpatrick, *Folklore*, p. 72.
21 Niditch, *Oral World*, pp. 120–5.

Carr locates the context of transmission in the education of elites, in which texts would be passed on orally and memorized, but with a written version available for reference.[22] Literary texts may have begun to be written under the monarchy of David and Solomon, but this did not mean that oral transmission ceased.[23]

Moreover, the assumption that pre-monarchic Israel was entirely illiterate is not correct. There have been finds in widespread locations of short texts using a version of the alphabet on durable materials from the Late Bronze and Iron I periods.[24] Their purposes are practical. The use of perishable material like leather for recording longer, perhaps literary or historical, texts is not to be excluded, but it is not very likely. It is hard to see where the demand might come from for such a thing in a decentralized tribal society.

The limitations of oral tradition

Assuming, then, that any possible memories from times before the monarchy would have been transmitted orally for the most part, what might one realistically expect from it? Conservative scholars confidently assume that reliable memories may be handed down over hundreds of years.[25] Appeal is made to the skills of accurate memorization alleged to prevail in oral societies. Scholars in the opposing camp deny that oral memories can give any reliable information beyond a few generations in the past. Kirkpatrick, on the basis of a survey of folklore and ethnographic literature, puts the limit at 150 years (though, as Hendel points out, other information in her book points to individual memories surviving for considerably longer).[26]

Jan Vansina, who has studied the history of several African societies on the basis of their oral traditions, has written a thorough guide to the use of oral tradition in history, and we may take this as our guide also.[27] The most fundamental point he makes is the same as that which Assmann makes about cultural memory in general: that the past is remembered not for its own sake but for the sake of the present, to explain and justify the current ordering of society. Thus oral tradition does not just forget and distort events in a random manner – though of course a great deal more is forgotten than remembered – but deliberately selects and structures what is remembered. Accounts that are believed to be true are less subject to alteration at will than tales understood to be fictional, but they may still be altered for good reason. Only certain types of information are useful for

22 Carr, *Writing*, pp. 111–73; see above, pp. 91–2.
23 Carr, *Writing*, p. 163.
24 Sanders, *Invention*, pp. 101–13.
25 E.g. Hendel, *Remembering Abraham*, p. 55; Cross, *From Epic*, pp. 22–52.
26 Kirkpatrick, *Folklore*, p. 114; cf. p. 104.
27 Vansina, *Oral Tradition*.

current purposes. Inconvenient facts may be suppressed. What is left is given a memorable structure: often reigns are arranged in pairs, a warlike king followed by a peaceful one, for example. Events are reattributed to a more suitable king's reign. Chronology is vague. The more artistic an account is, the less likely it is to be an accurate rendering of a historical situation, and this is especially true for remote events.

According to Vansina, the only type of tradition with substantial time depth is the official history of a centralized society, a state, for unofficial family or local traditions never go back much more than a century. But even official traditions are subject to severe loss of information as they go back into the past. There will be a wealth of detail about the last two to four generations. There will also be much apparent information about the initial founding period of the society (and the world), the stories of origin. In between there is what Vansina calls the 'floating gap', floating because it moves forward as real time goes on. Here the information is thin and sketchy, if it exists at all. But the stories of origin are more subject to idealization and mythicization than any others. Genealogies may give true information, and may go back centuries, but they are subject to manipulation as current relationships of groups in society change, and they may also be telescoped over the floating gap.

Despite all these limitations, Vansina considers that oral tradition does provide valuable information for the historian who knows how to use it. Although it does reflect the present, it will also exhibit traces of past conditions. 'A body of tradition therefore reflects both the past and the present.'[28] The historian needs to eliminate what is likely to represent the present in order to identify the traces of the past – this recalls what is known in Gospel criticism as the 'criterion of dissimilarity'. Confirmation from another source is also valuable, whether external written records, archaeology or natural events such as eclipses or volcanic eruptions that are referred to in the traditions. Information given unintentionally in other types of tradition such as tales and songs is more reliable than the overt message of historical tradition, which always has a purpose governed by the present.[29]

Application to the Pentateuch

Vansina makes several points that are relevant to the Pentateuch. But we need to realize that there is a difference between what an ethnographer like Vansina does in using live oral tradition to write history – he or she is the first person to write any of it down, and can sift it to ensure that only tradition regarded in the society as historical is used – and the work of an ancient historian on existing written documents that are *believed* to rely on

---

28 Vansina, *Oral Tradition*, p. 122.
29 Vansina, *Oral Tradition*, pp. 92–3.

THE HISTORICITY OF THE PENTATEUCH

oral tradition. As we have already discussed, it is uncertain to begin with whether they do represent oral tradition and to what extent. It may also be unclear what genres of oral tradition have been drawn on. Although the *written* Pentateuch is certainly intended to be historiographical, we do not know how far the earliest material was originally regarded as historical. It certainly contains folktale and mythical motifs: Jacob can be seen as a trickster, a typical folktale character, while the visit of three divine beings to Abraham is characteristic of myth; YHWH's use of the sea to destroy the Egyptian army redeploys motifs of the ancient myth of a god's battle with the sea; and so on. The story of Joseph is certainly not a folktale, but is often understood as a 'novella', a fictional story by an author.

Where historical tradition may have been used, we can easily recognize where the factors mentioned by Vansina have affected it. The whole of the Pentateuch consists of origin traditions, and is therefore subject to idealization. The traditions answer to the concerns of a later time in the way illustrated above. They are not likely to represent recent historical memory at the time they were written down, though we do not know when traditions began to be more or less fixed through the use of writing. We can also see where genealogies have been artificially constructed, for example, by connecting the three ancestors originally venerated in different parts of the country as father, son and grandson. Most of the accounts throughout Genesis, Exodus and Numbers are artistically composed and less reliable on that account.

Can anything then be made of them for history? The criterion of dissimilarity needs to be applied, using features of the traditions themselves that do not conform to the current norms of any likely time of writing and give no support to institutions of later times.[30] This does not mean that everything that could fit into a later time is not historical, only that there is no way of showing that it is, unless we find confirmation in sources external to the Pentateuch, such as archaeology and written records. However, we are not here attempting to write history, supposing that to be possible on the basis of the Pentateuch's accounts. We are only asking to what extent these may be seen as historical. The usefulness of these methods is unaffected by whether anything in the Pentateuch represents oral tradition or not.

---

30 Cf. Malamat, 'Proto-History'.

Finding historical traces in the Pentateuch

Time chart (showing persons and events mentioned in the text only)

Years BCE (approx.)	Archaeological periods (Palestine)	Coastal Syria and Palestine	Egypt (dates of kings as in ABD)	Upper Mesopotamia and Syria
2000–1500	Middle Bronze (MBA)			Amorite dominance
1500–1200	Late Bronze (LBA)	Egyptian control 1483–c. 1150 Ugarit Amarna letters from Canaanite kings to Akhenaten Exodus?? 'Israel' on Merneptah's stele	Akhenaten 1350–1334 Ramesses II 1279–1212 Merneptah 1212–1202	
1200–1000 or 900	Iron Age I	Highland settlements; beginnings of states in Israel, Moab, Ammon, Edom Philistines from c. 1150 David c. 990? Sheshonq I (Shishak) invades c. 925	Sheshonq I 945–924	Aramaeans

The traditions of the ancestors

The archaeological discoveries of the twentieth century produced apparent parallels to some features of the ancestral narratives that led a large body of scholarly opinion in mid-century to regard the 'patriarchal age' as securely established, probably in the Middle Bronze Age.[31] A relatively small

---

31 For a useful survey of the changes in scholarly opinion, see G. I. Davies, 'Genesis'.

band of conservatives has continued to hold out for this. The majority of scholars, however, have realized that that optimism was to a large extent based on misinterpretations of the evidence, or neglect of other possibilities.[32] More fundamentally, it depended on the prior assumption that there was such a period, leading to the attempt to find evidence to date it more precisely. But the fact that a period can be found that is not incompatible with the kind of migrations that the ancestors are said to undertake in no way proves that the 'patriarchs' existed, or that anything in Genesis actually took place. Moreover, the suggestion of the early second millennium produced the particularly improbable result that the tradition of the ancestors would have been accurately preserved for up to a thousand years. Nothing in Vansina's arguments suggests such a possibility. As a result, many or even most scholars today dismiss the possibility of finding any traces of history in these narratives.

As both Graham Davies and Ronald Hendel have suggested, this may be a hasty conclusion. It may be possible to salvage something with the methodology I have outlined, which is similar to Hendel's.[33]

The ancestors as migrants

Applying the 'criterion of dissimilarity', the most obvious way in which the ancestors differ from their descendants is that they live largely in tents and move from place to place with their large households and flocks and herds. It is inaccurate to describe them as nomads, as is so often done. The way of life pursued by nomad sheep-herding tribes in the arid regions of the Near East involves moving within a wide but circumscribed area from winter to summer pasture and back again. The ancestors' movements are nothing like this. They are better described as 'migrants'. Moreover, nomads generally live in tribal groups, whereas Abraham is represented as living as the head of a single extended but isolated family; similarly Isaac, and Jacob after he leaves Laban's household.[34]

There must have been a migratory or nomadic phase in the early history of Israel. For the settlements in the central highlands of Canaan, which are reasonably regarded as the core of early Israel, are very few in the Late Bronze Age and increase rapidly in Iron I.[35] This is more than can be accounted for by the natural increase of population. Either people came from somewhere and settled there, or they were already roving in the area.[36] Where they came

---

32 Thompson, *Historicity* (1974), and Van Seters, *Abraham* (1975), mark the turning point. De Vaux, *Early History*, writing in 1971, assumes historicity, but is already skeptical about some of the links made with cuneiform records: vol. 1, pp. 241–59.

33 Davies, 'Genesis', pp. 122–34; Hendel, *Remembering Abraham*, p. 47.

34 Van Seters, *Abraham*, pp. 13–20.

35 Finkelstein, *Settlement*.

36 Egyptian records represent the population of the highlands of Canaan in the Late Bronze Age period as 'transhumant pastoralists' (Redford, *Egypt*, pp. 268–9).

from is a matter of acute debate among historians.[37] Hendel argues that one group came from as far away as the upper Euphrates valley, which the narratives repeatedly refer to as the homeland of Abraham and the place whence Isaac and Jacob must get their wives.[38] There is no obvious reason for this in later conditions; it may conceivably be a true recollection. According to Hendel, an updating of the tradition in line with first-millennium conditions accounts for the reference to the area as Aram and the ancestors' relatives as Aramaeans, as this ethnic group had taken the area over by then.

Thus the picture of Israel's ancestors as migrants bears some relation to the facts. It does not necessarily mean that the actual migrations described are historical; but the way of life pictured is plausible. And the period it points to is not a remote era but the time at which Israel itself probably emerged, in the thirteenth and twelfth centuries, or even later. The time gap is one over which it is plausible that some general recollection could have survived, on the basis of which stories might be elaborated.

The names in Genesis

The ancestral names

It has been held that the names of the patriarchs – Abram, Abraham, Isaac, Jacob, Israel, Joseph – are of forms that are characteristic of the 'Amorites' who lived in the Syria-Mesopotamia area in the Middle Bronze Age. The 'Abram/Abraham' type, however, is common at all times.[39] De Vaux points out that names like the others are not found in Israel after the time of David until shortly before the exile.[40] Thus the names show that the traditions about these figures pre-date the monarchy. It is hardly possible to say more than that.

The ancestral names and the religion of the ancestors

Pursuing the criterion of dissimilarity, Hendel points out that not a single personal name in Genesis is formed with the name of YHWH, unlike all the following historical books, in which names beginning with *Y(eh)o-* (*J(eh)o-* in English versions) or ending with *-yah(u)* (*-iah*) are increasingly common.[41] However, there are many names with *-el*, such as Ishmael, Bethuel and

---

37 For a recent discussion, see Faust, *Ethnogenesis*, pp. 170–87.
38 Hendel, *Remembering*, pp. 52–4.
39 Thompson, *Historicity*, pp. 22–36.
40 De Vaux, *Early History*, p. 198.
41 However, they are extremely rare in the Pentateuch. The only possible ones seem to be Jochebed (Exod. 6.20), which is dubious, and Joshua.

of course Israel. Correspondingly, there are several occasions in Genesis 12—36 where one of the characters acknowledges God as El, usually with some epithet attached. El Shaddai is distinctive of P, but in the older sources we find El-roi (Gen. 16.15), El-'olam (21.33: 'the Everlasting God'), Beth-el as the name of a place (28.19), and most significantly El-elohe-Israel, 'El the god of Israel' (33.20). Except for the last name, these are all identified with YHWH in the context. El is the common noun for 'god' in most Semitic languages, but in the West Semitic area, as for example at Ugarit, it is the proper name of the supreme god.

Despite the identification with YHWH, which is surely the work of the authors who developed the tradition (the 'J' of the Documentary Hypothesis), such a distinctive usage points to a context where El, *not* yet identified with YHWH, was the principal god. And this context must have embraced that in which the name 'Israel' emerged, first mentioned on the stela of Merneptah at the end of the thirteenth century BCE.[42] Whatever group this refers to, it is reasonable to suppose it was one of the antecedents of the later nation of Israel. Yet, their god was El, not YHWH, since it is El's name that features in their own.[43] This could be, as the 'P' (Exod. 6.3) and (perhaps) 'E' traditions suggest, because YHWH was not yet known, or it could be that at first only a few people were YHWH-worshippers. Eventually the veneration of El was absorbed into the worship of YHWH, and El became simply a title of YHWH.[44] The theory of Exodus 6.3 reflects both this identification and the earlier distinction, mediated to the priestly writer through the early traditions of Genesis. Thus the divine and human names in Genesis reflect an important aspect of religion in the formative period of Israel and perhaps for some time afterwards.[45] Once again, we find a true reflection of a historical situation in the ancestral narratives, but it is the situation of early Israel, not of a hypothetical situation hundreds of years earlier.[46]

The religion of the ancestors

R. W. L. Moberly notes a number of other features of the religion of the ancestors as depicted in Genesis that are different from Yahwism as understood in the rest of the OT, especially in Deuteronomy.[47] It is not exclusive, or in conflict with the religion of their neighbours, who can even be

---

42 Miller and Hayes, *History*, pp. 39–42.

43 It is also worth noting that there are no place names in the land of Israel that are formed with YHWH, but quite a number with El, not only Bethel but also Jezreel, Penuel and others.

44 Cf. Moberly, *OT of OT*, p. 87.

45 See Miller and Hayes, *History*, p. 102; Day, *Yahweh*, pp. 13–42, esp. p. 16.

46 Hendel's conclusion that it points to the 'pre-Israelite period' (*Remembering*, pp. 49, 52, 55) is not warranted.

47 Moberly, *OT of OT*, pp. 85–104.

portrayed as in communication with God (*elohim*) in the same way as they are. They have no cultic centre, but build altars at various places. Trees and standing stones play a role in their cult. There is no hint of Sabbath observance or dietary codes. They have no need of priests or prophets to mediate between them and their God. The land plays no part in their religion. Their religion has little moral content. And the concept of holiness, with its ritual and moral connotations, is entirely absent. Moberly's point is that because of the traditions with which they were working the writers conceived of the ancestors' religious context as being different from what was inaugurated with Moses. Is this another archaic feature?

Most of the features of 'Mosaic' religion negated in this sketch can be connected with the innovations of Deuteronomy and P. This is not true of priests and prophets, admittedly. But these are connected to a large extent with the state institutions of monarchy and temples. From an archaeological point of view, Faust has shown how striking is the absence of cultic buildings in Israelite villages of both Iron I and Iron II compared with their Bronze Age predecessors.[48] It is not unreasonable to see the portrayal of 'patriarchal' religion as a sketch, mostly purified of polytheistic elements, of the local or family religion of rural Israel and Judah in the time of the monarchy.[49] In the original traditions, the ancestors are naturally seen as honouring their God in the same ways as contemporaries. In the final structuring of history in the Pentateuch, these ancestors had to be placed before Moses.

The conclusion is that although there is no way in which the personalities of Abraham, Isaac and Jacob, of Sarah, Rebekah and Leah and Rachel, and their stories, could be shown to be historical, the stories do embody some genuine information about social and religious conditions at an early phase of the settlement of the Israelite and Judaean tribes, as well as much that is later. However, nothing goes to show that they reflect anything dating from the Middle Bronze Age.

The tradition of the Exodus

Unlike the traditions of the ancestors, mainstream scholars today mostly tend to think there is a kernel of truth in the exodus story.[50] But is this simply an obeisance to its obvious importance in many parts of the Hebrew Bible, and its centrality in such summaries of faith as Deuteronomy 26.5–11? There is no direct contemporary evidence for it, no Egyptian inscriptions, no remains of camps in the desert. So-called 'minimalists' are content to view it as a legend, while conservatives such as Hoffmeier defend the entire story as

---

48 Faust, 'Israelite Cult'.
49 Compare the works mentioned by G. I. Davies, 'Genesis', p. 125.
50 See e.g. G. I. Davies, 'Was there an Exodus?'

historical, and even the huge numbers are given an explanation that brings them into the realm of the possible.[51]

Names of Egyptian origin

As with the ancestors, so with the exodus story: names may be significant, for though genealogies may be manipulated, they often preserve ancient names. It is universally recognized that the name Moses is of Egyptian derivation. It is the common termination of names like Rameses or Thutmosis, meaning 'child' of such-and-such a god. There is no sign that the Israelite storytellers were aware of this. It is given a Hebrew derivation in Exodus 2.10, and as so often this is playful rather than serious etymology. At the very least, this takes Moses' story back to the period of Egyptian domination in Canaan, before the mid-twelfth century. But this name does not stand alone. There is a whole series of names, mostly belonging to priests or members of the tribe of Levi, in the Pentateuch and also outside it, which can be traced to an Egyptian origin: they include Miriam, Phinehas, Merari, Hur and very likely Aaron.[52] It is possible that Canaanites in the Egyptian period took Egyptian names. But there is no sign of this in the Amarna letters, and it seems more likely that the Levites either originated or spent time in Egypt, where they acquired Egyptian names, and passed them by tradition to descendants as late as the time of Jeremiah. Of course, the story of the exodus in the text is the story of all Israel, not just one tribe; but this is the way cultural memory works. It may be compared to the way in which all Americans celebrate Thanksgiving, although very few of them are physically descended from passengers on the *Mayflower*. The founding story is the story of the whole nation, even if only a few literally experienced it.

Another feature of the story of Moses that is often quoted as unlikely to be made up in later times is his marriage or marriages to a foreigner: to the Midianite Zipporah in Exodus 2.21 and to a 'Cushite' in Numbers 12.1. There are several references to his Midianite father-in-law, but under a variety of names, and the Midianite connection is significant in view of the hostile attitude to Midian in other parts of the Pentateuch. It is true that the name Zipporah is Hebrew ('bird'), but tradition often invents names for originally nameless characters, which no doubt accounts also for her father's superfluity of names.

We can therefore already say that in early Israel there existed a tradition concerning Moses, who was an Egyptian or lived in Egypt, and who acquired a wife in Midian. This cannot prove the story true, but it brings it back to a very early period.

---

51 Hoffmeier, *Sinai*, pp. 153–59, dependent on Mendenhall, 'Census Lists'.
52 A complete list in Hoffmeier, *Sinai*, pp. 223–8, with derivations.

The circumstances of the exodus

But what about the exodus itself? – the slave labour, the plagues, the sea? It has often been pointed out that forced labour was used for state building work in ancient Egypt, and that under the New Kingdom it was frequently done by prisoners of war, as often as not Semites from the Levant. However, we lack parallels for the conscription of a group of resident Semites, especially one so integrated as to have Egyptian names.[53] Greta Hort tries to show that not only can each plague be given a natural explanation, but the order of the whole series can be explained as a natural sequence.[54] But it mistakes the character of the account to treat it as a report of natural events rather than a demonstration of the glory of YHWH. In any case, the explanation is purely hypothetical and, viewed as a natural series, exceedingly improbable.

The event at the sea is often seen as the original core of the exodus story. There has been much discussion of its location, but the usual tendency is to place it at one of the lakes through which the Suez Canal now passes, which may have been continuous with the sea at that period.[55] A rapidly returning tide over a shallow shelf with quicksands could have overwhelmed a small military force, and the miraculous conception of the event in which the Israelites walked between walls of water is only one of at least two presentations combined in Exodus 14.[56] A third is found in the poem of Exodus 15.1–18, which F. M. Cross argues to be a very ancient poem, dating to as early as the thirteenth or twelfth century.[57] He is certainly correct in arguing that it cannot be derived from either of the two conceptions in the prose account in Exodus 14 – the 'walls of water' in the 'P' account might conversely be derived from it – but the confidence with which he asserts its date is unwarranted. There is simply not enough evidence to reconstruct the early development of Hebrew poetry securely.[58] It is therefore precarious to assert that evidence of the tradition of the deliverance at the sea goes back to earliest Israel; but it is possible.

Another dubious piece of evidence that is often referred to is the names of the cities that the Israelite forced labourers worked on in Exodus 1.11, Pithom and Raamses. Raamses is generally recognized as Ramesses II's capital in the eastern delta, called after himself, and now securely located at Qantir. It was abandoned 100 years after his death, and it is often thought that the knowledge of its name would not have survived long after that, but this does not seem to be true. The issues are far too complex to discuss here;

---

53 Hoffmeier, *Egypt*, pp. 112–16. Hoffmeier asserts without evidence that 'the Israelites and other Semites already living in Egypt were treated likewise'.

54 Hort, 'Plagues'; cf. Hoffmeier, *Egypt*, pp. 144–55.

55 Hoffmeier, *Egypt*, pp. 199–222; *Sinai*, pp. 75–110.

56 See the commentaries.

57 Cross, *Canaanite Myth*, pp. 122–35.

58 Despite Robertson, *Linguistic Evidence*.

suffice it to say that the evidence is too insecure to base an argument on for the survival of a reliable tradition.[59]

Our conclusion has to be rather cautious. There is evidence that aspects of the exodus tradition go back to early Israel, therefore there is a substantial possibility that some of the ancestors of Israel, more specifically of the tribe of Levi, were residents of Egypt for more than one generation (hence the Egyptian names), who eventually made their home with other Israelite tribes in the highlands of Canaan. If this event was later than the original formation of Israel, this might explain why the Levites never gained a stake in the land and eked out a living as priests. But this in turn would have given them the influence particularly on Israel's religious development which led to the adoption of the exodus as the central origin story of the state.

The tradition of the theophany at Sinai

It is hard to show, and very widely dismissed, that the belief central to the Pentateuch that nascent Israel accepted the exclusive worship of YHWH, and that their later polytheism was a falling away from this, is historical fact as well as cultural memory. But it is at least worth noting that monotheism was in the air in the late second millennium as well as around 500 BCE.[60] And we should at least recognize the possibility that the later YHWH-alone movement had earlier roots in a section of Israelite society, perhaps the Levites, who we have seen probably had a distinctive origin.[61]

It is clear that the worship of YHWH was virtually confined to Israelites (including Judah)[62] and among them only appears after the time of settlement. From where did it originate? Our earlier investigations have shown that it is improbable that a covenant between YHWH and Israel is an old tradition, and the doctrine of the covenant is bound up with the YHWH-alone struggle in the late monarchy and the exile.[63] However, the dramatic context in which accounts of the meeting with YHWH and the making of the covenant are set is so remarkable, and so different from the circumstances of Israel's life in the land, that it has a fair claim to be ancient. Pilgrimage to the mountain might have been a feature of religious life in monarchic times, as the story of Elijah's journey to Horeb (1 Kings 19) suggests. There are ninth- or eighth-century graffiti connected with the worship of YHWH at a way station, Kuntillet 'Ajrud, in the modern 'Sinai' not far from the present border between Israel and Egypt, and this could have been used by pilgrims. But even then it would need to be explained why a site far

59 See: (a) in favour: Hoffmeier, *Egypt*, pp. 116–21; Davies, 'Was there an Exodus?', pp. 28–30; (b) against: Redford, 'Exodus I 11'; Van Seters, 'Geography'.
60 See de Moor, *Rise of Yahwism*, esp. pp. 41–102.
61 Cf. Cook, *Social Roots*.
62 Insignificant exceptions mentioned by Grabbe, *Ancient Israel*, p. 153.
63 See pp. 100–1.

from Israel's own land was a pilgrimage site. We are unable to say where exactly the mountain was, and the various traditions of the Pentateuch do not even agree on its name, but it is clear that it was deep in the southern wilderness.[64] YHWH is connected with the region of the far south in poetry such as Judges 5.4–5, Deuteronomy 33.2–3 and Habakkuk 3. The first two refer specifically to Sinai, and like Exodus 19 and 24 all the poems speak of an awe-inspiring theophany. Some now unidentifiable site in this area could have been the place of a religious experience that inspired the 'mountain of God' tradition in Exodus and perhaps later pilgrimage.

The tradition of the Tent of Meeting

In its present form, the P narrative of the building of a tent shrine for YHWH may be the latest of the major origin traditions to take shape, and the plan is clearly that of a type of permanent temple standard in Canaan. But it is unlikely that the whole idea of a tent shrine was an invention. There is the parallel account of a 'tent of meeting' in non-P sources in Exodus 33.7–11 and Numbers 11—12. Do these accounts also reflect a tradition about religious customs in Israel's early days?

This is at least possible. Tent shrines are known in various contexts. In Israel we hear of a tent pitched by David for the Ark in Jerusalem (2 Sam. 6.17). Reference is often made to tent shrines among the pre-Islamic Arabs. It is more relevant to note the conception at Ugarit that El dwelt in a tent and the gods met in one.[65] This is relevant not only because of the cultural closeness of Ugarit, but also because, as we have seen, El was the earliest god of Israel and later identified with YHWH. According to the Ugaritic conception, the heavenly dwelling of a god corresponded to his earthly temple. No temple of El has been found at Ugarit, and in view of this principle, it may be that his temple was a tent. Thus there is some indication that not only was early Israel familiar with tent shrines, but it could be that the normal or 'proper' sanctuary of their God was conceived to be a tent. Perhaps 2 Samuel 7.6 reflects such an ideology.

Conclusion

Thus although there is no way of authenticating the historical actuality of most of the Pentateuchal narrative, it contains material standing out in contrast against the background of historical Israel and suggesting links with earlier conditions. This enables us to say that it preserves a few genuine reminiscences of the period during which the groups whose descendants

---

64 Detailed discussion of the location in Hoffmeier, *Sinai*, pp. 111–48.
65 Brief discussion in Propp, *Exodus 19—40*, pp. 703–5; earlier, Clifford, 'Tent of El'.

formed the states of Israel and Judah were settling in the highlands of Canaan: say the thirteenth and twelfth centuries BCE. Among one or more of these groups it is possible that the seeds of exclusive Yahwism were germinating.

Would it matter if none of the events of the Pentateuch happened in reality? If so, why? Discuss in class, and try to answer both for yourselves and from the point of view of a Judaean or Samarian of the fifth century BCE.

Further reading

On the theory of cultural memory

Assmann's *Cultural Memory and Early Civilization*, now in English, is the classic work. In Part II, Chapters 4, on Egypt, and 7, on Greece, may be skipped, but not Chapter 6, which continues the discussion of Israel and Judaism begun in Chapter 5.

There is a useful summary of Assmann's argument, with an application to the Deuteronomistic History, in Rogerson's *Theology of the Old Testament*, pp. 13–41.

P. R. Davies's *Memories of Ancient Israel* is a more popular summary and application.

On oral tradition

Niditch's *Oral World and Written Word*, and Carr's *Writing on the Tablet of the Heart*, both discuss the relation of orality and writing, but from very different points of view.

Vansina's *Oral Tradition and History* is a systematic study of the use of oral tradition for the study of history. Its examples are drawn from *exclusively* oral societies, mostly in Africa.

Kirkpatrick's *The Old Testament and Folklore Study*, despite its title, applies only to the ancestral traditions in Genesis. It has been overtaken by Niditch and Carr, but is valuable for its discussion, with negative results, of how to identify oral tradition in the Bible.

On history in the Pentateuch

The older confidence in historicity is illustrated in de Vaux's *Early History of Israel*, which is still useful for its large collection of material. Volume 1 deals with the Pentateuchal traditions.

The ancestral traditions were still being defended in 1980 in the volume of essays edited by Millard and Wiseman, *Essays on the Patriarchal Narratives*.

The exodus and wilderness traditions are defended in their entirety by Hoffmeier, *Israel in Egypt* and *Ancient Israel in Sinai*. These books are also useful for their extensive collection of material.

The traditions are treated more cautiously but still positively by G. I. Davies, in 'Genesis and the Early History of Israel' and 'Was there an Exodus?'

Hendel, in *Remembering Abraham*, argues for the antiquity of some aspects of the Pentateuchal traditions (not only those about Abraham).

Among many other works, one of the best expositions of the case *against* relying in any way on the biblical text for the history of early Israel is Lemche's article 'Israel, History of – Premonarchic Period' in *ABD*.

Entirely negative about the ancestral narratives, and almost entirely about those in Exodus, are most recent histories of Israel, for example the second edition of Miller and Hayes's *History*, pp. 61–83; see also Grabbe, *Ancient Israel*, pp. 52–5, 83–8. Liverani attempts to show how the traditions emerged in much later times: *Israel's History*, pp. 250–91.

Part C

8

The Pentateuch in Judaism and Christianity

The final section of this book is concerned with what has been called 'the world in front of the text', the ways in which the Pentateuch has been taken by its readers and how it has influenced them. One traditional task of the commentator on the biblical text has been the 'history of interpretation', which at its most basic means a review of positions taken by earlier commentators. In the last 20 or 30 years interest in the history of readers' relation to the text has broadened and become much more widespread. A discipline called 'reception history' has developed. This is distinguished from the history of interpretation in that its focus is on how the text has influenced its readers and how it has been taken up and used by them, as illustrated in a great range of cultural expressions, such as liturgy, sermon, art, literature or film, as well as more directly exegetical works. As Scott M. Langston expresses it in his book on Exodus, 'This is a book about how readers have experienced the book of Exodus. It is about the intellectual, aesthetic, spiritual, religious, political, emotional, and social experiences generated by' the text of Exodus.[1]

But it is not possible to draw a clear distinction between these two disciplines, as Langston's book illustrates; it surveys much work that would normally be classed as 'interpretation', as well as work of other kinds that uses the text. Interpretation has never, at least traditionally, been undertaken for its own sake but for an ulterior purpose: to expound the faith, to justify doctrine or practice, to comfort the faithful, to solve difficulties; and in its turn it has influenced, often profoundly, the way in which the text has been 'experienced'; while artists, for example, who have painted scenes from the Bible have, until modern times, understood themselves as interpreters of the text as much as 'users' of it – in other words, the prime purpose of their art has been the edification of believers rather than its aesthetic impact.

It is not possible within the limits of three short chapters to deal with the whole range of responses generated by the text of the Pentateuch. As the majority of readers of this book will be interested in the Pentateuch for its theological and religious significance, we shall regretfully leave on one side most of the literary and artistic work of modern times, interesting though it is. This chapter will be concerned with the way in which the Pentateuch has

---

1 Langston, *Exodus*, p. 1.

helped to shape Judaism and Christianity, and conversely the way in which the understanding of the Pentateuch has been shaped in those two religions. In the following chapter we shall look at examples of the range of lively recent responses to the Pentateuchal text from readers' particular positions, sometimes within a religious context, but often not. The final chapter will address the question of how a modern reader, aware of all this, might write a theology of the Pentateuch.

The Torah in Judaism

The Torah in Jewish life

Those texts that a community views as sacred may be celebrated in four different ways, and all of these are evident in Jews' relation to the Torah.

First, the text is an *icon*, a sacred object. This is clearly true of the scroll of the Torah in a synagogue, which is treated with the utmost reverence. The *tefillin* worn by Jewish men when saying the Shema, containing the texts recited, are another example, as are the *mezuzot* affixed to their doorposts.

Second, the text is *read*, especially aloud. In Judaism the Torah is read from the scroll in the synagogue in its entirety in one year in a regular sequence. Texts from the Torah are used in private prayer and public liturgy. It is also read privately in copies that are not iconic and studied in classes.

Third, the text is *interpreted*. Much of this section will concern the manifold ways in which the Torah is interpreted. Normally this has the effect of contemporizing the text, making it comprehensible in contexts far from those in which it originated. It also frequently makes it clear how it may be applied in those new contexts. Traditional Judaism takes two essential lessons from the Torah: the first is that God has chosen Israel, and the second is its consequence, that they must obey God's commandments. These two aspects, election and law, belong together in a single pattern of religion that E. P. Sanders has called 'covenantal nomism'.[2]

Fourth, the text is *applied* in life. In the case of the Torah much of it is understood to consist of the commandments of God, which are there to be obeyed. Most of the distinctive observances of Jewish life are, in outline though not necessarily in detail, fulfilments of Pentateuchal laws: they are *mitsvot* (commandments): the circumcision of male infants, the observance of the Sabbath, eating kosher, and most of the festivals – the only important ones that have no basis in the Torah are Hanukkah and Purim. And in the Torah itself these are all framed in one way or another as expressions of Israel's election: circumcision marks the covenant between God and Abraham (Gen. 17.10–14); the Sabbath commemorates the exodus (Deut. 5.15); the avoidance of unclean food is a requirement of Israel's holiness to God

---

2 'Nomism' from the Greek *nomos*, law: Sanders, *Palestinian Judaism*, p. 236.

(Lev. 11.44–45; Deut. 14.2–3). Among the festivals it is Passover that has the most intimate relationship to the Pentateuchal narrative: not only does it commemorate the night of the exodus according to the Torah (Exod. 12.14), but the way it has traditionally been celebrated is explicit about it: the story of the exodus, with blessings and hymns and the traditional questions, the whole so-called Passover Haggadah, is told at the *seder*.

> We were Pharaoh's slaves in Egypt, and the Lord our God brought us forth from there with a mighty hand and an outstretched arm. And if the Holy One, blessed be he, had not brought our forefathers forth from Egypt, then we, our children, and our children's children would still be Pharaoh's slaves in Egypt.[3]

Needless to say, these are only the most prominent of the Torah-based ritual observances. In theory the entire body of commands in the Torah is to be obeyed. They have been numbered: there are believed to be 613 of them, and it is often said that they are all of equal importance.[4] In practice many of them must be treated as dead letters, for example, since 70 CE, all those concerned with the cult.

Halachah

But despite the central importance of the Torah, Orthodox Jewish practice is actually defined not directly by it, but by the agreed *halachah* (literally 'walking', that is, behaviour). Its definitive statement is the Mishnah (*c.* 200 CE), which is arranged thematically, and does not explain its own basis in the written Torah. But most *halachot* have at least some relation to the Pentateuch, even if the connection is not immediately obvious in some cases. Some of the provisions without an obvious basis there are simply stated to be 'Torah by the hand of Moses from Sinai'. The theory was that Moses received not only the commandments that are found in the Pentateuch, the 'written Torah', but also an oral Torah transmitted to the Rabbis by tradition. Although this means that the Pentateuch is not in fact the source of every traditional Jewish practice, the attribution of the oral law to Moses and Sinai is an acknowledgement that that is the proper source of it. The theory is usually regarded as going back before the common era. Jesus' polemics in the Gospels against 'the tradition of the elders' (for example Mark 7.1–13) may have an early version of the oral law in view.

---

3 *Passover Haggadah*, pp. 26–7.
4 E.g. 4 Macc. 5.19–20

Ancient Judaism

But in the ancient period of Judaism (before the fall of Jerusalem in 70 CE), there were many divergent parties and sects each with its own *halachah*. The Rabbis of the Mishnah, the so-called Tannaim, are generally regarded as the heirs of the Pharisees – which does not mean that any particular Mishnaic ruling must represent Pharisaic *halachah*. Assuming the Qumran community was Essene, Essene *halachah* is preserved to some extent in their writings, particularly the Damascus Document, the Manual of Discipline, 4QMMT and the Temple Scroll, although the last may not have been composed within the community. The motivation of Essene rigour is to preserve the holiness of the chosen people. The Temple Scroll, discovered in Cave 11 at Qumran, sets out a utopian vision of the Temple and City in which the holiness of each successive space, moving outwards, is rigidly guarded against contamination from outside. It is not permitted even to relieve oneself within the City: there are to be toilets a mile away![5] The intense concern with holiness naturally leads towards sectarianism, as shown in the Damascus Document. 'But with *the remnant* that held fast to the commandments of God he made his covenant with Israel for ever.'[6]

But halachic writings are not the only ones that appeal explicitly or implicitly to the Torah's teaching. Wisdom writings concerned with ordinary morality also do so. Ben Sira, for example, the author of Sirach (or Ecclesiasticus, c. 180 BCE), does not allude to any distinctively Jewish practices, but he puts the law of God at the head of the list of knowledge that the ideal scribe should be familiar with (Sir. 39.1), and identifies God's cosmic wisdom with 'the book of the covenant of the Most High, the law that Moses commanded us' (24.23). Sir. 29.8–10, on loans to the poor, parallels Deuteronomy 15.7–11, twice using a word for 'poor', and describing the poor person as a 'brother and friend'. To help the poor person with a loan that is in effect a gift is 'for the sake of the commandment'. It seems to me that it is above all Ben Sira's study of the Torah that leads him to lay stress on the duty of protecting and helping the poor.[7]

Rabbinic writings

Beginning not later than 70 CE, the rabbis devoted much of their exegetical effort to elucidating the basis of the *halachah* in the written Torah. This can be seen in the early midrashim, commentaries on the Pentateuch from the early centuries CE, the Mekilta on Exodus, Sifre on Leviticus and Numbers and Sifra on Deuteronomy. It can also be seen in the Babylonian and Jerusalem Talmuds, which are vast compendiums of comment on the Mishnah,

---

5 11QT 46.13–16 (Vermes, *Dead Sea Scrolls*, p. 207).
6 CD 3.13 (Vermes, *Dead Sea Scrolls*, p. 131; my italics).
7 Houston, 'The Scribe and His Class'.

completed about the fifth or sixth century CE. These works derive *halachah* from the text by a set of hermeneutic rules applied in ways that often appear to us arbitrary and even bizarre, ignoring the context and often dependent on small features of the text.

As an example, the law thrice repeated in the Pentateuch, 'You shall not boil a kid in its mother's milk',[8] is taken to support the rule that meat of any kind (even fowl) and milk or milk products (for example cheese) may not be eaten at the same meal or even touch each other, which requires a kosher kitchen to have separate sets of utensils for meat and dairy products.[9] It may originate simply in the desire to make absolutely sure that this law is not broken, as a 'fence about the Torah'.[10] But the detailed elaboration of the rule, forbidding meat to be cooked in the milk even of another species, is supported in the Mekilta and the Talmud by reference not only to this law, taking its repetition as reinforcing it in various ways, but to others, for example the law against cross-breeding (Lev. 19.19).[11]

The completion of the Talmud and the midrashim did not put an end to rabbinic work on the written Torah and *halachah*, but it was seen as definitive. When Rashi (Rabbi Solomon ben Isaac, 1040–1105 CE, northern France) deals with the legal passages in his (still today) very popular commentary on the Pentateuch, his comment is normally 'almost completely identical with the halakhic Midrash', despite his concern for the plain meaning of the text.[12]

A somewhat different approach was taken by Maimonides (Moshe ben Maimon, *c.* 1135–1204, Spain and Egypt). His most important work is his *Guide for the Perplexed*, in which his object is to show that the Jewish faith, and especially the biblical text, is in harmony with reason, as represented especially by the newly dominant Aristotelian philosophy. As far as the *halachah* is concerned, he therefore discusses what the *reasons* for the divine commands may be, rather than simply accepting them as inscrutable. For example, he explains the commandment against the consumption of blood (Lev. 17.10–12 – key to kosher slaughter) on the grounds that pagans believed that blood was the food of spirits, and the eating of blood would lead to the worship of spirits.[13] The distinctiveness of Israel's practice is rooted in their chosenness as the people of the one true God.

---

8 Exod. 23.19; 34.26; Deut. 14.21.

9 *Mishnah*, Hullin 8 (Danby, p. 524).

10 So *Mishnah* (Danby, p. 524, n. 1). But Milgrom (*Leviticus 1—16*, pp. 741–42) traces both the narrow biblical law and the broader rabbinic one to the same principle, that that which sustains life should not be used in association with an animal's death.

11 *Babylonian Talmud*, Hullin, 8; *Mekilta*, tractate Kaspa, ch. 5 (Lauterbach, vol. 2, pp. 186–96).

12 Grossman, 'Literal Jewish Exegesis', *HBOT* I:2, p. 336.

13 Maimonides, *Guide*, ch. 46, p. 362.

Telling and retelling

The insistence in the Bible and in Judaism on the avoidance of idolatry and the importance of the word of God has turned Jewish interpretive and artistic expression sharply towards verbal forms and away from the visual. But this does not seem to have been true at all times and in all places. For example, in the synagogue at Dura Europos in Syria on the Euphrates, dating from the late second or third century CE, the walls were covered with paintings of scenes from the Bible, including such episodes from the Pentateuch as the Akedah, the finding of baby Moses, the passage through the Red Sea, and Moses receiving the tablets of the law: essentially the story of salvation. The impulse to visual expression arises again repeatedly: in the twentieth century in the art of Marc Chagall, for instance.

However, the primary mode of interpretation of the Pentateuchal story in Judaism is to retell it in words. Traditional Jewish interpretation is classified under the headings of *halachah* and *haggadah*, literally 'telling', that is story. The mode of exegesis in the haggadic midrashim may frequently be that of retelling the story, filling in its gaps, and telling other stories which help to illuminate its meaning. But its object is homiletic: to teach theology and ethics, to encourage faith in God's love for God's people, and readiness to obey the commandments. This is also largely true of earlier 'retellings'.

Biblical and other ancient writings

The retelling begins in the Bible itself. We have noted above that there are parts of the Prophets and Writings that in retelling the story of the Pentateuch probably depend on it in more or less its present form.[14] Psalm 105 is founded on the conviction that YHWH has chosen his people (vv. 6 and 43). It is expressed in his covenant with the ancestors (vv. 8–11), and implicit throughout. And the final object of their election (v. 45) is 'that they might keep his statutes and obey his commandments'. Election and law! Psalm 106 takes us to the other side of the Pentateuchal story, and shows that even in the face of Israel's disobedience to God's will, YHWH still works out with them the purpose of their election. It selects all the major episodes in the Pentateuch in which Israel disobeyed God or complained. The consequences are twofold: punishment of course, but beyond that YHWH 'remembers his covenant' and rescues them in his mercy (vv. 44–47). The prayer in Nehemiah 9 covers both aspects and reaches beyond the Pentateuch. There are several word-for-word quotations, beginning with creation and then laying emphasis on the choice of Abraham and covenant with him (vv. 7–8), and specifically mentioning the giving of the law on Sinai (vv. 13–14). This sets the scene for what follows: a review of the people's disobedience to YHWH and YHWH's long-suffering forgiveness and mercy.

---

14 Above, p. 122.

The climax of Ben Sira's book is the chapters on the heroes of Israel's past. Sirach 44.16—45.26 is based on the Pentateuch. The description of Israel's ancestors in 44.19–23 repeatedly emphasizes God's 'covenant' (vv. 20, 23) or his 'oath' (v. 21), to multiply their seed and give them possession of the land; then it is said of Moses that 'he (God) put the commandments in his hand, the law of life and understanding, to teach his statutes in Jacob and his testimonies and judgements to Israel' (45.5, Hebrew text). Thus, although this passage is a celebration of national heroes, it does not fail to give emphasis to the central themes of the Torah.

Hellenistic Judaism

Jewish works written in Greek in Alexandria in the last two centuries BCE and the first CE include the Wisdom of Solomon, the 'Epistle of Aristeas',[15] which purports to describe the translation of the Pentateuch into Greek by the '72 interpreters', and the works of Philo of Alexandria. 'Aristeas' and Philo both use, not exclusively but very largely, an allegorical mode of exposition, a widespread mode of interpreting the poems of Homer in Alexandrian scholarship, which enabled sophisticated academics to give an uplifting and philosophically respectable meaning to trivial, unedifying and polytheistic stories. For Philo, living in an educated Gentile environment, the Scriptures had to have a meaning compatible with a contemporary philosophical understanding of the world. The spiritual world was the real world, consisting of the original forms of truth, goodness, justice and so forth, and this physical world presents mere shadows of them; the philosopher must rise from being absorbed by the world of shadows to contemplate truth itself. Moses, and therefore his people, are glorified by the demonstration that long before the Greeks he set forth true wisdom.

> *Allegory.* An allegory is a story or other text in which all the characters and details have a meaning in a context different from the one explicit in the text. *Animal Farm* appears to be a fairy story about talking animals, but is actually about the history of the Soviet Union and the corruption of the communist ideal, and many of the characters can be identified as particular members of the Soviet leadership. Allegorical interpretation means treating a text which may or may not be intended as an allegory as if it were one, usually out of context.

Philo allegorizes both narrative and legal material, but (unlike later Christian allegorists) he does not imply by finding an allegorical meaning in the law

---

15 Or Aristaeus (Siegert, 'Early Jewish Interpretation', *HBOT* I/1, p. 145 and n. 75). Shutt, 'Letter of Aristeas'.

that it did not need to be fulfilled in practice. The story of Adam and Eve he interprets as God's creation first of the mind and then of the senses. The mind abandons its father, God, and its mother, the virtue and wisdom of God, in order to cling to the senses, and together, through the medium of the senses, they are seduced by pleasure, under the form of the serpent.[16] (Feminists have not overlooked the pejorative reading here given to the woman's role.)

The haggadic Midrash

The haggadic and homiletic work of the Rabbis who worked in the two centuries after the compilation of the Mishnah, known as the Amoraim, is collected in the volumes called Midrash Rabbah. Midrash Rabbah on Genesis is mostly a verse-by-verse commentary, but the other four Pentateuchal volumes do not comment on every verse separately. A flavour of the Midrash may be suggested by an extract, commenting on the Binding of Isaac (Gen. 22).[17]

> Isaac and Ishmael were engaged in a controversy: the latter argued, 'I am more beloved than thou, because I was circumcised at the age of thirteen'; while the other retorted, 'I am more beloved than thou, because I was circumcised at eight days.' Said Ishmael to him: 'I am more beloved, because I could have protested, yet did not.' At that moment Isaac exclaimed: 'O that God would appear to me and bid me cut off one of my limbs! then I would not refuse.' Said God: 'Even if I bid thee sacrifice thyself, thou wilt not refuse.'[18]

The offence of Abraham's readiness to sacrifice an unknowing child is implicitly circumvented by arguing that Isaac is in fact 37. This is deduced from the immediately following Genesis 23.1 – Sarah was 127 when she died, and 90 when she bore Isaac (Gen. 17.17). Here he takes adult responsibility for his sacrifice. The solution of a problem in the text is not the only reason for this midrash. More important is the heightening and emphasizing of the ancestors' commitment to their God, and hence the justice of God's choice: the trial in the land of Moriah tested Isaac's faith as well as Abraham's.

---

16 Philo, *Legum Allegoria*, ii (Yonge, pp. 38–49).
17 Compare the narrative treatment above, pp. 32–5.
18 *Midrash Rabbah Genesis* 55.4 (Freedman and Simon, pp. 484–5).

Hebrew poetry

The imaginative retelling of the Pentateuchal story is not confined to the Midrash or even to prose. From the early centuries CE down to the fifteenth century the liturgy of the synagogue was enriched with poetical compositions, written in Hebrew like the standard elements of the liturgy. These were known as *piyutim* (singular *piyut*). Many of them retold and reflected on the Torah reading of the day. Forms and styles were enormously varied, but what they have in common is the drive to intensify the emotional impact of the narrative. T. Carmi's collection includes a beautiful rendering by Amittai ben Shephatiah (south Italy, ninth century) of the creation and Garden stories as the account of a marriage preceded by the construction of the bridal canopy, which is the entire creation: Adam and Eve are of course 'the bridegroom and the bride'.[19]

Among surviving *piyutim*, the subjects of the Akedah and the crossing of the Sea are popular. The Akedah is presented with a powerful concision exceeding the original in 16 three-word lines in an early anonymous *piyut*. In contrast, Ephraim of Bonn (1132–1200), who lived through the massacres of Jews in Germany that accompanied the Crusades, develops the tale over 26 stanzas of four mostly four-word lines, each stanza ending with a quotation from the Bible (mostly not from Genesis 22). He employs the midrash quoted in the last section, but more remarkably has Isaac slain and resurrected and then Abraham prepare to slaughter him over again, until at the pleading of the angels he is swept away into Eden. At the end, Ephraim prays that the merit of the fathers might 'answer for us': 'Remember, in our favour, how many have been slaughtered (literally 'how many *akedot* [there have been]'), pious men and women murdered for Your sake.'

Medieval literal interpretation

The tendency among the great exegetes of the Middle Ages was to turn from the imaginative exegesis of the Midrash to the literal interpretation of the text, and the growth of expertise in Hebrew grammar encouraged and assisted this development. However, Rashi, the founder of the school, included many carefully selected midrashim in his exposition; only about a quarter of his commentary on the Pentateuch is his own work.[20] This partly accounts for its popularity, in that it 'lend[s] the text depth and meaning and enrich[es] readers' intellectual and emotional worlds'.[21]

Rashi begins by asking why the Torah starts with the account of creation: it is so that when criticized for conquering the land of the seven nations, Israel may be able to answer that God the creator may give the earth to

---

19 Carmi, *Hebrew Verse*, pp. 235–7.
20 Grossman, 'Literal Jewish Exegesis', p. 335.
21 Grossman, 'Literal Jewish Exegesis', p. 345.

whomever he wills.[22] Thus at the very outset Rashi makes it clear that the Torah is about Israel's election: it is in that context that it can also command Israel's obedience. If this idea is somewhat midrashic, it is immediately followed by one of the most incisive and influential of Rashi's literal readings: he argues that Genesis 1.1–3 should be translated, 'At the beginning of the creation of heaven and earth, when the earth was desolate and void ..., then God said, "Let there be light."'[23] He has been followed in this reading by such modern versions as the NEB and the NRSV.

The flourishing of Torah study in the early Middle Ages was encouraged by the prosperous state and relatively liberal climate for the Jews in Europe and North Africa. From the thirteenth century onwards the position in Europe worsened, and this led partly back to the comfort of the Midrash, and partly to the development of the Kabbalah, a mystical reading of the Torah in which every letter was given significance in relation to the attributes of God.

Although we terminate our survey at this point that does not mean that creative work has not been done on the Torah in modern times by Jews writing as Jews rather than as academic scholars, but the material with which they were to work was already there.

The Pentateuch in Christianity

The Pentateuch does not have a unique position in Christianity as it does in Judaism. It is a part of the Old Testament, no more significant than any other part of that body of Scripture, which makes up the Bible alongside the New Testament. The modes of scriptural presence as icon and recitation are applied to it only as part of the Bible, while its application is a particular issue that we shall deal with below.

Many of the stories of the Pentateuch, especially of Genesis, are known and loved by Christians, but much if not most of the legal material is rarely read in church and virtually unknown to most. Theologically, the 'Law' has presented a particular problem since Paul, but parts of the narrative, varying somewhat in different Christian traditions, have been of vital significance in supporting doctrinal positions. In common with much of the rest of the Old Testament, hermeneutical methods such as allegory and typology have been used, especially but not only in ancient and mediaeval times, to read it as a *Christian* text, referring to Christ and the Church.

---

22 Rashi on Genesis 1.1 (Rosenbaum and Silbermann, p. 2).
23 Rashi on Genesis 1.1

Typology. When an Old Testament character or event is read as foreshadowing, in its historical setting, a character or event of the New Testament, it is said to be a *type* of the latter, which is its *antitype*. For example, in John 6 the manna, the 'bread from heaven' in Exodus 16, is treated as a type of Christ, the 'true bread from heaven'. Typology is distinct from allegorical interpretation in that in the latter the focus is on the text rather than on what it (literally) refers to, and the text is generally taken out of context.

The Pentateuch in the New Testament

The literature both on the use of the Old Testament in the New and on the question of the Mosaic law in the New Testament is vast, and here we can only make a few basic points.

In the Synoptic Gospels, disputes about the Sabbath or purity can easily be understood within the setting of first-century Judaism. It is not a question of whether the Sabbath should be observed but of how, nor of whether the Torah's teaching on kosher should be observed, but of the validity of additional traditions, in other words disputes about *halachah*.[24] Mark's aside that Jesus' teaching on the spiritual meaning of impurity 'rendered all foods clean' (Mark 7.19) must be mistaken, and clearly arises from the environment of the Gentile church.[25] Attempts to present Jesus as overthrowing the laws of purity in a revolutionary way are misguided. There is no reason to suppose that Jesus encouraged his hearers to disregard the Torah, or did not observe it himself.

The break from the Jewish setting came, naturally, with the Gentile mission, and with the admission of Gentiles into the Church by baptism without asking them to become Jews, so that the Jewish law did not apply to them. The full theological implications of this development are worked out by Paul, especially in Galatians and Romans. It is important for our purpose here, and was vital for the future of the Christian Church, that the Pentateuch, as well as the rest of the Hebrew Bible, continues to be Scripture for Paul, and can be quoted as authority, indeed as of divine authorship (1 Cor. 9.9). But the way in which it functions religiously for Paul is entirely different from the way it does in Judaism.

Those who have been saved by faith in Christ and live by the Spirit are not subject to the law's demands: this applies to Jews as much as Gentiles. The law then was a temporary measure (Gal. 3.19—4.7; Rom. 5.20).

---

24 Bockmuehl, *Jewish Law*, pp. 4–8; Sanders, *Jesus*, pp. 245–69, esp. pp. 264–7.

25 Sanders, *Jesus*, p. 266. Sanders considers that the Sabbath disputes are likely to have the same background. The teaching itself (Mark 7.15) probably does not deny the validity of the dietary laws but asserts the greater importance of moral purity.

Clearly this does not mean the Pentateuch as a whole, but the command-ments. Romans 5.20 appears to suggest it functioned to make sins deliberate 'transgressions' and therefore create all the more need for grace (cf. Gal. 3.19, 22 and Rom. 7). But in fact Paul has more positive things to say about it. The ritual laws may have no more significance for the Christian (Gal. 4.10), but the law taken as a whole is holy (Rom. 7.12) and is a source of the moral teaching by which the Spirit-filled Christian should live. 'The whole law can be summed up in one word: "You shall love your neighbour as yourself"' (Gal. 5.14, citing Lev. 18.19); this commandment is quoted again in Romans 13.8–10, alongside some of the Ten Commandments; 'love is the fulfilment of the law', and fulfilling the law is implicitly a good thing.

But besides all this, Paul finds in the Pentateuch, 'the law' in a wider sense, the theological resources to marginalize the law in the narrow sense. Abraham, whose 'faith is reckoned to him as righteousness' (Gen. 15.7), receives this blessing long before the giving of the law and while still un-circumcised (Rom. 4.10), and the promise that he received is for all those who believe like him (Rom. 4.13–24; cf. Gal. 4.21–31). Abraham is the *type* of the Christian believer. The other important part of the Pentateuch that functions typologically for Paul is Genesis 3. The effects of the transgres-sion of the one man Adam, which brought sin and death into the world, are reversed by the obedience of the one man Jesus Christ (Rom. 5.12–19. Verse 19 gives the clearest antithesis; cf. 1 Cor. 15.44b–49). Paul uses the word 'type' (Greek *tupos*) in Romans 5.14; and see 1 Corinthians 10.6, 11.

These themes – the impossibility of being saved by the law, the uselessness of observing the ritual law, the value of the moral law, and the typological significance of Adam and of Abraham, and in fact of all the characters and events of the Pentateuch (and the Old Testament as a whole) – largely deter-mine the way in which the Pentateuch is interpreted in most of the rest of Christian history. The Old Testament is read as a Christian book, which in veiled and obscure ways speaks of Christ and his work. The challenge of Marcion (*c.* 150 CE) threatened the rejection of the Old Testament. If these Scriptures, on which the Church had been nurtured, were to be retained, they had to be shown to have a Christian meaning.

Because the narrative and legal material are treated in such different ways, it will be convenient to divide our account between them.

The Pentateuchal narrative in Christian teaching

The 'senses' of Scripture

The Penteuchal narrative can be seen to be integrated into Christian think-ing in three important ways. It can be read *historically* as the first stage of the 'history of salvation'. Although some Old Testament theologians have spoken of 'saving history' as a construal of the (mainly) Pentateuchal narrative,[26] it is a Christian and not a Jewish idea. The events and characters of the Pentateuch can be viewed *typologically* as foreshadowing Christ. And finally they could (generally no longer) be read *allegorically* as representations or symbols of various aspects of Christian faith and life.

This does not exhaust the ways in which the Pentateuch has been interpreted in Christianity. Most stories can be read as moral teaching. How should one classify a modern interpretation such as is given to the exodus story in liberation theology? As biblical interpretation became more of an expert business in the Middle Ages, it became the accepted doctrine that every biblical text had four 'senses'. A well-known Latin couplet summed them up:

Littera gesta docet, quid credas allegoria,
moralis quid agas, quo tendas anagogia.

That is: 'The literal sense teaches what happened, allegory what you should believe, the moral sense what you should do, anagogy where you are going (that is, the eschatological sense).' But typology was subsumed under the literal sense, as it takes the supposed historical context seriously, and the three types of interpretation listed above are the primary ways in which the Pentateuch became part of the Christian world-view.

The Pentateuch as the history of salvation: Augustine

Augustine's interpretation (354–430) has been immensely influential among both Catholics and Protestants. Books 13 to 16 of *The City of God* (CD) are a continuous paraphrase and interpretation of Old Testament history up to the end of Judges, with an emphasis on the literal meaning, understood as historical, but also using typology and allegory where appropriate. Almost all of it is based on Genesis, and half of it, books 13 and 14, concerns the fall (that is, Gen. 3). Exodus, Numbers, Joshua and Judges are dispatched in a single chapter (CD 16.43). The interpretation broadens out again when Samuel and the story of the Messianic ancestor David are reached. This gives a fair impression of the relative importance attributed to the various parts of the Old Testament history in traditional Christianity, except that usually more attention is paid to the deliverance from Egypt. Augustine defines the aim of the inspired author as

to arrive at Abraham through a succession of certain generations descended from a single man, and then to proceed from the seed of Abraham to God's people, which was set apart from the other nations and would serve to foreshadow and foretell all things that relate to the city

---

26 Particularly von Rad; see below, Chapter 10, pp. 212–13.

whose kingdom will be eternal and to its king and founder Christ. (*CD* 15.8)

This clearly emphasizes the historical process as well as the typological understanding of the Old Testament.

In books 13–14, along with his works in the Pelagian controversy and his several commentaries on Genesis 1—3, Augustine established what was to be the orthodox western Christian view of the meaning of Genesis 3 for 1,400 years, and until today in more conservative circles. He insists that the Garden of Eden was a real historical place in which real historical events took place, against the view that the story is merely symbolic (*CD* 13.21). Of course he believes it is symbolically important as well. Adam and Eve were created capable of immortality. Their disobedience led to death, both spiritual and physical, and created a flaw in their nature which was transmitted to all their descendants, such that without God's grace they were mortal and bound to sin. Thus one could say that in Genesis Augustine found the origins of the problem to which Christ was the solution, and clearly identified them as subsequent to God's original creation, which was without a flaw, as Genesis also testified.

Most Christians came to agree with him, and this accounts for the extraordinary salience of this narrative in Christian readings of the Pentateuch and indeed the Old Testament generally. It appears at or near the beginning of many liturgical and artistic sequences on the history of salvation, though the specific scene used may be the cursing of the serpent (Gen. 3.15), read allegorically as a prophecy of the defeat of the devil by Christ. For example, the *Biblia Pauperum* (Poor People's Bible), a block-printed pictorial production widely circulated in Europe in the fifteenth century, arranged typologically, with two Old Testament scenes set alongside a central New Testament one on each page, on its first page sets the Annunciation alongside a combined picture of Eve's temptation and the denunciation of the serpent, with Gideon's fleece on the other side.[27] The York cycle of Corpus Christi 'mystery plays' (also fifteenth century, the most complete of the surviving English cycles) devotes no fewer than four of the 49 plays to the Genesis 2—3 story,[28] and there are only five other plays derived from the Old Testament, all from the Pentateuch: Cain and Abel, Noah and the Flood (two plays), Abraham and Isaac, Moses and Pharaoh.

Augustine makes the age of Abraham the beginning of a new era (*CD* 16.12), and directs attention to God's blessing on him in Genesis 12.1–3, especially the last words, 'And in you shall all the tribes of the earth be blessed' (this is the sense of the Old Latin translation used by Augustine), which he takes to refer to 'all peoples who follow in the footsteps of his faith' (*CD* 16.16). Clearly he is here simply following Paul (Gal. 3.8). Abra-

---

27 *Biblia Pauperum*, p. ii.
28 Purvis, *York Cycle*, pp. 25–40.

ham is here more than a typological precursor of those who have faith in Christ; he is their father, there is a historical process leading from Abraham to Christ. At the same time Augustine does not neglect the reference to Abraham's physical descendants, who are to occupy the land of Canaan (he believed they would continue to do so 'to the end', CD 16.21), for these are 'the people of God', from whom will come the Christ.

The Reformation

Medieval interpreters were readier to follow Augustine in his use of allegory and typology than to centre their thinking in history. A change came with the Reformation, which rejected the use of allegory, at least in principle, insisting that the literal was the only meaning, while retaining typology as a way of understanding the historical meaning. Calvin, closely followed by the Anglican formulary,[29] sees both Testaments as bearing witness to a single covenant, by which God for the sake of Christ grants eternal life to believers,[30] and frequently refers to the people of Israel as 'the Church'. Although old and new covenants are in substance the same, they differ in 'administration': thus the 'fathers' received earthly promises, but they were meant to point them on towards heavenly blessings, and since their earthly lives were utterly miserable (Calvin vividly, and with perhaps unconscious humour, describes the vicissitudes of the lives of Abraham, Isaac and Jacob),[31] the promises must, as Hebrews 11 declares, be fulfilled only in Christ and his heavenly kingdom. Exodus 6.7, 'And I will take you for my people ...', is 'a statement of the beginning of the history of salvation that has its goal in Christ'.[32] Thus the whole biblical history is, as Peter Opitz puts it, 'an unfolding history of liberation'.[33]

The modern critical approach

This understanding of the Pentateuch as the beginning of a continuous history of salvation continues to define the modern, especially the critical, view, expressed in the work of biblical theologians such as Gerhard von Rad. His *Old Testament Theology* (first published 1957–62) is clearly meant as a (Christian) *theological* work in the proper sense of the word. The emphasis, while not neglecting Genesis, has shifted on to the events of the deliverance from Egypt and the giving of the law and covenant.[34]

---

29 Book of Common Prayer, 'Articles of Religion', VII 'Of the Old Testament'.

30 Calvin, *Institutes*, ii.10.

31 Calvin, *Institutes*, ii.10.10–11.

32 Opitz, 'Exegetical and Hermeneutical Work', *HBOT* II, p. 446, based on *Calvini Opera* 24, p. 80.

33 Opitz, 'Exegetical and Hermeneutical Work', p. 446.

34 Von Rad, *OT Theology*, vol. 1.

But of course there is a great difference between the Reformation and the critical views. 'Saving history' (*Heilsgeschichte*) for von Rad is not history as the historian would reconstruct it. 'We are of course thinking, when we speak of divine acts in history, of those which the faith of Israel regarded as such ... and not of the results of modern critical historical scholarship.'[35] The subject of a theology of the Old Testament is 'a world made up of testimonies' – testimonies to a real historical experience, even if the stories in which it is encapsulated are legendary.[36] Thus modern Christianity, to the extent that it is influenced by critical scholarship (admittedly not very far!), is related to the Pentateuchal narrative in a way unlike any of the ways followed by traditional Christianity.

In its turn, the shift in emphasis enabled the birth of such radical interpretations of the Pentateuchal narrative as are found in liberation theology, where the exodus becomes the centre of the entire story and the essential expression of the purpose of God, and thus gospel for today's oppressed peoples. J. Severino Croatto has devoted an entire book to explicating the meaning of the exodus from the point of view of the oppressed peasants and working class of Latin America.[37]

The Pentateuch is thus understood much more in its actual proportions, while at the same time it is seen as preparing for the redemption by Jesus Christ. This depended unavoidably for its meaning on the context of the Israelite people, who understood themselves as redeemed by God and in covenant with God. It also enables the Pentateuch to be seen as preparing for the social and political redemption of the oppressed in today's world.

Typological interpretation

This kind of interpretation is ubiquitous in traditional Christian reading of the Old Testament, not least of the Pentateuch, summed up pictorially in such late mediaeval productions as the *Biblia Pauperum* or the windows of King's College Chapel in Cambridge (1515–31), which pair an Old Testament scene, most often from the Pentateuch, with a New Testament one in each window.[38] It is prepared for in such New Testament passages as 1 Corinthians 10.1–11 and Hebrews 11.

Melito of Sardis

Characteristic of early Christian typology is the sermon or poem of Melito, Bishop of Sardis (second century CE), *Peri Pascha*, which may be translated

---

35 Von Rad, *OT Theology*, vol. 1, p. 106. See further below, pp. 212–13.
36 Von Rad, *OT Theology*, vol. 1, p. 111.
37 Croatto, *Exodus*.
38 Harrison, *Windows*.

either 'on Passover' or 'on Easter'. For Melito there is no difference, since his church, in common with other churches of Asia in the first couple of centuries, celebrated Easter at the same time as the Jews were eating the Passover, on the night of 14 Nisan of the lunar calendar, and this gives point to Melito's systematic exposition, probably given at the celebration, of the Exodus story as the type of the redemption worked by Christ. He compares a 'type' with an architect's preliminary model for the construction of a building: 'When the thing comes about of which the sketch was a type, that which was to be, of which the type bore the likeness, then the type is destroyed, it has become useless, it yields up the image to what is truly real.'[39]

> This [Jesus] is the one who clad death in shame and, as Moses did to Pharaoh, made the devil grieve. This is the one who struck down lawlessness and made injustice childless, as Moses did to Egypt. This is the one who delivered us from slavery to freedom, from darkness into light, from death into life, from tyranny into an eternal Kingdom, and made us a new priesthood, and a people everlasting for himself.[40]

He also includes other typological connections: 'This is the one who was murdered in Abel, tied up in Isaac, exiled in Jacob, sold in Joseph, exposed in Moses, slaughtered in the lamb, hunted down in David, dishonored in the prophets.'[41] The Isaac story in particular becomes an important typology in Christian biblical interpretation and theology.[42]

San Vitale

A different typological scheme is exhibited in the mural mosaics of the church of San Vitale at Ravenna (c. 540–50 CE).[43] Here there is no pairing between Testaments: instructed worshippers are meant to make the connections for themselves between the paired Pentateuchal scenes on the walls and the celebration of the Eucharist at the altar, which represents the sacrifice of Jesus on the cross. (There is no representation of the crucifixion itself in this church.) On one side, Abraham is shown twice: presenting his three guests (understood to represent the Trinity) with the slain calf (Gen. 18) on the left, and about to sacrifice Isaac (Gen. 22) on the right. Above him to the right, Moses receives the Commandments (Exod. 31.18). Opposite, Abel's sacrifice of a lamb (Gen. 4.4) is shown alongside Melchizedek's offering of bread and wine (Gen. 14.18). The table between them is clearly a eucharistic

---

39 Melito, *On Pascha*, ch. 37 (Stewart-Sykes, p. 46).

40 Melito, *On Pascha*, ch. 68 (Stewart-Sykes, p. 55). There is an echo here of the Passover haggadah.

41 Melito, *On Pascha*, ch. 69 (Stewart-Sykes, p. 56)

42 See above, p. 32, with literature mentioned there.

43 Splendidly reproduced in Toesca, *San Vitale*.

altar. Moses appears again to the side, pasturing his sheep at Horeb, and, above, taking off his sandals to approach the revelation of the Logos in the burning bush (Exod. 3).

Typology appeared to be moribund in the modern period, but was revived in the biblical theology movement of the mid-twentieth century. It was argued that it is entirely reasonable to see correspondences between the way God acted in Christ and the way the same God acted at an earlier point in the history of salvation.[44] But we should note that this is not typology as traditionally conceived, in which God ordains specific persons, events or institutions to prefigure Christ and his work.[45]

Typology continues to be important in liturgy. The order for baptism in the Church of England's *Common Worship* includes the words: 'Over water the Holy Spirit moved in the beginning of creation. Through water you led the children of Israel from slavery in Egypt to freedom in the Promised Land.'[46] The latter sentence picks up a very ancient connection made in the context of baptism, as we see in the next section.

Allegorical interpretation: Origen

One extended example will suffice to show how allegory tends to work. It is Origen's fifth homily on Exodus (early third century), 'On the setting out of the children of Israel', on Exodus 12.27—14.31, which interprets the exodus from Egypt and the event at the sea in relation to the experience of the Christian convert approaching baptism.[47] Origen maintained that anything in Scripture that is impossible or morally problematic should be allegorized, but the reach of his allegorizing goes far beyond that, for neither of those considerations applies to this passage, at least not to the believer in miracles. The distinction between typology and allegory can be seen not only in the way details are treated – for example, all the place names are interpreted according to their Hebrew etymology, real or supposed – but especially in the fact that the account is applied to personal spiritual experience rather than to events of the gospel. Origen takes 1 Corinthians 10.1–4 as his motto and condemns the Jews for reading the account literally.

The Christian convert must leave behind wealth, symbolized by 'Raamses' (Exod. 12.27), supposed to mean 'fluttering of a moth', which points to Matthew 6.20, 'where moth and rust corrupt', and the desires of the body, indicated by 'Succoth' (13.20), meaning 'booths' or 'tents' and referring to 2 Corinthians 5.4. He or she must then 'pitch at Ethan', read with different vowels in the LXX which make it look like the Hebrew for 'signs', that is, the sacraments, which Pharaoh, that is, the devil, had not permitted them

---

44 See Lampe, 'Reasonableness'.
45 See Puckett, *Calvin's Exegesis*, p. 135.
46 *Common Worship*, p. 364.
47 Origène, *Homélies sur l'Exode*, 5.5, pp. 168–9.

to partake of. The great temptation comes at 14.11–12, where the Israelites complain it would have been better to remain in Egypt than to die in the wilderness. Origen replies it would be much better to die en route to the perfect life than to die in Egypt, in the life of sin. The strange words of God in 14.15, 'Why do you cry to me?', when Moses has not done so, Origen confidently interprets via Romans 8.26–27: the reference is to the silent cry of the heart uttered to God by the Spirit. The crossing of the sea is of course the act of baptism, whereby all the works of darkness (Pharaoh's army) are extinguished. And he concludes: 'We can even see Pharaoh himself drowned, if we live with such faith that God tramples Satan quickly under our feet, through Jesus Christ our Lord' (see Rom. 16.20).

The Pentateuchal law in Christian Teaching

Early years

What were Gentile Christians to do with the Mosaic law? Paul himself, for all his radical views, attempted to keep together Jewish Christians of the Diaspora, observing the law, with Gentile ones not observing it (see Rom. 14.1—15.6). The failure of this strategy was probably due to the crushed Jewish revolts of 66–70 CE and 132–5 in the land of Israel and of 115–17 in Egypt and Libya. This led to a revulsion against the Jews in the Roman empire, and inevitably this affected Gentile Christians.[48] Jewish Christians, at least outside Palestine, were under pressure to decide whether to be Jews *or* Christians.[49] Some highly negative views of Judaism, and of any literal observance of the law, emerged in the late first and early second century. A good example is the so-called 'Epistle of Barnabas'.

The 'Epistle of Barnabas'[50]

In this anonymous work (attributed to Barnabas in tradition; between 70 and 140 CE) the Israelite people are held to have been finally condemned in the episode of the golden calf, and the covenant passed to the Christians (Ep. Barn. 4.7–8; 14.1–4). The entire ritual law, as well as several narrative episodes, is read allegorically. The sacrificial rituals, especially the scapegoat and red heifer, are types of Christ's passion (chapters 7—8). Circumcision and the dietary laws are read as moral allegories, much as Philo had done, but with the crucial difference that 'Barnabas' believes they were never intended to be observed literally (chapters 9—10). An 'evil angel' misled

---

48 See Goodman, *Rome and Jerusalem*, pp. 445–585, esp. p. 583.

49 The obscure problem of the parting between Jews and Christians in this era is studied in detail by Dunn, *Partings*. See p. 311 for 'Barnabas'.

50 *Apostolic Fathers*, vol. 1, pp. 335–409.

the Israelites to interpret them in the obvious sense (9.4)! The Sabbath is interpreted eschatologically, and the writer says it is impossible to observe it at present 'with clean hands and a pure heart' (15.6); it has evidently already been supplanted by the Lord's day, which is the eighth day of creation (15.8–9).

Augustine

'Barnabas' already assumes Christian praxis much as it will continue, but it is hermeneutically naive. Later writers were forced to consider more seriously what was of moral value in the Mosaic law, as well as how to deal with what was apparently not. Augustine again consolidates the theological gains made in the first 300 years of Christian thought. In *Contra Faustum Manichaeum* (*CF*), one of his main tasks is to demonstrate the value of the Old Testament. He draws a distinction between commandments that *shape* life, for example 'You shall not covet', and ones that *signify* life, for example 'You shall circumcise every male'. The first kind is a continuing obligation, the second is not (*CF* 6.2). 'What in the Old Testament's own day was a precept is now a testimony' (*CF* 6.9).[51] In other words, the ritual laws always had symbolic value, expressed in their observance as much as in their words, and even if they are no longer observed their words retain their value as testimony to Christ. It must be doubted whether the symbolism is as effective once the commandment is reduced to a mere text. But the distinction between what came to be called 'moral' and 'ceremonial' laws was established. Generally the moral law was identified with the Ten Commandments.

Mediaeval interpretation: Thomas Aquinas (1224–74)

The context of Thomas's teaching is in the new universities of the late Middle Ages, and so he presents it in systematic form and in dialogue with secular, Muslim and Jewish philosophers, Aristotle, Avicenna and Maimonides. He devotes a long discussion to what he calls 'the old law', in contrast with the new law which is the law of grace in Christ.[52] So far from thinking that the Jews were misled into observing it literally, like 'Barnabas', he sees that it was given to them to observe because of the special holiness of the people who had received the promise of Christ, and was needed to lead towards Christ. However, it was not able to achieve its proper end as God's law, which was the perfection of human beings for eternal happiness. That required the gift of grace, and once that had come, the commands distinctive

---

51 D. F. Wright, 'Augustine', *HBOT* I:1, p. 715.

52 Thomas Aquinas, *Summa Theologiae*, IaIIae, 98–105 (Blackfriars vol. 29; McDermott pp. 294–302).

to the old law were no longer needed. But its essential demand of love for God and for fellow humans is part of the 'law that is in us by nature',[53] and so are all the moral laws, which are specifications of the demand for love, and exemplified especially in the Decalogue. None of these are outdated. But there are also specifications that can be dispensed with or replaced by new ones: ritual injunctions, specifications of love for God, which have symbolic meanings pointing to Christ and are replaced by new ones once Christ has come; and 'judicial injunctions', which are practical more than symbolic, ordering God's people in justice. His threefold distinction between moral laws, ritual or ceremonial laws, and judicial or civil laws, became established, and was accepted by the Reformation, as in Article 7 of the Church of England.[54]

The Reformation

The Reformers, whose concerns were pastoral rather than academic, dismissed the teaching of the 'schoolmen', and their reliance on secular philosophy. Nevertheless, they retain the basic distinctions found in Thomas's work. The use of the Decalogue as one of the bases of catechetical teaching gains a higher profile with the abandonment of scholastic teaching about the cardinal virtues and deadly sins. Both Luther's catechism and Reformed catechisms, for example the Westminster catechism (1649), are based on the Apostles' Creed, the Lord's Prayer and the Ten Commandments. This is still true of at least one modern Reformed catechism, that of the Presbyterian Church (USA) (1998).[55]

The Reformers agreed that the moral Law had three functions. In Calvin's listing, the first was to convict humanity of their sinfulness and condemnation and therefore drive them to realize their need of grace. The second was to restrain, by threatened punishment, the wickedness of those who despised God's will. And the third, which was only effective for believers, who had the gift of the Holy Spirit to enable them to want to obey God, was to teach them the will of God and to encourage them in obedience.[56] It is this function that explains why the Decalogue should be taught to new believers. Luther rather emphasizes the Christian's freedom from the necessity to obey the Law, but retains the Decalogue in his teaching because it embodies 'natural law'.[57] Calvin agrees that it does: the unacknowledged debt to mediaeval thinking is clear.[58] This concept of the natural law does not imply

53 McDermott's translation.
54 *Book of Common Prayer*, 'Articles of Religion', VII 'Of the Old Testament'.
55 http://www.presbyterianmission.org/ministries/theologyandworship/catechism.
56 Calvin, *Institutes*, ii.7.6–15; cf. Raeder, 'Martin Luther', *HBOT* II, pp. 383–4.
57 Luther, 'How Christians'.
58 Raeder, p. 384; *Institutes*, ii.8.1.

that people know it instinctively, but that it is the proper expression of their nature as created by God; they still need to be taught it.

Calvin's interpretation of the commandments, followed in the Reformed catechisms, is that in each the root principle should be discerned; this enables us to see that when something is prohibited, the opposite is commanded, and vice versa. 'You shall not commit murder' implies not only that we should avoid any action, or thought (Matt. 5.22), which might lead to the death or injury of another, except for a lawful reason, but also that we should make every effort to preserve and defend the life of others.[59] In this way the Decalogue becomes the basis of all morality.[60] In his commentary on the Pentateuch,[61] Calvin identifies many of the moral and civil laws as implications of the Ten Commandments. Some should remain in force for Christian society, while others are 'political laws' in the sense that they apply only to a particular 'polity', that of the Jews. An example would be the remission of debts in the seventh year.[62] Calvin's ethics were consciously related to the new commercial society of European cities, but it was only in later Protestantism that it was silently or openly agreed that the laws on economic justice were no longer relevant.[63]

Modern teaching

The tendency in recent years in large parts of the Church has been to forget the Ten Commandments in favour of the two 'greatest commandments' (still Pentateuchal!) as identified by Jesus. The obvious danger is that much self-serving behaviour may masquerade under the guise of 'love'. But it has been recognized by some that the Torah, as well as the New Testament and the rest of the Old Testament, contains a great deal of other material, beyond the Ten Commandments, offering useful moral guidance, and ideas on how morality may be expressed in society, in other words on justice.

Some argue for the law in its total religious and social environment in ancient Israel to be taken as a 'paradigm' for modern society, without necessarily applying the laws directly. This is argued by Christopher Wright, and with an effort at practical application in UK society by the Jubilee Centre in Cambridge.[64] Obvious weaknesses attend this position. It assumes that there really was a time when all the laws of the Torah and all the institutions assumed by it, especially the extended family, were in operation at the same

---

59 *Institutes*, ii.8.9, 40.

60 The Westminster and PCUSA catechisms are more extensive on the topic than Calvin's relatively brief observations.

61 Calvin, *Four Last Books*.

62 For Calvin's teaching on economic morality and practice at Geneva, see Tawney, *Religion*, pp. 111–33.

63 Tawney, *Religion*.

64 C. J. H. Wright, *OT Ethics*, esp. pp. 48–99; http://www.jubilee-centre.org/; Schluter & Clements, 'Jubilee Institutional Norms'.

time, which is historically most unlikely, and that somehow this paradigm can be expressed in our own society.

Most scholars and theologians who are convinced that the Torah has relevance for Christians find that relevance not in comprehensive paradigms, let alone in the direct application of individual laws, but in the moral power of particular ideas and images of justice and morality and certainly not in separation from the rest of the Bible. John Rogerson argues that what the Bible offers us is 'example, not precept': the example is of moral discernment exercised in particular situations, which we may imitate without, in our situation, necessarily coming to the same conclusion.[65] Johanna van Wijk-Bos, in her exposition of the Torah for Christians, does not separate its moral teaching from its story. Her main point is that Christians are impoverished in their moral resources by not being aware of the teaching of the Torah; but certainly they should not be bound by it in a legalistic way. She comments on the unfortunate effects of the translation of *torah* as 'law' which we looked at above.[66]

Read one of the salient passages from the Pentateuch focused on by one of the interpreters who have been discussed above. Then read the interpreter's work (see 'Further reading' for a list of accessible editions or translations), and try to answer the following questions:

1 What questions is the interpreter trying to answer about the passage?
2 Why do you think those particular questions are the ones focused on? How and why are they different from the ones you would focus on? Some knowledge of the interpreter's context would help here.
3 Only after thinking about the questions, think about the answers the interpreter gives. How does he or she arrive at that answer? What does that tell you about the assumptions of the work?

If you have time, you should repeat the exercise, once with a Jewish and once with a Christian source.

Further reading

There are several large encyclopedia projects, complete or in progress, on reception history. The three volumes of *Hebrew Bible/Old Testament* (ed. Magne Sæbø) serve as a history of the interpretation of the Old Testament up to about 1800. But there is little on Eastern Orthodoxy, and it is largely limited to formal interpretation; similarly Reventlow's *History of Biblical*

---

65 Rogerson, *According to the Scriptures?*, pp. 80–6.
66 Van Wijk-Bos, *Making Wise*, pp. 276–7; above, pp. 42–3.

Interpretation. The two volumes so far published of the 30-volume *Encyclopedia of the Bible and its Reception* (ed. Klauck et al.) concentrate, like this chapter, on the reception of the biblical text in religion. Hayes's *Dictionary of Biblical Interpretation* comes up to the present day and takes in scholarly, theological and artistic interpretation.

More directly related to our theme are the volumes in the Blackwell Bible Commentaries series, 'Through the Centuries'. At the time of writing only one volume concerned with the Pentateuch has been published, Langston's *Exodus through the Centuries*. This contains a great deal of information about the interpretation and use of Exodus in both Judaism and Christianity, with a bias, in the modern period, towards their history in America. Two volumes on Genesis and ones on Numbers and Deuteronomy may appear in the next few years. There is a narrower focus in each of the two series 'Ancient Christian Commentary on Scripture' and 'Reformation Commentary on Scripture'. These give ample passage-by-passage Christian comment from their respective periods. There are three volumes of the former series on the Pentateuch: *Genesis 1—11* (Louth), *Genesis 12—50* (Sheridan) and *Exodus, Leviticus, Numbers, Deuteronomy* (Lienhard); the latter had no volumes published at the time of writing. Other individual works are worth reading on the way in which parts of the Pentateuch have wrought on the imagination of believers. Here I will just mention three: Anderson, *Genesis of Perfection*, on Adam and Eve; Cohn, *Noah's Flood*; and Larsson, *Bound for Freedom*, on Exodus.

Although John Rogerson's *According to the Scriptures?* concerns the use of the Bible in general, and approaches the subject mainly through a historical survey, it majors on the question of the continuing validity of the Old Testament law for Christians, and this is studied at greater length than I have been able to do above, though still briefly.

On the subject of the reception of the Ten Commandments in Christianity, see Brown, *Ten Commandments*. Its Section 1 (pp. 33–129) includes both extracts from the sources – Thomas Aquinas, Luther, Calvin and others – and essays by modern scholars on them.

It is important to observe the reception of the scriptural text in the original sources. Use the footnotes to this chapter, with the Bibliography, for details. But here are some of the most important sources in their most accessible English-language editions. Bibliographical details are in the Bibliography.

Geza Vermes, *The Complete Dead Sea Scrolls in English.*
The Works of Philo, tr. C. D. Yonge.
Rabbinic sources:
The Mishnah, tr. Herbert Danby.
Mekilta de-Rabbi Ishmael, ed. and tr. Jacob Z. Lauterbach
The Babylonian Talmud, Soncino edition (many volumes).
The Midrash Rabbah, tr. and ed. H. Freedman and Maurice Simon, five volumes.

Rashi: *Pentateuch, with... Rashi's Commentary*, ed. and tr. M. Rosenbaum and A. M. Silbermann.

Maimonides, *The Guide for the Perplexed*, tr. M. Friedländer

Melito, *On Pascha*, tr. Alistair Stewart-Sykes.

Augustine, *City of God*, tr. Henry Bettenson.

Thomas Aquinas, *Summa Theologiae: A Concise Translation*, ed. Timothy McDermott.

Luther, 'How Christians should regard Moses', in *Luther's Works* (Muhlenberg), vol. 35.

Calvin, *Institutes*, tr. Henry Beveridge.

Von Rad, *Old Testament Theology*, vol. 1.

Croatto, *Exodus, a Hermeneutics of Freedom*.

9

The Modern Reader and the Pentateuch

Reading from this place

The critical interpreter

Throughout history, most readers of the Bible, and within it the Pentateuch, have been content to be guided in their understanding of the text and
their responses to it by the religious teaching they have received, the kind
of teaching surveyed in the previous chapter. But many readers in modern
times have chosen to take a more critical view, both of such teaching and of
the text itself, daring to ask how true or acceptable it is for people in their
position, as women, or black, or Palestinian, or in relation to a particular
concern of theirs, such as the environment. The basis of their position is
that no one can survey the text with a totally objective eye; everyone has a
point of view which is shaped by their context and their interests, whether
they admit it or not, and the difference in this way of reading the text is that
this point of view is admitted and made the starting point for interpretation.
Even more important, perhaps, is that interpretation of the text is allied to
action and becomes part of the armoury of a cause in the modern world.

Writers, context and ideology

Not everyone who uses the Bible in such a cause finds reason for critique of
the text's own stance. Many readers find in the Hebrew Bible powerful support for the cause of the poor and oppressed in the modern world, and we
shall refer to some readings of this kind below. But others note that it must
have been written by the relatively few people who could read and write.
These were male, at a distance from poverty and hard labour, and largely
in the service of rulers and their interests, and what they write serves those
interests.

There is here a difference in perception, but also a question of fact about
the social context in which the texts were composed, which I have explored
myself in another work.[1] My conclusion is that while the texts were indeed

---

1 Houston, *Contending*, esp. pp. 4–16; *Biblical Challenge*, pp. 10–12.

composed by or for members of the ruling class, it was quite possible for some of them to speak on behalf of the less privileged, and further that, because their rule needed popular support, its legitimating ideology included ideas of social solidarity and traditions of deliverance from oppression that were part of the cultural memory of the people. But in any case, groups such as women or gays, let alone the natural environment, do not get even so much recognition in the text.

Ideology. This is a word used in a number of different ways. Here, it refers: (a) in a society to the beliefs and mindset whereby the existing social and political arrangements are taken for granted, including the dominant and subordinate roles of groups such as men and women or rulers and subjects; and (b) in a text to the way it is shaped to present these arrangements as natural.

Hermeneutic of suspicion

Readers who perceive that voices supporting their cause are marginalized or suppressed in the text operate with a *hermeneutic of suspicion*. Less technically, some speak of 'reading against the grain', that is, with concerns and assumptions that run contrary to the rhetoric of the text itself. However, this is not a fully adequate description, as many of the readings explored in the previous chapter may be said to be 'against the grain' of the text, where midrashic or allegorical methods are used to extract a meaning far from the plain sense of the text.

In the most general terms, a hermeneutic of suspicion is one that refuses to accept the text's assumptions and rhetoric as a starting point, refuses, that is, to be led in the direction that the implied author intends the reader to take.[2] This may be because of the kind of commitment I have referred to, or because of a general belief or suspicion that texts are untrustworthy and meaning always indeterminate, and that binary distinctions always undermine themselves: the hypotheses of *deconstruction*. The next section offers an example of a reading of this kind.

More commonly, it is because the reader is committed to a point of view, such as one of those above, that leads her to *suspect* that the text promotes an opposed point of view, and often to find that the text reflects the same kind of conflict in which she is herself involved. Study of the text may then lead in one or more of several directions. One is to expose its contradictions, which enables the interpreter, if she wishes, to opt for one or other of the

---

2 See my discussion above in Chapter 2, pp. 21–34.

> *Deconstruction*. The philosopher Jacques Derrida developed the method of deconstruction as a critique of philosophical ideas, by which he claimed to show that the way in which ideas are described tends to include or imply contrary ideas, so that structures of thought based on oppositions between two ideas, such as matter and spirit, are undermined and fall apart. The method, or at least the word, has been taken over by literary critics, including some biblical critics, who have argued that texts (according to some, all texts) contradict themselves by including hidden implications that undermine their rhetoric.

distinct points of view exposed. Another is to find that it is indeed committed to an opposed point of view as a whole. A third is to find within the text a point of *identification*, a character or situation with which the reader can experience sympathy, and from there go on to *retrieve* a point of view suppressed or obscured in the text, perhaps the viewpoint of a character subordinated or ignored.[3]

My general principle in this book is to read the Pentateuch as a whole, but the principle is sorely tested in this chapter, because nearly all readings of this kind examine quite restricted passages. I hope that those selected here will cast light on the interpretation of the Pentateuch as a whole. The first certainly does so.

Reading for contradiction

In his essay 'God in the Pentateuch', David Clines points up tensions within the text's portrayal of God. He asks who really saves Noah and the inmates of the ark in the Flood. God does nothing, but simply instructs Noah what to do, so that 'the actual saving *acts* are those of Noah'. Yet the Flood story is generally considered to relate not only God's acts of judgement, but also his salvation.[4] (I should point out that this language is not used in the text itself.) Again, in Exodus, God is presented as delivering the Israelites from Egypt; but who was it who brought them into Egypt in the first place? Genesis 37—50, which emphasizes the providence of God (Gen. 45.8; 50.20), seems to be absent from the narrator's memory in Exodus 1—15, after Exodus 1.8.

It makes a difference ... whether the deliverance from Egypt is a sheer act of divine grace ... or whether it is a way of undoing the damage done

---

3 Habel, *Birth*, pp. 8–14, describes the process of suspicion, identification and retrieval systematically.

4 Clines, 'God in the Pentateuch', pp. 193–4.

to the Hebrew people by engineering their descent into Egypt in the first place.[5]

Clines is not the first to note ambiguity in the narrative of the plagues of Egypt,[6] but he notes particularly how God's hardening of Pharaoh's heart works against God's ostensible purpose of liberating the people of Israel, constantly deferring the moment of deliverance, and leaving them under the lash of the overseer in the meantime, and all, according to Exodus 10.1–2, in order to show the Egyptians 'these signs of mine' and that the Israelites may pass the story to their descendants, 'that they may know that I am YHWH', though this would have been unnecessary if YHWH had not hardened Pharaoh's heart.[7] We can agree that two divergent motives are attributed to YHWH in the plagues narrative: to bring the Israelites out of Egypt, and to demonstrate his own glory. Eventually both ends are achieved, but only at the expense of a confusion between YHWH's role as the God of his chosen people and that of divine ruler of the world.[8]

But the fact that YHWH does have both these roles is Clines's clinching point: should the judge of all the earth have favourites? 'If we do not actually *approve* of a universal deity having one favourite race, we are bound to take a different view of that deity's character from a reader who happily embraces the ideology of the text.'[9] Clines's point is that what we find in the text depends to a large extent on what we bring to it, that we may 'embrace the ideology of the text' or take a critical view of it, in which case the coherence seen in it by those who accept its ideology begins to fall apart. In practice such a critical stance is usually the result of the adoption of a definite viewpoint different from that of the text. And whereas Clines's reading is purely literary, readers concerned with interpreting the text as an expression of their social or political commitment are frequently interested in the text itself as a social and political product.

Feminist readings

In sheer numbers feminist readings outweigh all the rest, and this is not surprising, for there are probably more women of feminist consciousness professionally engaged in the study of the Bible – and few non-professional readers write this sort of study – than there are people from other self-conscious groups.[10]

---

5 Clines, 'God in the Pentateuch', pp. 194–5.
6 See Gunn, 'Hardening'.
7 Clines, 'God in the Pentateuch', pp. 195–9.
8 Houston, 'Character of YHWH', pp. 20–5.
9 Clines, 'God in the Pentateuch', p. 201.
10 For a useful overview of feminist biblical criticism, see Shectman, *Women in the Pentateuch*, pp. 9–54.

Patriarchal and *androcentric*. Strictly speaking, the word 'patriarchal' applies to societies and their ideologies, though it is sometimes also applied to texts, and 'androcentric' to texts. In social anthropology, a 'patriarchal' society (Greek *pater*, 'father', and *arche*, 'rule') is one in which power lies in the hands of the male heads of extended families. More loosely, it is applied to any society in which power and influence lies primarily with men. An 'androcentric' text is one, normally arising from a patriarchal society, in either sense, that is *centred* on men (Greek *andres*) and their interests, and reflects their dominance.

The point of view from which feminist reading begins is that society through-out history has been organized in a manner dominated by men (normally men of a ruling class or caste), in which women have been given a sub-ordinate place defined by their domestic roles as childbearers, mothers and homemakers; and the suspicion, normally confirmed, is that the Bible as a product of society reflects this 'patriarchal' organization in its ideology and assumptions, and often promotes it.

Theological feminism

Whether feminists go on to 'retrieve' anything depends more on their assumptions and approach than on objective features of the text; not all wish to do so. Phyllis Trible illustrates an approach taken by many feminists with a religious commitment. In her watershed essay, 'Depatriarchalizing in Biblical Interpretation', she starts by affirming, against the rejection of the Bible as irredeemably patriarchal, 'that the intentionality of biblical faith, as distinguished from a general description of biblical religion, is neither to create nor to perpetuate patriarchy but rather to function as salvation for both women and men'.[11] It is then natural that in Genesis 2—3 she finds that the *'adam* or 'earth creature'[12] first created is both male and female and does not signify the priority of the male.[13] Sexuality only emerges in the complementary words 'man' and 'woman' in 2.23. Moreover, 'if the woman be intelligent, sensitive, and ingenious, the man is passive, brutish, and inept'.[14] Subordination only emerges as a result of the couple's sin. 'Of special concern are the words telling the woman that her husband shall rule over her (3.16). This statement is not license for male supremacy, but rather

---

11 Trible, 'Depatriarchalizing', p. 31.

12 Trible, *God*, pp. 76, 98.

13 Trible, 'Depatriarchalizing', p. 35. All these points on Genesis 2—3 also in *God*, pp. 72–143.

14 Trible, 'Depatriarchalizing', p. 40.

it is condemnation of that very pattern. Subjugation and supremacy are perversions of creation.'[15]

Working with a similar approach, Cheryl Exum in one of her early works looked at the first two chapters of Exodus – a passage that is of significance in setting the scene for the central plot of the Pentateuch – and noted what a significant role was taken in this prologue to the story of the exodus by women, no fewer than five of them, who in their different ways contributed to the frustration of the Pharaoh's plan of genocide and succeeded in preserving the future liberator of Israel.[16] Women appear here as 'defiers of oppression ... givers of life ... wise and resourceful', and they should be looked for in such roles in the rest of the story.

Critique of ideology

Exum's later work on the same text demonstrates a very different approach, which well illustrates changes in feminist interpretation in general, as well as perhaps in her personal viewpoint.[17] Her previous method she characterizes as 'pluck[ing] positive images out of an admittedly androcentric text, separating literary characterizations from the androcentric interests they were created to serve'.[18] Now, her object is to uncover the ideology of the text, which determines the roles that women may be allowed to play in patriarchal society. All these women's activity is directed to the preservation of men, and in particular one man, who alone is destined to be the deliverer, and none of them steps outside the roles that patriarchal society allots them, as respectively midwives, mother and daughter. In the text's ideology they can either receive honour (Exod. 1.21) as the reward for staying in their place, nurturing and protecting the lives of men, who alone can take authority and leadership roles, under their 'male-identified' God; or they may be denounced, punished and expelled for daring to claim authority themselves, as happens to Miriam (Num. 12; see v. 2; Aaron and Miriam both challenge Moses, but only Miriam is struck with 'leprosy').[19]

Exum, and feminist critics in general, have thus moved from highlighting positive portrayals of women in action to discerning the ideology which, in the text as in life, determines how women both act and suffer, and how they are portrayed as doing so. The initial motivation for Trible and many others was theological.[20] The text had been used for centuries to demean and disempower women; they needed to show that this was a misreading of a text they accepted as canonical and authoritative. Many feminist critics

---

15 Trible, 'Depatriarchalizing', p. 41.
16 Exum, 'You shall let every daughter'.
17 Exum, 'The Hand that Rocks'; also earlier 'Second Thoughts'.
18 'The Hand that Rocks', p. 81; 'Second Thoughts', p. 76.
19 'The Hand that Rocks', pp. 99–100.
20 Shectman, *Women in the Pentateuch*, p. 15.

more recently have been motivated very differently: by the concern to show how the text itself is involved, through its ideological representations, in the subjection of women to patriarchal authority. They have thus felt less of a need to engage in retrieval, and are more inclined to critique the text as a whole. The method used by most remains literary. Though some, such as Carol Meyers, have tried to read the text against the actual social context in history,[21] most feminist critics of narrative – Exum is a good example – have employed an ideological critique which exposes the social assumptions of the text without needing to go behind it to explore the social reality. Interpretation of the laws is a slightly different matter (see below).

Reading for the victims

Danna Nolan Fewell and David Gunn illustrate a different variety of this approach in their provocative study of Genesis to Kings, one of the rare extensive studies of biblical material from a feminist point of view.[22] More than half of the book is concerned with the Pentateuch, but this is because of the detailed attention given to Genesis with its prominent female characters; the books from Exodus to Deuteronomy are treated much more sketchily. The subtitle, 'The Subject of the Bible's First Story', refers not to the sub-ject-*matter* of the so-called Primary History but to the personal Subject of the story, 'the governing consciousness … the point of view whose interest this text expresses, or better, constructs', which turns out to be, of course, 'the male Israelite' (more precisely the free adult male Israelite), and along with him the male God YHWH; and this consciousness defines women, or foreigners, slaves or children, as the Other.[23] A common strategy deployed by the authors is to expose the self-seeking, deceit or immorality used to maintain the authority of this Subject, including YHWH. Despite their stringent ideological critique, they aim for retrieval by looking for the women and reading the story as if woman were the Subject in this sense. Sometimes reading in this way undermines the clear definition of women as Other by revealing their (informal) power; more often, the apparently sympathetic portrayal of (a) woman is undermined by the patriarchal context in which she has to operate.

A few examples from the book will illustrate these abstract considerations. Fewell and Gunn are unsparing in their condemnation of Abraham's cowardice and lack of concern for Sarah, or indeed anyone except himself and his promised male descent line. This is shown in his manoeuvring over Sarah with foreign kings and his willingness to expel Hagar and Ishmael to die of thirst, barring the divine intervention that the story relates. The

---

21 See Meyers, *Discovering Eve*.

22 Fewell and Gunn, *Gender*. Newsom and Ringe, *Women's Bible Commentary*, covers the whole Bible but usually only gives brief comments on any one passage.

23 Fewell and Gunn, *Gender*, pp. 16–17.

climax comes in his willingness to sacrifice Isaac. The authors ask whether the purpose of the 'test' was 'to see just how far Abraham will go' in sacrificing members of his family to his own interests, in this case out of fear, as referred to by the voice from heaven, 'Now I know that you fear God' (Gen. 22.12).[24]

The destruction of the Cities of the Plain offers the opportunity for a devastating deconstruction of the concern for justice that apparently animates Genesis 18.16–33. Verses 20–21 speak of a 'cry of distress' (Heb. za'aqah) coming up from Sodom. 'Implied by the term "cry for help" are many who are oppressed. Are they all at the same time and equally oppressors who deserve destruction?'[25] And in Genesis 19.4 all the *men* of the city surround Lot's house. But where are the women and children? Some or all of these are *innocent* (a connotation of Abraham's term *tsaddiq*, usually translated 'righteous'). Yet, all together, men, women and children, are destroyed. Where is the *justice* in that?[26]

The third term in Fewell and Gunn's title, *Promise*, alludes of course to the major theme of the Pentateuch. Their investigation may be judged to show just who the promise is for. Israel's male God gives it formally to Israel, but effectively to their adult male family heads. The women, children, slaves and alien settlers are formally included and occasionally given particular attention, but they are marginal to the project.

Patriarchy in law

What about the laws? A question considered by many feminist commentators is: who is the addressee or 'Subject' of the Decalogue?[27] Grammatically the commandments are written in the second person singular masculine, but it is inconceivable that women are not expected to observe them. The answer is that, as Brenner puts it, 'I am a sub-category' of the addressees, 'indirectly implicated but never directly addressed'. The Sabbath commandment uses a list of those subject to the law similar to those in the cultic laws in Deuteronomy. Here 'you' (singular), the law's addressee, is distinguished from others who must also rest on the Sabbath (Exod. 20.10; Deut. 5.14). The glaring omission from the list is 'your wife', and it is argued by some that she is directly addressed along with the master of the house.[28] She does have authority over children and servants, and is to be honoured by her

---

24 Fewell and Gunn, *Gender*, pp. 53–5. On the point of 'fearing God', Fewell and Gunn have ignored the normal contextual meaning of this phrase, discussed by Moberly, *Bible*, pp. 80–97 (see above, p. 34).

25 Fewell and Gunn, *Gender*, p. 65.

26 Fewell and Gunn, *Gender*, pp. 66–7.

27 Fewell and Gunn, *Gender*, pp. 94–5; Clines, *Interested Parties*, pp. 26–45; Setel, 'Exodus', p. 33; Frymer-Kensky, 'Deuteronomy', pp. 53–4; Brenner, 'Afterword'.

28 Frymer-Kensky, 'Deuteronomy', p. 54.

children along with her husband. But it seems more likely that she is simply 'sub-categorized'. The inconsistency is the inevitable effect of the patriarchal context. All should obey, but the patriarchal bias ensures that only male householders are addressed.

Representative of feminist work on the laws is Harold Washington's study of the Deuteronomic laws of war and sexual violence.[29] Following Michel Foucault, he starts from the premise that the way in which people understand such concepts as gender, masculinity and rape is culturally determined, made to appear natural by cultural products such as the laws of Deuteronomy. He rightly does not assume that these laws were practically enforced, but points out that even if they were not, they affected attitudes to gender and violence by existing and being read. In many societies, certainly including that of the Hebrew Bible, there is a close connection assumed between masculinity and violence. Men are assumed to practise violence, women to suffer it. The laws of war in Deuteronomy 20 are often described as humanizing warfare, but this is only so if one identifies with the aggressors: in fact they legitimize killing and enslavement by regulating them. The decree in verse 7 that gives Washington his title, rather than being 'humane', protects the soldier's right to possession of the woman he has acquired at home. Likewise the law of the female captive in Deuteronomy 21.10–14 legitimizes marriage by capture, which for us is rape, for the woman cannot be assumed to consent; and the laws in Deuteronomy 22.23–29 authorize sexual violence according to circumstances.

The laws in general image the community as one of male heads of family, called 'neighbours' in the Decalogue and the Book of the Covenant and 'brothers' in Deuteronomy. Others are not directly addressed, however closely they may be concerned. Carolyn Pressler's study of the family laws of Deuteronomy, done from a legal–historical rather than an explicitly feminist point of view, provides strong backing for such an approach as Washington's.[30] Where women are specifically mentioned, principally in the family laws, it is as members of a male-headed household. A woman is under the control of her father while unmarried, and a married woman's sexuality belongs exclusively to her husband. The only area in which a woman exercises authority and has parity with her husband is in relation to their children. The laws do give protection to vulnerable women, but this is required largely because of the hierarchical structure of the family that it is Deuteronomy's purpose to confirm.[31]

29 Washington, '"Lest He Die in the Battle"', in Matthews et al., *Gender and Law.*
30 Pressler, *View of Women.*
31 Pressler, *View of Women*, esp. pp. 96–105.

Queer readings

Readings of the Bible looking for the suppressed voices or presence of those whose sexual leanings or practice is different from the majority are just beginning to make their appearance. Theodore Jennings writes on the Hebrew Bible, but the bulk of the book refers to the Prophets and Writings, and the Pentateuch becomes significant only towards the end. [32] As he notes, most people thinking about the Hebrew Bible in relation to homosexuality regard it as homophobic (or condemnatory of unnatural sex, according to your outlook) because of two laws in Leviticus, 18.22 and 20.13, but he rightly insists that texts in the legal collections are no guide to attitudes in the rest of the Hebrew Bible or in ancient Israelite life. In his view, these laws contradict a more relaxed attitude that he has found in many places later in the canon, but probably earlier in date. The laws are in H, the latest of the Pentateuchal collections, [33] and there is no interest in the subject in earlier ones. Careful attention, says Jennings, to the text of Leviticus 18.22 (literally 'with a male you shall not lie the lying of a woman') suggests that what it is actually prohibiting is a man's assuming the woman's role, thereby challenging the social construction of masculinity. [34] This is the ideology that has led to the persecution of gay men throughout Christian history; but it is not necessarily representative of the whole Hebrew Bible.

More unsettling is Jennings's treatment of the text alluded to in his title, Jacob's struggle with God in Genesis 32.22–32. The attack by an unknown assailant in the darkness of the night is reminiscent of a sexual assault, particularly as 'Jacob's wound' is at a site close to the buttocks; a violent sexual assault might strain the sciatic nerve, the traditional identification of the 'sinew' mentioned in 32.32. [35] The assailant is then revealed as God (vv. 29–30). This would align the attack with other attacks by God with sexual overtones in the Hebrew Bible, notably the mysterious attack on Moses in Exodus 4.24–26 or Jeremiah's complaint against YHWH in Jeremiah 20.7.

Readings from a class point of view

The presupposition of feminist readings is that women are oppressed in patriarchal society; but here we are concerned with oppression as it manifests itself between classes in society. The sufferings in view are those of slaves and of rack-rented peasants, and of workers ground down in the early stages of industrialization. The readings here go under a variety of names according to the precise point of view and method: thus we have liberation

---

32 Jennings, *Jacob's Wound*.

33 See above, p. 133.

34 Jennings, *Jacob's Wound*, pp. 202–18. For a wider range of ideas, see Guest et al., *The Queer Bible Commentary*, pp. 96–9.

35 Jennings, *Jacob's Wound*, p. 253.

readings, including readings in the tradition of black theology; materialist or Marxist readings; and ideological criticism.

Exodus: naive readings

Readings of the Exodus story from various points of view will illustrate the variety. For many this is the classic biblical story of liberation, and it can be broadly understood as the substance of the Pentateuchal narrative as a whole. The simplest, one might say most naive approach does not employ a hermeneutic of suspicion at all. The singers of black spirituals saw one thing in the story, that in it God delivers people from slavery:

> Go down, Moses!
> Way down in Egypt's land!
> Tell old Pharaoh,
> Let my people go.[36]

James Cone reproduces in his theology the unsuspicious hermeneutic of Exodus characteristic of black American preachers. The Old Testament

> tells the story of the divine acts of grace and of judgment as God calls the people of Israel into a free, liberated existence ... In the Exodus event, God is revealed by means of acts on behalf of a weak and defenseless people. This is the God of power and strength, able to destroy the enslaving power of the mighty Pharaoh.[37]

Cone does not refer to YHWH's pre-existing commitment to Israel. On the contrary, 'Historically, the story began with the Exodus.'[38] This makes it easy to universalize YHWH's commitment to the poor and oppressed. Nor does he address the problem of the displacement, involving massacre, of the existing population of Canaan.

Liberation theology: Pixley

The Latin American liberation theology movement uniformly takes the story of the exodus as one of its foundations. The most systematic study of the book of Exodus itself in that tradition is George V. Pixley's commentary *On Exodus*. It is somewhat more sophisticated than Cone's work, displaying some signs of a hermeneutic of suspicion. He expounds the book as a text that describes and promotes revolution in the specifically Marxist

---

36 See Kirk-Duggan, 'Let My People Go!'
37 Cone, *God of the Oppressed*, p. 58.
38 Cone, *God of the Oppressed*, p. 58.

sense of a transformation of social and political relationships through the insurrection of the oppressed classes. But he does not naively claim that this is all there is to the book. He sees that two non-revolutionary ideologies can be detected in it: one, found in J and E, supporting the monarchy of Israel, the story of 'a national liberation struggle – no longer a class struggle'; and another priestly one coming in after 'the identity of the Jewish people had become purely religious' under the Persian empire, which makes the exodus an act of YHWH demonstrating his divinity and sovereignty, the foundation of Judaism as the monotheistic religious community that we know.[39] For example, the puzzling 'hardening of Pharaoh's heart' by YHWH is an 'ideological rereading' of the plagues narrative, undertaken because it is 'more important to demonstrate the unsurpassable greatness of YHWH than it is to proceed forthwith to the liberation of Israel. Politics has become secondary to religion.'[40]

The revolutionary point of view to which Pixley is committed would be characteristic only of a hypothetical substratum in the book. Yet, he claims to be able to retrieve the 'authentic' class struggle from the text.[41] He explains much or even most of it as an account of class struggle and revolution, followed by the foundation of a classless society through the giving of the law. Right at the beginning, he declares that Exodus 1.8–14 reveals a situation of class (rather than national) conflict. The Pharaoh's 'we' means the dominant class, and the 'slavery' is the standard conscript labour service imposed on the whole peasant population by ancient Near Eastern kings.[42] The First Commandment (Exod. 20.3) establishes YHWH in the position held by kings in other societies, and forbids the worship of gods who would legitimize kingship; thus Israel becomes a stateless and so classless society.[43]

Pixley thus expounds the text of Exodus, whose 'plain meaning' concerns a struggle between YHWH, on the side of the oppressed *nation* Israel, and Pharaoh along with the Egyptians, *as if* it were an account of a class struggle. Some parts of the exposition work well, but this is because there is an analogy between the situations. But when, for example, he suggests that the death of the firstborn may have been 'a terrorist action – inspired by God' he is substituting a groundless hypothesis for what the text says.[44]

---

39 Pixley, *On Exodus*, pp. xviii–xx.

40 Pixley, *On Exodus*, p. 39.

41 Pixley, *On Exodus*, p. xix.

42 Pixley, *On Exodus*, p. 3.

43 Pixley, *On Exodus*, p. 119. Cf. Gottwald, *Tribes*, p. 693.

44 Pixley, *On Exodus*, p. 80; and in Gottwald and Horsley, *Bible and Liberation*, p. 91.

YHWH the Conqueror

Pixley's hermeneutic of suspicion, it is clear, is inadequate. At key points either the text's national orientation is ignored or it is artificially reinterpreted as reflecting a class conflict. He would perhaps have done better to adopt a more robust hermeneutic of suspicion such as that of the more consistently Marxist Itumeleng Mosala. Mosala criticizes black theology in South Africa in the era of apartheid, which was very similar to American black theology, for accepting the Bible as a whole as the 'Word of God', although conflicting social and political interests are encoded in the text itself and many texts 'emanate from the biblical counterparts of our contemporary oppressors and violators of ... human rights. The biblical story of the settlement of the Israelite tribes in Canaan, for example, is totally oblivious of any understanding of human rights' – until, he says, it is 'rescued' by Norman Gottwald's reassessment of the history.[45] But it is hard to see how the story is rescued by any view of the actual history: it remains a story of massacre and occupation, justified by the danger posed by the inhabitants' religion. This story is the essential pendant to the story of the exodus. Consider only Exodus 3.8. There is no 'bringing out' without a 'bringing in' to the land of 'the Canaanites, the Hittites' and the rest. Thus, for any serious theology of liberation, the story of the exodus ought to be deeply problematic, and the fact that generally it is not points to the superficiality of much of its biblical work.

This consideration is far from academic, as is well brought out by Robert Allen Warrior, a Native American writer of the Osage nation.[46] Who are the Native Americans to identify with in the biblical story but the Canaanites? – just as women readers will identify with women characters. And in doing so they find themselves standing in the place of peoples the God of the exodus commands to be annihilated (Deut. 7.2; 20.16–18). It does not matter, Warrior emphasizes, that historians have decided that this genocide did not actually take place. It is still there in the text. 'People who read the narratives read them as they are, not as scholars and experts would *like* them to be read and interpreted.'[47] And white Americans have applied these texts to the native peoples of the continent: Warrior mentions Puritan preachers who referred to Native Americans as Amalekites and Canaanites. If genocide did not take place in ancient Canaan, it certainly did on the North American continent, and the texts in Deuteronomy and Joshua were often taken to legitimate it. This also happened in Hispanic America and on a less comprehensive scale in South Africa and in modern Palestine.[48] Therefore,

---

45 Mosala, *Biblical Hermeneutics*, p. 29, referring to Gottwald, *Tribes*.
46 Warrior, 'Canaanites'.
47 Warrior, 'Canaanites', p. 237.
48 Prior, *Bible and Colonialism*.

'as long as people believe in the Yahweh of deliverance, the world will not be safe from Yahweh the conqueror'.[49]

Laws for the poor?

Equally with the story of the exodus, the commandments of the Torah are commonly taken as proclaiming a preferential option for the poor. But the justice and generosity urged in these commandments has to be read in the context of the unequal, stratified society which they mostly take for granted, as I have argued.[50] The laws – moral teachings might be a better term, except for the few which propose national institutions – appear to protect poor and marginal persons from exploitation, regularly cancel debts, return alienated land and ensure that the community supplies the poor with an adequate livelihood. However, they would rely essentially on the goodwill of the well-to-do to work. We need not assume that this was not forthcoming, if only because of the sanction of shame. But the laws mostly assume that the stratification of society is a given, and by their very existence they confirm and support it. There will always be poor, as Deuteronomy 15.11 says explicitly, and correspondingly, if less explicitly, there will always be rich; and indeed there will always be slaves.

The only law that seems not to accept this is the jubilee law in Leviticus 25. The law in verses 8–22 would not work without fair initial shares; and the series of individual cases that follows in verses 23–55 avoids the use of any noun or adjective meaning 'poor', instead using a verb meaning to become low, or, as we sometimes say, to be in reduced circumstances; poverty is a temporary accident rather than as is assumed elsewhere a permanent condition.[51] This is clearly unrealistic, and obscures the reality of an unequal society.

The effects of inequality may be softened if the commandments are observed, but to do so is in itself to underline the superiority of those who are in a position to do so; to accept charity can be demeaning to one's dignity, and even the humblest have their pride. As if to emphasize this point, the laws in Deuteronomy and Leviticus 25 refer to the person to be helped as 'your brother' (obscured in some inclusive language translations), implying that he or she is to be treated as a member of the family, a community of equals. This appeals to an ancient sense of solidarity within the clan in an attempt to make the reality of a class society more acceptable. It is in profound tension with the assumption that 'the poor will never cease out of the land' and even more so with the continuation of debt slavery: 'to take the meaning of the rhetoric seriously is to see that there cannot be masters

---

49 Warrior, 'Canaanites', p. 241.
50 Houston, *Contending*, pp. 105–18, 169–203; and see above, pp. 63–7.
51 Houston, *Contending*, p. 198.

and slaves within a family of brothers'.[52] The lesson for our present socio-economic order is that the neglected principle of 'fraternity' – 'solidarity' would be a better term today – is needed if liberty and equality are to be held together.

Postcolonial readings

A growing feature of literary criticism, and hence of biblical interpretation, is so-called 'postcolonial' theory and criticism, the effect of the increasing number of scholars based in the former colonies of European powers. This approach identifies the effects of colonialism both in the modern world (and so in the use and interpretation of the text) and in the text. It notes that the cultural products of subject peoples under colonialism tend to display the impress of both their national traditions and the ideology of the colonizing power, since people educated under colonial rule tend to internalize much of the colonial world-view, but also sometimes express resistance to their colonization, perhaps in disguised form. Thus it expects to find in a text like the Pentateuch, which was shaped to a significant extent under the rule of the Persian empire, both the ideology of the conqueror, justifying the subjection of the native peoples, and their own distinct traditions.

Gale A. Yee applies these ideas to Exodus.[53] She suggests that a function of Exodus 1—2 may be to poke fun at the Egyptians as stupid, a regular feature of colonialist ideology, as for instance in English jokes about Irish people. Pharaoh's plan of forced labour has exactly the effect it was intended to prevent (Exod. 1.10); he orders the killing of the wrong element of the Hebrew population if he wanted to reduce their numbers (he should have massacred women of childbearing age); and his daughter unbeknown to him brings the future deliverer of the Hebrews into his own palace.[54] She may, however, be mocked herself. She is conned into paying wages to the child's own mother, and may even be mocked for her bad Hebrew: *mosheh* should mean 'drawing out' not 'drawn out' (Exod. 2.10).[55] (An improbable suggestion – explanations of names in Hebrew narrative pay little attention to grammar, even when Hebrews are speaking.)

In the broader context, Yee goes on to point out, there are features of the Pentateuchal narrative that are derived from imperialist ideology. One is the vassal treaty model of the covenant texts, in which Israel is delivered from Egyptian slavery only to become slaves of YHWH. Another is the promise of the land to Abraham, regardless of the fact that it has inhabitants.

---

52 Houston, *Contending*, p. 188, and the whole context, pp. 180–90.
53 Yee, 'Postcolonial Biblical Criticism'.
54 Yee, 'Postcolonial Biblical Criticism', pp. 216–22.
55 Yee, 'Postcolonial Biblical Criticism', p. 221, referring to Ackerman, 'Moses Birth Story', p. 93.

The straightforward acknowledgement in [Gen. 15.18–21 and Exod. 3.8] that the land is *already* populated calls attention to God as the magisterial regent, sanctioning and sanctifying brutal acts of imperialism ... The Israelites are given a religious warrant to conquer indigenous peoples, colonize their lands, and abolish their gods.[56]

Ecological readings

The growth in recent years in our consciousness of environmental degradation caused by human activity has inevitably led to reflection on the relations between humanity and nature in the Bible, and the primeval narrative in Genesis 1—11 is at the heart of this reflection.

Lynn White

An article by the historian Lynn White as long ago as 1967 asserted that the interpretation of this passage in Christian tradition, especially of the apparent charter for humanity's domination of the earth in Genesis 1.26–28, lay at the root of the arrogant assumption in modern western civilization that the earth could be exploited without limit.[57] The article stirred up a number of defensive responses claiming that the text did not mean that – though the important point was not what it may have originally meant, but what it had been taken to mean, as was later pointed out by Peter Harrison.[58] The debate failed to make progress at the time, and since then a number of studies of the theology of creation in the Old Testament have been published, affirming a positive, non-violent understanding of this text and of the creation narratives as a whole.[59]

The Earth Bible project

The question has been re-opened and the field of inquiry greatly widened by the 'Earth Bible' project, led by Norman Habel, which is very much a project of the hermeneutics of suspicion. The obvious weakness in expecting ecological perspectives to make their way into the company of feminist and liberationist ones is that, unlike these, they do not represent the interests of a specific human group anxious to better their position. To overcome this problem, those involved in the Earth Bible project have developed a set of precise 'ecojustice principles' that hermeneutically commit them to making

---

56 Yee, 'Postcolonial Biblical Criticism', p. 224.
57 White, 'Historic Roots'. See also Cohen, *'Be Fertile'*.
58 P. Harrison, 'Subduing'.
59 See, e.g., Brown, *Ethos*, esp. pp. 43–6; Fretheim, *God and World*, esp. pp. 48–53. See also Brett, *Decolonizing*, pp. 32–9.

Earth's voice audible.[60] Earth is treated as a character in the biblical story, and therefore has a proper name, capitalized and without article, and is sometimes referred to as 'she'. The voice of Earth is usually suppressed in the story but may be retrieved by careful exegesis, so that Earth may speak for herself of her oppression and mistreatment. It is extremely clear in this project that the 'ecojustice principles' are accepted prior to the interpretation of the Bible, which then turns on whether these principles can be discerned in the text.

Habel's own most recent expression of this approach is in his commentary on Genesis 1—11.[61] Here Earth is deliberately made the subject of the story, against the apparent intention of the text, which, after describing its 'birth' in Genesis 1.9, subordinates its fate to that of humankind. In each passage he exposes the way in which Earth is made an object and used in pursuit of God's purposes with humankind; the exposition of each section concludes with a piece headed 'retrieval', which is an imaginative rendering of Earth's commentary on the episode from Earth's point of view, usually plaintive rather than angry, complaining of the injustice of her treatment, until the lifting of the curse at 8.21–22.

Habel renews the critique of Genesis 1.26–28, finding it in literary terms an interruption of the symmetry of the account of creation, and ideologically the intrusion of a contradictory myth which is concerned not with Earth and the successive emanation of creatures from Earth but with the glory and power of humanity.[62] From the point of view of Earth, the episode is the imposition of an alien creature, who is given the command to subdue her with violence and to dominate her children.[63]

Thus Habel's reading of the overt thrust of the primeval story in Genesis, as distinct from what he can 'retrieve' from it, is that it is not really interested in Earth, except as a backdrop, stage or prop for the drama played out between God and humans, or at most God and humans and animals ('all flesh' in Gen. 6.12–13). God is presented as indifferent or hostile to Earth, and for this reason any attempt to call Genesis in support of an idea of environmental justice must be problematic, despite the eventual assurance in 9.9–17.

Not all readers concerned about human abuse of the earth would concur with Habel's reading.[64] Moreover, the feminine language used in places of Earth runs the risk of aligning it with the subordination of women in human society. Habel is aware of this danger;[65] but it is difficult in English to insist on an entity being a person and at the same time not use 'he' or 'she' of it.

---

60 The full list of principles is given in all the volumes from the project.

61 Habel, Birth.

62 Habel, Birth, pp. 25–7. In fact only the creatures of the third and sixth days 'emanate' from Earth.

63 Habel, Birth, pp. 35–40.

64 See the works mentioned in n. 59; also Houston, 'Justice and Violence'.

65 Habel, Birth, p. 10.

Nevertheless, Habel's reading could be appropriately extended to the story of the Pentateuch as a whole, for where the earth and its creatures appear in this, they have a subordinate and instrumental role, and, as in the plagues of Egypt, the crossing of the sea, or the manna and the quails, may be used abnormally and violently to deal with an issue between God and God's people or God and their enemies.

After reading a sample of one of the approaches discussed in this chapter, try your hand at applying it to a text not dealt with in the sample. The following are suggestions of possible texts to look at, chosen because they may be interesting and fruitful. None of them are dealt with above. Some could be looked at from more than one point of view. You can probably find studies from the chosen point of view of all of them somewhere, but the point is to work out your own approach. Don't fly blind, however; use the commentaries, whatever their orientation.

- Feminist criticism: Genesis 29.15—30.22; Genesis 39; Exodus 21.2–11; Leviticus 18.6–18; Numbers 25.
- Interpretation from a class point of view: Genesis 47.13–26; Exodus 21.2–11; Exodus 22.21—23.13; Numbers 18.21–32; Deuteronomy 14.22–29.
- Postcolonial interpretation: Numbers 33.50—34.15; Deuteronomy 20.
- Ecological interpretation: Exodus 7—10; Leviticus 11.1–23; Deuteronomy 28.15–52.

Further reading

General

The Postmodern Bible, by the Bible and Culture Collective, gives a useful introduction to various recently developed ways of interpreting the Bible in general that have in common their orientation towards the reader. The chapters most relevant to the concerns of this chapter are Chapter 3, 'Post-structuralist Criticism' (that is, deconstruction and the like), Chapter 6, 'Feminist and Womanist Criticism'[66] and Chapter 7, 'Ideological Criticism'.

Certain chapters of *The Oxford Handbook of Biblical Studies* (Rogerson and Lieu), which is much more recent, may also be found useful. *The Cambridge Companion to Biblical Interpretation* (Barton) has a similar range, but is shorter and somewhat older. All the dictionary-type works on reception history mentioned in the previous chapter have relevant material.

---

66 'Womanist' is a label adopted by black feminists concerned with the double impact of gender and racial oppression.

The series Methods in Biblical Interpretation aims to cover every book of the Bible, dealing with both 'classical' and more recent methods. The only volume on a book of the Pentateuch that has appeared at the time of writing, so far as I know, is Dozeman (ed.), *Methods for Exodus*. Besides the chapter by Yee on postcolonial criticism discussed above, this includes Pixley on liberation criticism and Naomi Steinberg on feminist criticism.

Deconstruction

Much criticism of this kind is impenetrable to the uninitiated, but David Clines's work, much of which may loosely or precisely fall into that category, is lucid and provocative. *Interested Parties* includes two essays on Pentateuchal themes, one on the Decalogue, and 'God in the Pentateuch' discussed above.

Feminist criticism

Brenner and Fontaine's *A Feminist Companion to Reading the Bible* is a substantial introduction to the general issues and methods of feminist criticism and interpretation. Shectman, *Women in the Pentateuch* (pp. 9–54), gives an overview of feminist work, especially on the Pentateuch, drawing distinctions between different approaches. Eskenazi and Weiss's commentary, *The Torah*, presents 'postbiblical interpretations' and modern feminist reflection alongside 'the original author's views'. The volume *Torah* (eds Fischer and Navarro Puerto), in the series 'The Bible and Women', includes a number of studies on the Pentateuch from various points of view.

The work of Phyllis Trible, however much overtaken today, was important in inaugurating modern feminist work on the Hebrew Bible. Her 'Depatriarchalizing' and *God and the Rhetoric of Sexuality* continue to be worth reading, and so does her *Texts of Terror*.

Athalya Brenner has edited two series of *Feminist Companions* to different books or parts of the Hebrew Bible, collecting significant essays by feminist scholars. (See the Bibliography for details.) The essays in the four volumes on the Pentateuch come from a wide range of positions under the broad feminist umbrella. Exum's *Fragmented Women* has three essays on Pentateuchal passages. Fewell and Gunn's *Gender* is the one book offering some approach to a continuous interpretation of the Pentateuch (with the Former Prophets) from a feminist point of view.

Queer readings

Not much has been published in this line, but there is Guest et al. (eds), *Queer Bible Commentary*, which has an interesting range of comments on all the books of the Bible. Each of the chapters on the Pentateuchal books is by a different author. Jennings, *Jacob's Wound*, is discussed above. Stone, *Practicing*, has discussions of the Eden story and the food and sex laws.

Liberation, ideological, materialist, etc., criticism

Most interpreters from these points of view see the actual social situation at the time of the writing of the text as significant; so their interpretations are vulnerable to changes in views of the date and circumstances of writing. Works written before about 1995 have to be treated with caution. I have mentioned Pixley's *On Exodus* simply because it is one of only two works in the liberation movement to give *extended* attention to that book; the other is Croatto's, which has less on the text itself. However, the large collection of essays and other materials in Gottwald and Horsley (eds), *Bible and Liberation* (1990), is still a useful introduction to the variety of approaches in question here. A more up-to-date one, with its own particular point of view, as all the writers are based in what was still (in 2006) called 'the Third World', is the collection edited by Sugirtharajah, *Voices from the Margin*. Part Three of this collection, with six articles, is focused on Exodus.

Mosala's *Biblical Hermeneutics and Black Theology* does not contain much significant exegesis of Pentateuchal texts. There are relatively recent approaches to understanding the Pentateuch, especially the laws, in class terms in Sneed (ed.), *Concepts of Class*, in Knight, *Law, Power and Justice*, and in my *Contending for Justice*.

The defunct journal *Semeia* gave much space to ideological reflection on the Bible. Each issue was devoted to a particular topic. Issue 87 (1999) was on 'social world' studies of the Hebrew Bible. This means not simply study of objective social situations, but the way in which society is represented ideologically in the texts. There are several articles relative to the Pentateuch in this issue.

Postcolonial criticism

R. S. Sugirtharajah has been a prime mover in ensuring that the voices of scholars and theologians with a postcolonial viewpoint are heard in the West. *Postcolonial Criticism* surveys the field. *Voices from the Margin* has been mentioned above; some of the contributions are explicitly 'postcolonial', and most can be seen in that light. *Semeia* volumes 75 (1996) and 88 (2001) are on this topic. Mark Brett's *Decolonizing God* is a contribution from Australia with a different approach; several of the studies here have relevance to the Pentateuch.

Ecological interpretation

This field has recently been dominated by the Earth Bible project. This began with the Earth Bible series, including *Readings from the Perspective of Earth* and *The Earth Story in Genesis,* and has now gone on to the Earth Bible Commentary, beginning with Habel's *The Birth, the Curse and the Greening of Earth.* A further volume of essays, *Exploring Ecological Hermeneutics,* contains four essays on Pentateuchal themes. All these books are written or edited by Habel, with or without assistance.

It would be important to look also at an approach independent of this project. Ellen Davis's *Scripture, Culture and Agriculture* would be a good choice, or Horrell's *Bible and Environment.*

10

The Theology of the Pentateuch

The nature of the task

We have left until last what I expect many readers will see as the most important thing they would hope to gain from a book like this. You are a theologian, or studying theology (doesn't that make you a theologian?), and your reason for studying the Pentateuch is because it is a theological writing and you expect it to contribute to your own theology. But that raises the issue of what we mean by 'the theology' of a book or part of the Bible, or of the commoner terms 'Old Testament theology' or 'biblical theology'.

Exegesis and biblical theology

The question is addressed at a basic level by Rolf Knierim, who argues that exegesis on its own cannot give the biblical truth that may confront us today, because exegesis shows only the multiplicity of ideas and theologies in the Bible or the Old Testament. What biblical theology must do is to establish how all the various theological ideas are related to each other systematically, and which is the most fundamental, the criterion of truth for all the others (for him the fundamental idea of the Old Testament is 'the universal dominion of YHWH in justice and righteousness'). Only after we have done this can we ask how this might be truth for us, the hermeneutic task.[1]

Against this, how we establish the systematic relationship of all the ideas of the Pentateuch is not a purely logical exercise: it will depend on our own assumptions, including how we perceive the significance of the ideas to ourselves. There is bound to be disagreement between biblical theologians, not just on details, but at this most basic level. We shall come back to this point in a moment. Again, Walter Brueggemann contends that the typical mode of theologizing in the Old Testament is through dialogue. One idea is pitted against another, and each must be taken seriously. If this is so, the Pentateuch must resist any attempt to systematize it, and Brueggemann rejects that term for his own work.[2]

---

1 Knierim, *Task*, pp. 1–21.
2 Brueggemann, *Theology*, pp. 83–4, 267–8 and elsewhere.

'What it meant and what it means'

Biblical theology is distinct not only from exegesis but also from 'dogmatic' or 'systematic' theology, which describes what Christians believe, or ought to believe.[3] But the two are closely related. Virtually all the biblical theologies that have been written are the work of Christians. Although Jewish biblical theologies have been written,[4] Jon Levenson shows that generally Jews have no interest in the exercise, for good reasons;[5] and it is clear that scholars confessing no faith are also generally uninterested.

One way of relating biblical and systematic theology is suggested by the New Testament scholar Krister Stendahl, who coined the memorable slogan, 'What it meant is not what it means'. He argues that while the biblical scholar may synthesize the variety of statements in the Old Testament, for example, into a *descriptive* theology of the Old Testament, that cannot function as a theology for the present day without what he terms 'translation' into modern thought-forms appropriate to a modern world-view.[6]

Nicholas Lash's objections are multiple.[7] First, the 'description' that biblical theology offers is itself the result of an act of imaginative interpretation.[8] In the act of interpretation, the interpreter's presuppositions – for the biblical theologian, Christian ones – come into play, as everyone now recognizes. When we are dealing with a biblical theology, which systematizes a range of ideas, the interpreter's imagination and presuppositions are even more significant than in the exegesis of a single text.

Second, Stendahl never explores what he means by 'meaning'; but this is not a simple idea. It cannot be restricted to the intention of the author, and may have multiple variations even for a single text. Many today consider that the reader is as important as the author in creating the meaning of a text. Third, the metaphor of 'translation' is inappropriate for work that brings in other ideas, perhaps conceptually distinct from the biblical text. The fourth point is that the traffic between biblical scholarship and modern theology does not go one way only: there is a relationship of mutual dependence between them. 'If the questions to which ancient authors sought to respond in terms available to them ... are to be "heard" today ... they have first to be "heard" as questions that challenge us with comparable seriousness.'[9]

If these points are well taken, the 'what it meant – what it means' model of the relationship is neither useful as a programme for how to write biblical theology nor accurate as a description of how it has been written. Although

---

3 See Barr, *Concept*, p. 62; Hayes and Prussner, *OT Theology*, p. 63.
4 Barr, *Concept*, pp. 286–91.
5 Levenson, *Hebrew Bible*, pp. 33–61.
6 Stendahl, 'Biblical Theology, Contemporary'.
7 Lash, 'Martyrdom', pp. 77–82 (in *Emmaus*).
8 Cf. Barr, *Concept*, pp. 204–5.
9 Lash, 'Martyrdom', p. 81.

in simple terms biblical theology is an attempt to state the 'meaning' of the Bible, or part of it, that meaning is arrived at in the light of the scholar's own concerns and convictions and in the hope that the result will be of value in relation to those concerns. This is the approach of the recent movement of 'theological interpretation'.[10]

Our chapter on 'the theology of the Pentateuch' thus appropriately stands in Part C as an aspect of 'the world in front of the text', alongside traditional Jewish and Christian interpretation and the hermeneutic of the suspicious reader.

The theology of the Pentateuch and Christian faith

Given, then, that biblical theology is mostly done by Christians and that it is related to the scholar's own convictions, should it be explicitly designed to engage with, or indeed to support, Christian faith and teaching?[11] For modern readers, it would be wrong to read Christian ideas into the Pentateuch,[12] but that does not exclude relating it to Christian faith. Two recent writers of Old Testament theologies, Walter Brueggemann and John Goldingay, have argued against this. Rolf Knierim, as we have seen, understands it as a separate task subsequent to systematizing the theology of the Old Testament.[13] Von Rad, however, in his *Old Testament Theology*, devotes Part Three of the book to the subject 'The Old Testament and the New'.[14] Here we are told that 'the most essential characteristic of the Old Testament is the way in which it points forward to the Christ-event of the New'.[15] When we read this, we can look back at Part Two (Section B for the 'Hexateuch')[16] to see how Von Rad has silently prepared for it. He has described the theology of the Old Testament as a repeated reuse and reinterpretation of the old traditions enshrined in the Pentateuch (or Hexateuch for von Rad), and he now argues that the Christian gospel is a reinterpretation of the Old Testament traditions in the same way, but 'on the basis of an entirely new saving event'.[17]

Childs's 'canonical' approach, rather differently, aims at first hearing the witness of Old and New Testaments separately and then reflecting on them both together as the whole witness of the (Christian) Bible. An example

---

10 In relation to the Pentateuch, see in particular Moberly, *Bible* and *Theology of Genesis*; and Briggs and Lohr (eds), *Theological Introduction*.

11 See Barr, *Concept*, pp. 62–76 and 253–65; in fact the whole work is more or less relevant.

12 Contrast the traditional readings we met in Chapter 8, pp. 172–9.

13 Brueggemann, *Theology*, p. 107 (but see pp. 311–12, 332, etc.!); Goldingay, *Israel's Gospel*, p. 35; Knierim, *Task*, p. 69.

14 Von Rad, *OT Theology*, vol. 2, pp. 319–409.

15 Von Rad, *OT Theology*, vol. 2, p. 389.

16 Von Rad, *OT Theology*, vol. 1, pp. 129–305.

17 Von Rad, *OT Theology*, vol. 2, p. 360.

relevant to the Pentateuch is his discussion of 'covenant, election and people of God'.[18]

> The Hebrew scriptures remain a lasting witness to the truth that Israel's existence depends solely upon the divine mercy and initiative ... (Deut. 7.7ff.) ... toward the purpose of shaping this people into a holy and right-eous vehicle by which to reconcile himself to the world (Gen. 12.1ff.).[19]

Given our earlier conclusion that the interpreter's own commitments and presuppositions are bound to be involved in the act of interpretation, it is not likely to be possible for a Christian interpreter to exclude a Christian angle altogether, and in my view it is better to acknowledge this openly. More generally, the whole of the traditions directly or indirectly dependent on the Old Testament – Judaism, Christianity, Islam – are relevant to its interpretation, including theological interpretation.

The theology of the Pentateuch and historical criticism

Biblical theology only exists because of historical criticism. The idea of draw-ing a distinction between the study of the Bible's theology as a historical study and dogmatic theology only emerged as the Bible came to be seen as a historical document. All biblical theologies that I am aware of make use of historical criticism. Therefore it comes as a surprise when two of them, Brueggemann's and Goldingay's, appear to take a stand against it. Goldingay's objection is simple: that historical criticism does not provide a secure enough basis for a theology, in view of the uncertainties it gener-ates.[20] Brueggemann's position is complex. He appears to confuse historical criticism as a method with certain views associated with some of its practi-tioners, especially the systematic disqualification of 'the witness of the text to the mysterious workings of God'.[21] Having thus apparently rejected it on theological grounds, he concludes that 'we continue to engage with such criticism, but with some vigilance about its temptation to overreach'.[22]

The fact is that both Brueggemann and other biblical theologians take for granted certain results of historical criticism, not all the same ones, of course, and use them in their theologies. Childs sees historical criticism as being unable to deal with Scripture theologically, but nevertheless puts more historical–critical argument in his works than most biblical theologians. He understands the canonical text not merely as a text but as the witness to an experience with God at a particular historical moment. This position

---

18 Childs, *Biblical Theology*, pp. 413–51.
19 Childs, *Biblical Theology*, p. 445.
20 Goldingay, *Israel's Gospel*, p. 40. See above, Chapter 5, for a proof of his words!
21 Brueggemann, *Theology*, pp. 103–4.
22 Brueggemann, *Theology*, p. 105.

is to be respected, but its weakness is the uncertainty of historical reconstruction that leads Goldingay to avoid relying on such reconstructions as far as possible. The great majority of published biblical theologies do rely on particular reconstructions, and generally aim to set forth 'the faith of Israel' or some similar term implying that the theology is the result of historical research. The historical–critical position adopted makes a difference to the way in which the theology is expounded. Good examples are the great twentieth-century works of Eichrodt and von Rad.

Walther Eichrodt

Eichrodt's *Theology of the Old Testament* can be seen as especially relevant to the theology of the Pentateuch, since he makes the relationship based on the covenant the central theme of the account in his first volume, concerned with God and Israel, and I have already argued that the covenant accounts are the key to the unity of the Pentateuch. The historical scholarship this book reflects is that of the early twentieth century,[23] and today appears highly conservative. Although the Pentateuch is compiled from several sources dating from the monarchy or later, it gives a faithful picture of the earliest days of Israel and the role of Moses. Yahwism goes back to a covenant adopted in Israel's wilderness period and mediated by Moses, expressed in terms of law in at least the Ten Commandments. The faith thus inaugurated had to struggle against the syncretistic tendencies encouraged by the Canaanite environment, but after the exile it became established and eventually hardened into Jewish legalism.

Now, at the beginning of his book, Eichrodt declares that 'it is high time the tyranny of historicism was broken'; the problem is 'to understand the realm of OT belief in its structural unity'.[24] But his argument is historical rather than structural; it is not that the ideas of the *Old Testament* depend on the covenant, though that is implied, but that the *life of Israel* was determined by the covenant. Despite Eichrodt's proclaimed aversion to 'historicism', he cannot escape thinking historically, and this is why he should be seen as dependent on historical criticism.

What Eichrodt says theologically about 'the covenant', which he always treats as singular, is closely related to how he understands it historically. It is not just a transaction, but a relationship. The establishment of the covenant 'emphasizes the factual nature of the divine revelation', as God 'breaks in on his people and moulds them according to his will'.[25] It is worked out in history, beginning with the deliverance from Egypt and the occupation of Canaan (both historical events for Eichrodt). It was later refashioned by the

---

23 The German original was first published in 1933.
24 Eichrodt, *Theology*, p. 31.
25 Eichrodt, *Theology*, p. 37.

biblical writers. Eichrodt mentions among these the three main groups of writers who created the Pentateuch, who emphasize election and grace. That Israel owes its existence to the gracious choice, blessing and deliverance of YHWH is absolutely central to the Pentateuch. Eichrodt grounds this in the character of the covenant God, whose will is absolute but far from all arbitrariness, who is trustworthy and ready to save and help his people but at the same time insistent that they should obey his will in all things.

Gerhard von Rad

Von Rad lays it down at the start that 'the subject-matter which concerns the theologian is ... Israel's own explicit assertions about Jahweh'.[26] This implies that what is expressed in the Old Testament is the faith of the people. Von Rad considered that the research done, principally by himself and Martin Noth, on the history of traditions, had demonstrated that the narrative of the Pentateuch especially (the Hexateuch for von Rad) could be traced back to distinct traditions preserved at the old sanctuaries, constantly expanded from their initial nucleus in such texts as Deuteronomy 26.5–9, and renewed in new contexts in the written sources.[27] This is the historical–critical basis of his *Theology*, and it determines the presentation of the material.

The proper subject matter of the theology of the Old Testament, according to von Rad, is what in German is called the *Heilsgeschichte*, usually given by his translator as the 'saving history'; 'history of salvation' is another common translation. This is the work of YHWH in calling and saving Israel. Israel presents her faith not systematically, but by continually retelling this history, and the theologian should do the same. 'Thus, re-telling remains the most legitimate form of theological discourse on the Old Testament.'[28] Von Rad's approach is thus sharply contrary to Knierim's.

But von Rad does not retell the story as the Hexateuch presents it.[29] Rather, he dissects the account into the traditions out of which he believed it had been composed. The headings are the successive main traditional 'themes' of the story: the primeval history, the history of the patriarchs, the deliverance from Egypt, the divine revelation at Sinai, the wandering in the wilderness, and the granting of the land of Canaan;[30] to these is added, before the last item, 'the conception of Moses and his office'. In each case he identifies what he sees as the original traditional nucleus of the theme, and then deals separately with the way it is 'recontextualized' and carried

26 Von Rad, *OT Theology*, vol. 1, p. 105.
27 See above, p. 97.
28 Von Rad, *OT Theology*, vol. 1, p. 121.
29 Von Rad, *OT Theology*, vol. 1, pp. 129–305.
30 These are the themes identified by Noth, in slightly different wording. See above, p. 97.

forward in each of the 'sources' of the Documentary Hypothesis. But large parts of the narrative are omitted, or only referred to casually. The total impression is far from a 'retelling' of the story. More than half of the discussion of the Hexateuch deals with 'the divine revelation at Sinai', and is devoted entirely to reflection on the various collections of commandments, starting with the Decalogue. This adds to the disjointed impression created by the separate treatment of the sources.

On the other hand, von Rad does explain clearly how the creators of the Pentateuchal sources linked together the various old local narratives of the ancestors *theologically*, 'by means of the constantly recurring divine promise', a promise claimed by the whole of Israel.[31]

Each of these examples of Pentateuchal theologies based on historical criticism has its own weaknesses, and of course the critical positions adopted by Eichrodt and von Rad are both outdated. The tendency in recent years, at least in English-language scholarship, has been to avoid relying too heavily on a particular historical reconstruction in writing the theology of the Old Testament; as Goldingay hints, this is insecure and too easily overtaken by the changing face of scholarship. The more serious problem with historical criticism is what it tends to imply about the *historicity* of the Pentateuch especially.

The theology of the Pentateuch and the historicity of the Pentateuch

Von Rad insisted that 'Israel's' narrative assertions were assertions about history, however embellished,[32] but he was so conscious of the difference between the history as told in the Bible and the history as reconstructed by modern scholars that he prefixed a sketch of the latter to his *Theology*. The cohabitation of these two incompatible approaches within the covers of one volume symbolizes von Rad's dilemma.

Eichrodt, on the other hand, tries to provide a basis for his theology in history, but he is equally unsuccessful. For example, his treatment of the laws lays it down that both the moral and the cultic laws flow from the direct will of God. This is no more than what the text says: Moses receives the law from YHWH on Sinai/Horeb. But Eichrodt, wishing to base this observation historically, weakens it theologically by explaining that 'the contemplation of the divine Being must have exercised a decisive influence on [the law's] formation'.[33]

The way in which the historical investigation of early Israel has gone since the times of Eichrodt and von Rad has only made the problem worse, so that while von Rad saw the Hexateuch as attributing certain historical events to the work of God, of course unprovably, many would now say that

---

31 Von Rad, *OT Theology*, vol. 1, p. 167.
32 Von Rad, *OT Theology*, vol. 2, pp. 418–25.
33 Eichrodt, *Theology*, p. 76.

the Pentateuch makes God the author of events that never happened. Can such be a 'saving history'?[34]

Understandably, therefore, recent Old Testament theologians evade the dilemma. Brueggemann, taking the speech of 'Israel' as the subject of the theology, says that 'in focusing on speech, we tend to bracket out all questions of historicity … To inquire into the historicity of the text is a legitimate enterprise, but it does not, I suggest, belong to the work of Old Testament theology.'[35] Goldingay says, even if we could establish the history in the face of all the uncertainties, 'the actual subject would still be the story'.[36] History as written in the Pentateuch is creative and imaginative rather than scientific. But according to Goldingay, 'we do have grounds for trusting God that the story they wrote was one that God meant us to have and from which God meant us to learn'.[37]

The theology of the Pentateuch and critical interpretation

In the twenty-first century, we cannot avoid the questions raised through the hermeneutic of suspicion by the critical interpreters whose work we explored in the previous chapter. In other words, we cannot avoid the question whether whatever we determine to be the theology of the Pentateuch is actually true or not. Most Old Testament theologians in the past either took it for granted that it was or did not raise the question. But today Walter Brueggemann, to take a prominent example, is very much alive to it. He sets out the approaches we have discussed as part of his survey of 'the contemporary situation'.[38] Later he has a chapter 'cross-examining Israel's core testimony', showing that the Old Testament itself questions the justice and faithfulness of its God, and going on to point, among other things, to the Holocaust as the 'unanswerable disruption' of the case for YHWH.[39]

Structuring a theology of the Pentateuch

The two main alternatives here are the narrative (however qualified) or canonical presentation, as exemplified by von Rad, and the thematic presentation, as exemplified by Eichrodt or Brueggemann, and indeed most Old Testament theologies, other than von Rad's, written before the 1990s. The canonical presentation enables us as readers to separate out easily what they say about the Pentateuch, but there seems to be no issue of principle giving an advantage to one mode or the other in the composition of a work

---

34 See above, Chapter 7.
35 Brueggemann, *Theology*, p. 118.
36 Goldingay, *Israel's Gospel*, p. 871.
37 Goldingay, *Israel's Gospel*, p. 883.
38 Brueggemann, *Theology*, pp. 98–102.
39 Goldingay, *Israel's Gospel*, p. 317–32.

on the Pentateuch alone. Since I have offered a narrative interpretation of the Pentateuch above in Chapter 2, it seems appropriate that I should conclude with a thematic interpretation of its theology.

The discussion so far has led to the conclusion that the composition of a theology of the Pentateuch will involve:

1 'an interplay between the biblical text and the questions [the interpreter] brings to it, questions that necessarily reflect the interpreter's own preconceptions and frame of reference.'[40] For the Christian interpreter, this frame of reference will include the New Testament and Christian tradition; and for the twenty-first-century interpreter, it must include the questions raised via the hermeneutic of suspicion.

2 Reflection on ways of reading the text adopted in the traditions that have flowed from it.

3 The systematization or at least 'thematization' (Brueggemann) of the ideas.

4 Only a modest and subsidiary role for any historical–critical theories.

5 The 'bracketing out' of the question of historicity.

A thematic outline of the theology of the Pentateuch

Obviously there is only room for a few of the aspects that might be expected under each heading.

God

The Pentateuch identifies the creator God who is called *elohim* in its first verse with YHWH the God of Israel. It is clear that various other designations in Genesis all apply to the same God, even though YHWH's assertion of identity in Exodus 6.3 only explicitly refers to *el shaddai*. It is this God who reveals the name YHWH to Moses, and it is this God who proclaims his nature as a God of mercy (first!) and justice in Exodus 34.6–7.

The Pentateuch thereby recognizes only one God, and on this is founded the essential belief of all three so-called Abrahamic faiths. This statement is surprisingly controversial. 'Monotheism' is a term avoided by many Old Testament scholars, or applied only to limited parts of the Old Testament.[41] They raise the objection that the existence of other gods is often assumed, as in the commandment, 'You shall have no other gods before me' (Exod. 20.3 = Deut. 5.7). But what follows identifies 'other gods' only as idols.[42] Nathan MacDonald rightly argues that Deuteronomy's emphasis on the

---

40 Moberly, *Theology of Genesis*, p. 157.
41 For a full discussion, see MacDonald, *Deuteronomy*.
42 See above, p. 46.

uniqueness of YHWH as God (Deut. 4.35, 39) has to do with love and commitment rather than with intellectual belief. But to proceed from there to exclude 'monotheism' goes too far. It is true that some passages hint at or assume the existence of other supernatural beings: the use of the plural 'we' in Genesis 1.26; 3.22; 11.7; or the reference to the 'sons of god', or divine beings, in Genesis 6.2 and Deuteronomy 32.8. But only YHWH can truly be described as God (*ha'elohim*, literally 'the god', Deut. 4.35, 39): this is MacDonald's own interpretation.[43] Or to put it another way, YHWH can be called *the* god, because the term 'god' does not properly apply to anyone else. MacDonald argues that this does not deny the existence of other gods. It may not deny their existence, but it does effectively deny their deity: it denies that they are gods. If 'heaven and the heaven of heavens and the earth and all that is in it' belong to YHWH (Deut. 10.14), what realm is left for these other so-called gods? Sovereignty belongs to YHWH alone.

And this is evident in the action of the Pentateuch. YHWH is the only person who *functions* as a god in the narrative, and we have seen that all the major events are YHWH's responsibility. The difference from polytheism is instantly apparent when one compares the founding narratives of other ancient peoples. It is particularly striking when Genesis uses the story of the Flood, which exists in several Mesopotamian versions. In all of these more than one god takes part, and one god is frequently set against another. In Genesis, however, the same God both brings the Flood and warns Noah; no other appears.

So it seems that the Pentateuch sets the scene for the problem of evil in the form in which we know it. If there is only one god, and that god is sovereign, then that god can be blamed (not necessarily rightly) for bad things as well as praised for good things; and this raises a question against YHWH's self-description as just and merciful. Cross-examination begins, not first in the book of Job, but already in the Pentateuch, in Genesis 18.17–33.[44]

God and the world: creation and blessing

The world and everything in it owe their being to God. This is assumed everywhere and stated in many places in the Old Testament. But the Pentateuch opens with a dramatic presentation of this teaching. Notable here are: the creative power of God's word; the basis of creation in the separation of realms within the world; the evaluation of the creation by God as good; and the close association of creation with blessing (Gen. 1.22, 28; 2.3). What we do not find here, or anywhere in the Pentateuch, is the connection of creation with conflict, the necessity for God to defeat hostile beings in order to establish creation securely, that is common in ancient Near Eastern myth and referred to in a number of places in Hebrew poetry (for example

---

43 MacDonald, *Deuteronomy*, p. 80.
44 For a thorough discussion, see Lindström, *God and the Origin of Evil*.

Ps. 74.13–14; 89.9–10).[45] But though God here reigns without challenge to create a good world, evil still finds its way in.

As the two blessings of creatures begin 'be fruitful and multiply', it is clear that blessing gives the creatures the power to reproduce, to carry forward the effects of creation continuously within their own being. Their response parallels the response of the earth and the sea to the command to bring forth life. The fact that the world is created by God does not mean that 'by his power, each tree and flower was planned and made', for the earth brings forth trees and flowers of its own accord in response to God's command (Gen. 1.11–12; cf. 1.24). Perhaps there is here a point of contact between the creation doctrine of Genesis 1 and a naturalistic view of life, though clearly evolution is not within the horizon of this account. Nevertheless, such texts as Exodus 4.11 and Numbers 16.30 (which uses the verb *bara'*, 'create', as in Genesis 1) show that the authors took for granted God's creative power in the present-day world and could always attribute direct creative action to God.

Similarly, God's blessing of human beings is the direct renewal by God of fertility in both humans and other creatures, as in YHWH's blessings of the ancestors (Gen. 9.1; 12.1–3; 17.16, 20; etc.). The covenant blessings of Leviticus 26.3–13 and Deuteronomy 28.1–14 are more complex, since they include political and military success. Claus Westermann comprehends the activities of God in the Old Testament under the headings of blessing and salvation, both of which are experienced by all creatures – and therefore, though Westermann does not say this, are the work of the creator God.[46] The political blessings are examples of salvation, and this will be dealt with below. The curses which follow in each case can be seen as corollaries of the power of the creator; they are God's 'strange work' in response to human disobedience, as are the plagues of Egypt, and, going back to the beginning, the sentences pronounced in Eden (Gen. 3.14–19), and above all the Flood. However, some of the language in the covenant curses and in Genesis 3 rather suggests an automatic working out of the consequences of evil conduct.[47]

God's assessment of the creation as 'very good' (Gen. 1.31) contrasts sharply with the later observation that 'the earth was ruined before God, and the earth was full of violence ... for every creature[48] had behaved ruinously upon the earth' (Gen. 6.11–12). Although God brings the Flood in response to this, there is no indication that the situation is altered as a result: on the contrary, the regime of fear to be imposed by humanity on the animals in Genesis 9.2–6 appears to be the permanent solution.[49] God, it

---

45 See Levenson, *Creation*.

46 Westermann, *What Does the OT?*, p. 28.

47 Klaus Koch discusses the issue in an important but one-sided and badly translated article, 'Is there a Doctrine of Retribution?'

48 Literally 'all flesh' (*kol basar*); not just all human beings, but all living creatures.

49 See Houston, 'Sex or Violence?'

appears, is not responsible for 'nature red in tooth and claw' – not, therefore, for the behaviour of the parasitic wasps that so distressed Charles
Darwin.[50] Although this theme in the primeval history is distinctive of P,
and the 'J' account is more exclusively focused on humanity, this too describes a corruption which remains unaltered by the Flood (Gen. 3.14–19;
6.5; 8.21).

Moberly argues that it is a misreading of the creation story 'to make
"God" into an "explanation" of the world in a way analogous to the scientific concern to explain the world'.[51] This leads into the blind alley of the
'god of the gaps'. Theology is concerned with 'understanding' rather than
'explaining', and with wisdom as the key to how to live. To affirm that
'God made me', and analogously made the world, is an affirmation of trust,
dependence and accountability in the here and now, as creature to creator.[52]
If my reading of Genesis 1—9 is correct, this can be made more precise. The
story affirms that we depend for life and blessing on God, and that violence
and fear are of our own devising. The path of wisdom, towards blessing and
away from curse (see Gen. 5.29), is the path of Noah, who was 'just and
perfect in his generations, and walked with God' (Gen. 6.9). It is appropriate that he is the recipient of God's covenanted promise that never again
will the earth be destroyed in the waters of the Flood (Gen. 6.18; 9.9–17).

God and Israel: election and promise

We have already noted the prominence of God's choice as a theme in the
Pentateuch.[53] All its major individual human characters are chosen by God
to be the bearer of God's blessing and covenant or for particular roles. Here
we are concerned only with that series of choices – of Abraham, Isaac and
Jacob – that can be summed up as the choice of Israel as God's people.
Divine choice only becomes an explicit theological theme in Deuteronomy
(7.6–8; 10.15, etc.), but in the choice of Israel Deuteronomy is only bringing
out the implications of the preceding narrative.

YHWH's choice is free and unconstrained. In Deuteronomy 7.8 Moses
explains the choice of Israel on the grounds that 'YHWH loves you and
is keeping the oath which he swore to your fathers'. Once the oath had
been taken, YHWH had no option but to choose Israel. But YHWH's
free will was exercised in choosing the ancestors. Paradoxically, therefore,

---

50 'I cannot persuade myself that a benevolent and *omnipotent* [emphasis Darwin's]
God would have designedly created the Ichneumonidae with the express intention of their
feeding within the living bodies of caterpillars.' Letter to Asa Gray, 22 May 1860. Quotation from Spencer, *Darwin and God*, p. 85; slightly misquoted ('with' for 'within') in the
quotation from Dawkins in Moberly, *Theology of Genesis*, p. 58.
51 Moberly, *Theology of Genesis*, p. 62.
52 Moberly, *Theology of Genesis*, pp. 64–5.
53 Above, p. 29.

the assertion of YHWH's unconstrained choice assures the Israelites of YHWH's commitment to them.

YHWH's choice may not be altogether unmotivated, but it is not because of any virtue of Israel's (Deut. 9.4–6). Genesis 22.16–18 is the only text in Genesis that offers a reason for the promise, 'because you have done this and have not withheld your only son'; but this comes long after YHWH's original choice of Abram, and after several reiterations of the promise. In general, Paul's judgement that the promise to Abraham was not on the ground of anything he had done is correct. It seems one function of the Akedah is to confirm the wisdom of YHWH's choice, as well as to enable Abraham himself to discover what it meant to 'fear God'.[54]

The episode in Genesis 17, where God states that he is giving Abraham his covenant, is distinctive within Genesis. Not only does it repeat the promises of progeny and of land (v. 8), but in v. 7 the content of the covenant is 'to be God to you and to your descendants after you'. In other words, the covenant does not merely bind God externally to give something to Abraham, it expresses personal commitment, the commitment of God's person, to Abraham and his descendants. When the covenant is recalled in Exodus 6, after the descendants have become a people, this phrase is expanded into a reciprocal statement: 'I shall take you to be my people, and I shall be your God', linked with the promise to deliver them from slavery in Egypt. This is often referred to as the 'covenant formula', and recurs, for example, in the covenant blessings in Leviticus 26.12, where the promise of deliverance in Exodus 6 is recalled.[55] It is this relationship of mutual commitment that Eichrodt, for example, understands as the covenant. But though the commitment is to be mutual, it is God who takes the initiative, makes the promise, and single-handedly creates the relationship.

This promise that embraces mutual commitment demands fulfilment in various ways. The promise of posterity begins to be fulfilled almost straight away, and by the beginning of Exodus the children of Israel are a people. The promise of land is still unfulfilled at the end of the Pentateuch. It will be shortly fulfilled, and yet the text gives one to understand that it will remain under question. Both Leviticus and Deuteronomy warn that failure to obey YHWH's commands will lead to expulsion from the land (Lev. 26.33–39; Deut. 28.63–68). But both also assure their hearers that YHWH will be open to hear them in the land where they have been deported. In Leviticus 26.40–45 YHWH says, 'I will remember my covenant with Jacob ... with Isaac ... and with Abraham; and I will remember the land.' In Deuteronomy 30.1–5 Moses assures them that if they return to YHWH, YHWH will bring them back to their land. We thus understand that the security of the land promise depends on the people's faithfulness; but that on the other hand YHWH will remain faithful to the covenant of commitment to be their God

---

54 See above, pp. 32–5.
55 See Rendtorff, *Covenant Formula*, and *Hebrew Bible*, pp. 442–4.

whether they are faithful or not. It is, as YHWH says to Abraham in Genesis 17.7 when making it, an enduring covenant.

Can the universal God show special favour to one people? – the question we saw Clines asking in the last chapter.[56] At Deuteronomy 10.17–18 it is asserted that YHWH does not show favouritism. The usual defence is that the election of Israel is for the sake of the world. Genesis 12.3 is appealed to. Yet the interpretation of this text is disputed.[57] It is better to appeal to the fact that monotheism and social justice in the whole world can be traced back to the Old Testament. Christianity has an important role in this process, but the Christian interpreter is faced with the question: does the covenant still endure, and if so how does this cohere with the conviction that the Christian community has a covenant with the same God? As we saw in Chapter 8, Christians for centuries took for granted that the Jews had been rejected and the Church elected in their place. How much blood and suffering the maintenance of this dogma in the very presence of Jews in every country of Europe has been responsible for cannot be counted.

In the aftermath of the Holocaust, Christian theologians have taken a new turn, to reject 'supersessionism'.[58] Are Israel and the Church two separate 'chosen peoples' with distinct covenants which will both endure to the end? 'Christian Zionism' is popular today among (chiefly) North American evangelicals.[59] This maintains a place for Israel in God's plans, but it also assumes that they will be converted to Christ in the end. Moltmann sets both Israel and the Church in the light of the hope for the kingdom of God. Each has a distinct calling: Israel in the observance of the Torah, 'for the Torah is the prefiguration and beginning of the divine rule on earth'; the Church in spreading hope for that rule among the Gentiles. Each in its own way expresses the spirit of the first three petitions of the Lord's Prayer.[60]

God and Israel: salvation

The deliverance of Israel from slavery in Egypt is narratively the central episode of the Pentateuch. We may argue that it is also central theologically, as in Exodus 19.4 YHWH brings it forward as the foundation for his call to obey his covenant, and it is repeatedly referred to in the laws, especially in Deuteronomy, as motivation for doing justice to slaves and other subordinate or marginal people. But of course it follows on from YHWH's commitment to Israel's ancestors. (See Exod. 2.23–25 and 6.2–8; Deut. 7.8–9; etc.) This is also implied when YHWH refers to Israel as 'my people' in Exodus 3.7. It is made plain that it is solely by the power of YHWH that

---

56 Above, p. 189.
57 See, e.g., Wenham, *Genesis 1—15*, pp. 277–8.
58 See Childs, *Biblical Theology*, pp. 441–51; Moltmann, *Church*, pp. 136–50.
59 Moberly demonstrates its rooting in Genesis 12.3: *Theology of Genesis*, pp. 141–8.
60 Moltmann, *Church*, pp. 147–8. See also Brueggemann, *Theology*, p. 449.

they are released from Egypt: the death of the firstborn and the drowning of Pharaoh and his army in the Red Sea are not achieved by human arms. This is recalled in Deuteronomy's repeated phrase 'with a strong hand and an outstretched arm, and with signs and wonders' (or variations: Deut. 4.34, etc.).

It is also the case that this central act of deliverance is paralleled by others both before and after: when the mother of Israel is rescued twice from being swallowed up in a king's harem owing to her husband's cowardice; when Jacob and his sons are rescued from famine by the wisdom of their brother Joseph – dreams play an important role in these cases, and as Joseph remarks (Gen. 40.8), the interpretation of dreams is a gift of God; in the sending in the wilderness of water and the manna, and in the turning of Balaam's intended curses into blessings. Thus YHWH displays a consistent will to save his people, except only at the two great crises of unfaithfulness after the exodus, those of the golden calf and the refusal to enter the land. In the case of the golden calf Moses' successful intercession for them hinges on his reminder of YHWH's promises to the ancestors (Exod. 32.13). In the second case he refers to YHWH's will to forgive sins that YHWH had himself announced after the first great apostasy (Num. 14.18 = Exod. 34.6–7).

We have previously noted that the story of the exodus is taken by liberation theologians as the foundation of the doctrine of God's preferential option for the poor. In other words, God's will to liberate Israel from oppression is universalized: God wills to liberate the oppressed as such. J. P. Miranda expresses this understanding in an exceptionally hard form. YHWH hears the cry of the oppressed Israel, which is the universal cry of the oppressed, and therefore 'we must completely exclude the possibility that Yahweh's "descent" to "deliver" in Exodus 3.7–9 should be attributed to the fact that it is "my people" who cry out'.[61] It is the result solely of YHWH's universal and impartial will for justice as God of the whole earth. I have discussed this issue elsewhere, and shown that there is ample evidence for YHWH's partiality as God of Israel in the Old Testament, and especially in Exodus 3, where YHWH refers repeatedly to his personal connection with Moses and his people.[62] The crucial point is that others are made to suffer for the sake of Israel. It is not simply that Pharaoh and his court and army, the oppressive ruling class, suffer deservedly.[63] The text makes a point of saying that the 'maid at the mill' and the 'prisoner in the dungeon' lose their firstborn just like Pharaoh (Exod. 11.5; 12.29). In other words, they suffer because they are Egyptians, not because they are oppressors.[64] We have noted in the previous chapter the inescapable connection between the deliverance of Israel and the eviction or massacre of the indigenous inhabitants of Canaan,

61 Miranda, *Marx*, p. 89.
62 Houston, *Contending*, pp. 207–14; 'Character of YHWH', pp. 18–20.
63 As claimed by Brueggemann, 'Pharaoh as Vassal'.
64 Houston, 'Character of YHWH', pp. 23–4.

which problematizes the use of the exodus as a theological model.[65] It also problematizes a purely systematic view of the theology of the Pentateuch: it does not appear to square with the 'universal reign of God in justice and righteousness'.

The universalization of the exodus model is thus not as easy as has been suggested. Yet, YHWH is *also* the impartial king of the whole earth – this necessarily follows from YHWH's position as creator and sole God – and his impartial benevolence is expressed in such a passage as Deuteronomy 10.17–18. Levenson argues that both universal and particularist perspectives are expressed in Exodus 2.23–25.

> What attracts God's attention and causes him to remember his long-neglected covenant is Israel's groaning, crying and moaning in bondage. These reach God independently of his remembering the covenant and even *before* he does so. The point here is that the pain of *any* slave can evoke sympathy in God.[66]

But is not the crucial word here 'can'? The pain of the slave who lost her firstborn does not in fact evoke sympathy: she is a victim to a 'higher' cause.

Levenson also points out that the 'liberation' of Israel is not political liberation as understood by modern radicals, as deliverance from dependence and oppression into self-determination or equality.[67] The exodus may provide a model for political revolution, and has done,[68] but in its full meaning it has to be understood differently. 'They are my slaves, whom I brought out of the land of Egypt' (Lev. 25.42, 55). They are freed from slavery to Pharaoh to become slaves of YHWH, maintaining YHWH's cult and obeying YHWH's commands. Of course, *this* slavery is to the one 'whose service is perfect freedom', unlike the exploitative slavery of Egypt. The only place where the word 'freedom' (*deror*) occurs in the Pentateuch is in the same chapter as that which proclaims the Israelites slaves to YHWH (Lev. 25.10). Obedience to God's commandments means true freedom.

The covenant of obedience

The covenant offered and accepted at Sinai does not *make* Israel YHWH's people, but inaugurates a new phase in the relationship. This phase is marked by a condition: '*If* you obey me and keep my covenant ...' But it is a reciprocal relationship. YHWH's part is already in process: 'You see what I have done to the Egyptians, and how I have borne you on eagles' wings and brought you to myself.' Israel, as an obedient people, will become a

---

65 Above, p. 198.
66 Levenson, *Hebrew Bible*, p. 152 (Levenson's emphasis).
67 Levenson, *Hebrew Bible*, pp. 140–51.
68 Walzer, *Exodus and Revolution*.

nation with a special relationship both to YHWH and to other nations. This conditional reciprocity is maintained throughout the subsequent narrative, especially in the covenant blessings of Leviticus 26 and Deuteronomy 28 and the repeated promises of blessing for faithfulness and obedience in Deuteronomy.

On the surface, it would appear that the Israelites are offered a choice, both here (with Exod. 24.3, 7) and in Deuteronomy 30.15–20 ('I have set before you life and death ... choose life!). The covenant formally enables the junior partner to consent to the conditions, but the appearance of choice is an illusion. In reality the commands of the new master are inescapable. The alternative, as Moses says, is death. Thus the pragmatic structure of the covenant closely parallels that of a vassal treaty, even if the formal structure of the document is hard to trace. This may be held to justify Yee's criticism of the covenant as 'imperial ideology'.[69] It would be more accurate to say that the instrument of imperial ideology is here turned to the ultimate end of the life and freedom of the 'vassal'.

The conditions are numerous, but it is easy to see that there is one leading stipulation, the command to have no god but YHWH. This heads the Decalogue, which alone, both in Exodus and in Deuteronomy, is spoken directly to the people by YHWH. And this is the issue that is at the root of the first great crisis in relationships between YHWH and Israel in Exodus 32. It could be argued that the people are intending to worship YHWH – see Exodus 32.5: 'Tomorrow will be a feast to YHWH.' But this is not how either the narrator or YHWH or Moses sees it. What they are committing is apostasy from their God.

Deuteronomy expresses the same stipulation in different terms: 'You shall love YHWH your God with all your heart, and all your soul, and all your strength' (Deut. 6.5). Though the argument has some traction that the term 'to love' here is derived from the terminology of the treaties, meaning simply 'to be faithful to your Lord',[70] in the context of the framework of Deuteronomy it surely means more than this. It is repeated several times, and in Deuteronomy it is an essential part of the reciprocity of the covenant. It is stated several times in the same context that 'YHWH loves you and is fulfilling the oath that he swore to your ancestors'. YHWH places his love upon Israel to the exclusion of other nations (which does not mean that other nations are not blessed; see, for example, Gen. 17.20). This makes a great difference from the vassal-treaty model. Human sovereigns do not have just one vassal: on the contrary, their glory increases according to the number of their conquests and dependants. The first commandment is inextricable from the structure of the election and covenant of promise. Israel is to love YHWH and serve YHWH alone, because YHWH loves them and has saved them alone.

---

69 See above, p. 200.
70 Moran, 'Love of God'.

Perhaps the best commentary on the first commandment remains Martin Luther's in his larger catechism:

What does it mean to have a god? or, what is God? Answer: A god means that from which we are to expect all good and to which we are to take refuge in all distress, so that to have a God is nothing else than to trust and believe Him from the [whole] heart; as I have often said that the confidence and faith of the heart alone make both God and an idol.[71]

The power of this definition in making the commandment applicable in a non-polytheistic environment is impressive. It does not attempt a philosophical definition of a god, but relates the idea strictly to the human will and heart. The pervasiveness of the worship of 'other gods' in the hearers' original context was an obvious temptation. But what Luther saw was that the tendencies in the human make-up that responded to that temptation still existed and responded to other stimuli. In his context he mentions riches and possessions, which he calls 'Mammon', individual talents, honour and so forth, and of course the veneration of the saints.

The limitation of this definition, to be expected in a catechism, is its exclusively individual orientation. The commandments are addressed to Israel and to individuals as members of Israel. Luther's definition does not allow for whole nations seduced by false gods, and though he undoubtedly believed that the Roman church had been so seduced, he restricts his comments to the individual's selection of a saint for private devotion. But in our own day we see clearly how whole nations or other groups may 'expect all good and take refuge in all distress' from false gods, whether a charismatic leader such as Hitler, or, increasingly, our technological civilization. The command to 'trust and believe with your whole heart' in the one true God remains the rock bottom of all three 'Abrahamic' faiths.

Themes of Torah

Here I select a few aspects of the legal and instructional material that have theological implications. It will be seen that they all imply a form of natural law[72] and immediately raise the issue of universal validity.

The Sabbath as acknowledgement of the order of creation

The command to observe the Sabbath day is the most frequently repeated in the Pentateuch, and some further places command observance of the sab-

---

71 Luther, *The Large Catechism*, p. 12.
72 See above in Chapter 8, p. 181.

batical year.[73] The great majority of the places belong to P or H, and must be seen in the light of the culmination of the creation account in Genesis 2.1–3. The blessing of the seventh day inscribes the Sabbath rest in the order of creation and underlines the perfection of the original created order in the fact that it was completed and that the Creator could cease from the work. God's creation thus exhibits a seven-day rhythm, which human beings and animals (Exod. 20.10; 23.12; Deut. 5.14) are called to share in by resting on the seventh day. In Exodus 23.12 and Deuteronomy 5.15 there is also an aspect of social justice to the commandment (see below). The seven-year rhythm is a development from this. It is no great discovery to point out that the way in which modern consumer capitalism has developed violates this rhythm of work and rest, and therefore justice, and that neither humanity nor the natural creation is the better for it.

Idolatry as falsity to God

The Decalogue prohibits the making of any kind of images for worship (Exod. 20.4; Deut. 5.8). Other sentences in the Torah are not so comprehensive, but equally clear: Exodus 20.23; 22.20 [19]); Leviticus 19.4; 26.1; Deuteronomy 16.21–22; 17.3; 27.15. Some of these go beyond the prohibition of images to the setting up of poles, trees or standing stones without imagery (Lev. 26.1; Deut. 16.21–22). Deuteronomy 17.3 further implies the prohibition of the worship of the heavenly bodies.

Usually images are associated with 'other gods', as in the Decalogue, rather than being raised as an issue in the worship of YHWH. But in Exodus 32.4–5 Aaron appears to understand the golden calf as an image of YHWH, in the same way as Jeroboam in 1 Kings 12.28. And Deuteronomy 4 reckons with this as a possibility in giving a reason for the prohibition of image worship: 'since you did not see any form when YHWH your God spoke to you at Horeb out of the fire' (Deut. 4.15). This is unlikely to be a denial that YHWH has any physical form, since that is implied elsewhere (for example Deut. 34.10). The point is rather that YHWH did not choose to be known in this way by Israel, but only through the word. (The frequent assertion that images were thought to enable the deity to be manipulated[74] lacks evidence.)

While the Ark of God seems to be understood in Numbers 10.35–36, as in the stories in 1 Sam. 4—6, to represent the presence of the divine in much the same way as images and standing stones do in polytheism, the main theological threads in the Pentateuch deny that the real presence of YHWH is bound to this manmade object. For Deuteronomy (10.1–5) it is simply a

---

73 Even if Genesis 2.1–3, Exodus 16.5, 22–30; 23.10–11, 12; 34.21; Deuteronomy 15.1–11 are set aside because they do not use the word 'Sabbath', there are still Exodus 20.8–11; 31.13–17; 35.2–3; Lev. 19.3, 20; 25.1–8; 26.2; Numbers 15.32–36; Deuteronomy 5.12–15.

74 E.g. Eichrodt, *Theology*, vol. 1, p. 215.

container for the tablets of the covenant (hence the Deuteronomistic name 'the ark *of the covenant* of YHWH'), while for P it marks the place where YHWH *chooses* to meet with Moses as the representative of Israel (Exod. 25.22). The actual loss of the ark may have made this partial desacralization easier to accept.

The frequent prohibitions in the Pentateuch suggest that the popular inclination was always towards making the incomprehensible presence of God graspable through the senses. Experience in the history of Christianity is similar. The vast majority of Christians in history have used images, whether two-dimensional as in Orthodoxy or in the round as in Catholicism. The wholesale destruction of religious art in the Swiss, Dutch, English and Scottish Reformations may horrify the cultured, but it demonstrates the serious intention to listen to the Word of God and understand God through that alone. It brings Reformed Christianity significantly closer to the position of Judaism and Islam.

The life of Israel with YHWH enabled by the Dwelling and its cult

In some tension with the tendency to desacralization just discussed stand the extensive instructions for the building and furnishing of the Dwelling for YHWH and the sacrificial cult in Exodus 25—31; Leviticus 1—7; 16. When these are complete, YHWH promises to 'dwell among you' (Exod. 25.8; 29.45–46[75]), and this promise is fulfilled, though the language is guarded, when 'the glory of YHWH fills the Dwelling' in Exodus 40.24. But this presence of YHWH, or YHWH's glory, among Israel, which is in principle a blessing to them, is also dangerous. 'The uncleannesses of the children of Israel and their transgressions, all their sins' (Lev. 16.16), if they pollute the Dwelling, will lead to their death (Lev. 15.31). For this reason, the Dwelling is guarded against any unauthorized approach (Lev. 10.1–2; 16.2), and the sacrificial system is directed towards atonement and purification (Lev. 1.4; 4–6; 16). The underlying rationale here is an opposition between the holy, the divine presence, and the unclean, the result of natural bodily processes, above all death (Lev. 12—15; Num. 19). Moses' obedience to the instructions enables Israel to live in YHWH's presence.

The priestly conception of holiness and uncleanness is one that is not shared with modern western culture, but it is familiar in its broad outlines to Islam as well as Judaism. Every mosque has facilities for ablutions so that the worshippers do not pray without having washed, and footwear is left at the door (cf. Exod. 3.5). Traditional Christianity also has its protocols that clearly separate the secular from the sacred: in Catholicism communion is (or was) taken fasting so that ordinary food does not come into contact with the body of Christ, while in traditional Reformed Protestantism the table

---

75 These passages appear to be H (Knohl, *Sanctuary*, pp. 63–5). P avoids saying simply that YHWH will dwell among Israel.

was fenced against 'notorious evil livers' and in sectarian versions against non-members. It is also true that, as with the teaching in Leviticus, the traditions display a certain misogyny: 'unclean' bodily processes are commoner in women than men, and such ideas have been the pretext for excluding women from priesthood and hence from authority.

But this is not a reason for rejecting ritual practice altogether. It is clear that wherever religion is affected by modern secularism, the practice of ritual and the sense of a presence that ought to be guarded against intrusion is diminished. What is lost in this process? I would suggest that what is lost is the sense of reverence before God and the attentive practice of the presence of God.

The practice of justice as the imitation of God

YHWH your God is the God of gods and the Lord of Lords, the great God, mighty and fearsome, who has no favourites and takes no bribes, who gives fatherless and widow their rights, and loves strangers, giving them food and clothing; and you shall love strangers, for you were strangers in the land of Egypt. (Deut. 10.17–19)

This remarkable text presents YHWH as the example for just conduct in Israel.[76] Three aspects of justice are attributed to YHWH in this brief, compressed characterization, and all of them are required of the hearers of the Torah in many texts here and elsewhere.

The first is concerned with judicial procedure: YHWH is not guilty of favouritism and cannot be influenced by bribery, but judges with strict impartiality and honesty (cf., for example, Exod. 23.6–8). The second is concerned with judicial outcomes: YHWH judges in favour of the vulnerable and marginalized and against those who oppress and exploit them (cf., for example, Deut. 24.17; 27.19). The third is concerned with distributive justice: YHWH gives the necessities of life to those who are without them (cf., for example, Deut. 14.28—15.11, the third-year tithe, the remission of debts and an exhortation to be generous to the poor). What is said here of YHWH is confirmed elsewhere in the Torah. YHWH loved Israel when they were aliens in Egypt, delivered them from slavery, and fed them in the wilderness; rescued Hagar and Ishmael when they were effectively widowed and fatherless after being driven out by Abraham (Gen. 21.9–21); and will condemn and punish his own people without favouritism (Deut. 28.15–68).

We have seen above how extensive and important the material on social justice is in the Torah. Brueggemann is precise and emphatic. 'It is difficult to overstate the pivotal importance for the rest of Israel's testimony of ... the commitment of Yahweh (and of Israel) to justice ... rooted in the character and resolve of Yahweh'; and this justice, to be precise, is distributive justice:

---

76 See also my treatment of this text in Houston, 'Character of YHWH', pp. 11–12.

'The intention of Mosaic justice is to redistribute social goods and social power.'[77] My own examination of texts concerned with justice between rich and poor in the Old Testament places a question mark against the latter part of that definition. A large number of texts mandate the redistribution of goods; most of them, however, do not address the question of power.[78] The revolutionary nature of their teaching does not lie in what they actually command, but in their assumptions. The key point is the insistence of all these texts on treating rich and poor, powerful and marginalized, as fellow members of the community of YHWH's people, who have an equal right to the bounty of YHWH. Thus the practice of justice in Israel looks not only to imitate YHWH's impartial justice as lord of the world, as 'God of gods and Lord of lords', but also to learn from the implications of YHWH's partial love of Israel as Israel's God.

While I question the accuracy of Brueggemann's characterization of the distributive justice demanded in the Old Testament, I dissent in no way from his passionate assertion of the importance of this teaching today, in a world where the unhindered march of modern capitalism has resulted in a world of extreme inequality both within nations and between them, and fragmented communities. 'This ideology is in the end deathly.'[79] We stand with Israel before Moses in the fields of Moab, as he sets before us 'life and good, death and evil' (Deut. 30.15). If we choose the dominant ideology we choose 'death and evil'. To refuse this choice and instead take the gift of life requires an act of faith, knowledge of our freedom from slavery, and a consistent will to be active in the cause of life. But this is not a topic for this book.[80]

Exercise for an individual student. Select an important topic or theme of the Pentateuch, such as one of those dealt with above, and read what is said about it in two or more of the works on the theology of the Old Testament or part of it mentioned in the reading list below (use the indexes as well as tables of contents to find out where it is dealt with). Then write an essay/ paper comparing the different ways in which it is treated.

Exercise for the class. After a similar reading exercise, discuss the different approaches of the writers, and consider how you might deal with the topic yourselves.

---

77 Brueggemann, *Theology*, p. 736.
78 Houston, *Contending*. See above, p. 67.
79 Brueggemann, *Theology*, p. 741.
80 See Houston, *Biblical Challenge*.

Further reading

No full-length self-contained work exists, so far as I know, offering a theology of the Pentateuch alone. Lohfink's *Theology of the Pentateuch* is a collection of essays written at different times on P and Deuteronomy separately. One or two of them contribute significantly to an understanding of the Pentateuch as a whole.

There are works concerned with the theology of individual books. Moberly's *Theology of the Book of Genesis* is well worth reading as a fine example of the approach of theological interpretation of which Moberly is a leading exponent. The series 'Old Testament Theology' to which his book belongs will in due course be enriched by volumes on the other four books of the Pentateuch. Briggs and Lohr (eds), *Introduction to the Theology of the Pentateuch*, is a series of five essays on the theology of the individual books.

The prime resource, therefore, must be those works offering a theology of the Old Testament (or the Bible), especially those that deal separately with different parts of it. For a fairly quick overview of the subject there are the shorter works of Westermann, *What Does the OT Say?*; Clements; and Zimmerli. But no serious student should evade the challenge of the big works – or at least one of them! I will mention six. The classic treatments are the two-volume works of Eichrodt (1933 originally) and von Rad (1957 and 1962). Von Rad's has the advantage for our purpose of being arranged, broadly speaking, according to the books or main parts of the Old Testament. The theology of the 'Hexateuch' is in volume 1.

A number of theologies have appeared more recently. Childs published more than one according to his canonical principles. I take it that his definitive statement is his *Biblical Theology of the Old and New Testaments* (1992). The brief treatment of the Pentateuch in part of Chapter 3 (pp. 107–42) is not exciting, but more important is Chapter 6, 'Theological Reflection on the Christian Bible', which follows the studies of the Old and New Testaments.

Brueggemann's distinctive and often exciting work (1997) could be said to be arranged topically. The topics are devised by Brueggemann to define the different ways in which the Old Testament bears witness to its God. In Chapter 4, 'Testimony in Verbal Sentences', the successive 'sentences' follow the narrative of the Pentateuch closely, though not all the material is Pentateuchal: 'Yahweh, the God Who Creates ... Makes Promises ... Delivers ... Commands ... Leads'.

In the present century, Rendtorff (original 2001) and Goldingay (2003, 2007, 2009) have not contented themselves with a single approach. Rendtorff follows a survey in canonical order with a thematic study of about the same length, and finishes with a short study of 'The Hermeneutics of an Old Testament Theology'. Goldingay has produced what must be the longest Old Testament theology ever written, three volumes of about

900 pages each. But they are very readable! *Israel's Gospel* is a narrative theology that follows the order of the narrative books; therefore it begins with the Pentateuch. *Israel's Faith* is based more on the other books, while *Israel's Life* uses the Torah among other material in a thematic study of ethics.

The journals *Biblical Theology Bulletin*, *Horizons in Biblical Theology* and *Journal of Theological Interpretation* may also be found useful sources of ideas.

It is not necessary to confine oneself to works with 'Theology' in the title. Some commentaries have significant theological weight. Obvious examples in relation to the Pentateuch are von Rad's commentary on Genesis and Childs on Exodus. In addition there are many works on particular theological themes, such as creation or covenant, too many to list here.

Bibliography

General works and commentaries

This is a selective list of some that may be found useful, including all that are referred to in the text.

Commentaries are classified as follows (though such categories overlap):

(A) Full academic critical commentaries. This does not mean these commentaries are not usable by students. It is always possible to skip the more technical parts.

(S) Less technical commentaries designed for students (among others). Some of these, notably the *Word Biblical Commentary*, have grammatical notes for those tackling the text in Hebrew.

(T) Commentaries primarily theological in focus.

Dictionaries

Anchor Bible Dictionary, Gen. Ed. David Noel Freedman, 6 vols, New York: Doubleday, 1992.
Dictionary of the Old Testament: Pentateuch, ed. T. Desmond Alexander and David W. Baker, Downers Grove, IL and Leicester: InterVarsity Press, 2003.
Encyclopedia of Bible and Law, ed. Brent Strawn, 2 vols, New York: Oxford University Press, 2013.
New Interpreter's Dictionary of the Bible, Gen. Ed. Katharine Doob Sakenfeld, 5 vols, Nashville, TN: Abingdon Press, 2006–9.

Internet resources

There are a great many websites devoted to biblical studies in one way or another. Many of them are unreliable, and it is hard for a non-expert to tell which ones can be relied on. The Society for Old Testament Study is developing its own Wiki at https://sots-ot.wikispaces.com/. This will consist of articles written by experts in the field, which will be added to the site as they are written over the next few years.

Commentaries on the Pentateuch or the whole Bible

The Torah: A Modern Commentary, ed. W. Gunther Plaut, New York: Union of American Hebrew Congregations, 1981. (S/T)
New Interpreter's Bible, 12 vols, Nashville, TN: Abingdon Press, 1994–2004. Commentaries on the books of the Pentateuch are in the first two vols. (S/T)
New Jerome Bible Commentary, ed. Raymond E. Brown, Joseph A. Fitzmyer and Roland E. Murphy, London: Geoffrey Chapman, 1991. (S/T)
Oxford Bible Commentary, ed. John Barton and John Muddiman, Oxford: Oxford University Press, 2001. (S)
Eerdmans Dictionary of the Bible, ed. James D. G. Dunn and J. W. Rogerson, Grand Rapids, MI: Eerdmans, 2003. (S)

All these whole-Bible commentaries have articles on the Pentateuch as well as commentaries on each book.

Commentaries on the books of the Pentateuch

Genesis

Brueggemann, Walter, *Genesis: A Bible Commentary for Teaching and Preaching* (Interpretation), Atlanta, GA: John Knox Press, 1981. (T)
Rad, Gerhard von, *Genesis: A Commentary* (OTL), 2nd edn, London: SCM Press, 1963. (T/S)
Sarna, Nahum S., *Genesis: The Traditional Hebrew Text with the New JPS Translation*, Philadelphia, PA: Jewish Publication Society, 1989. (S/T)
Skinner, John, *A Critical and Exegetical Commentary on Genesis* (ICC), 2nd edn, Edinburgh: T & T Clark, 1930. (A)
Wenham, Gordon J., *Word Biblical Commentary*, 1: *Genesis 1—15*, Dallas, TX: Word Books, 1991; 2: *Genesis 16—50*, Dallas, TX: Word Books, 1994. (A/S)
Westermann, Claus, *Genesis 1—11: A Commentary* (including Introduction), Minneapolis, MN: Augsburg and London: SPCK, 1984; *Genesis 12—36: A Commentary*, Minneapolis, MN: Augsburg, 1985 and London: SPCK, 1986; *Genesis 37—50: A Commentary*, Minneapolis, MN: Augsburg, 1986, and London: SPCK, 1987. (A)

Exodus

Childs, Brevard S., *Exodus: A Commentary* (OTL), London: SCM Press, 1974. (T/A)
Dozeman, Thomas B., *Commentary on Exodus* (ECC), Grand Rapids, MI and Cambridge: Eerdmans, 2009. (A)
Durham, John I., *Word Biblical Commentary*, 3: *Exodus*, Waco, TX: Word, 1987. (A/S)
Fretheim, Terence, *Exodus: A Bible Commentary for Teaching and Preaching* (Interpretation), Louisville, KY: John Knox Press, 1991. (T)
Houtman, Cornelis, *Exodus* (HCOT), vol. 1, Introduction and 1:1—7:13, Kampen: Kok, 1993; vol. 2, 7:14—19:25, Kampen: Kok, 1996; vol. 3, 20—40, Leuven: Peeters, 2000; vol. 4, Indexes, Leuven: Peeters, 2002. (A)

Propp, William H. C., *Exodus 1—18* (AB 2), New York: Doubleday, 1998, *Exodus 19—40* (AB 2A), 2006. (A)

Leviticus

Hartley, John E., *Word Biblical Commentary 4: Leviticus*, Dallas, TX: Word Books, 1992. (A/S)

Milgrom, Jacob, *Leviticus 1—16* (AB 3), New York: Doubleday, 1991, *Leviticus 17—22* (AB 3A), 2000, *Leviticus 23—27* (AB 3B), 2000. (A)

Wenham, Gordon J., *The Book of Leviticus* (NICOT), Grand Rapids, MI: Eerdmans, 1979. (S/T)

Willis, Timothy M., *Leviticus* (Abingdon OTC), Nashville, TN: Abingdon Press, 2009. (S)

Numbers

Budd, Philip J., *Word Biblical Commentary*, 5: *Numbers*, Waco, TX: Word Books, 1984. (S)

Davies, Eryl W., *Numbers* (NCB), London: Marshall Pickering and Grand Rapids, MI: Eerdmans, 1995. (S)

Gray, G. Buchanan, *A Critical and Exegetical Commentary on Numbers* (ICC), Edinburgh: T & T Clark, 1903. (A)

Levine, Baruch A., *Numbers 1—20* (AB 4), New York: Doubleday, 1993; *Numbers 21—36* (AB 4A), 2000. (A)

Deuteronomy

Driver, Samuel R., *A Critical and Exegetical Commentary on Deuteronomy* (ICC), 3rd edn, Edinburgh: T & T Clark, 1902. (A)

McConville, J. G., *Deuteronomy* (Apollos OTC), Downers Grove, IL; InterVarsity Press and Leicester: Apollos, 2002. (A/S)

Mayes, A. D. H., *Deuteronomy* (NCB), Grand Rapids, MI: Eerdmans and London: Marshall, Morgan & Scott, 1979. (S)

Nelson, Richard D., *Deuteronomy: A Commentary* (OTL), Louisville, KY: Westminster John Knox Press, 2002. (S)

Old Testament Guides

Introducing scholarship on the individual books, at a student level. All published by Sheffield Academic Press. In the next few years these will be gradually replaced by a new series, published by Sheffield Phoenix Press.

Clements, R. E., *Deuteronomy*, 1989.

Grabbe, Lester L., *Leviticus*, 1993.

Johnstone, W., *Exodus*, 1990.

Moberly, R. W. L., *Genesis 12—50*, 1992.

Rogerson, J. W., *Genesis 1—11*, 1991.

Wenham, Gordon, *Numbers*, 1997.

Ancient, medieval and Reformation texts in translation

There are alternative editions of many of these.

Apostolic Fathers, The, tr. Kirsopp Lake, 2 vols (LCL), London: Heinemann, 1912.

Aquinas, Thomas, *Summa Theologiae*, with translations, 61 vols, London: Black-friars, 1964–80.

Aquinas, Thomas, *Summa Theologiae: A Concise Translation*, ed. Timothy McDermott, London: Methuen, 1991.

Augustine, *City of God*, tr. Henry Bettenson, London: Penguin Books, 2003.

Babylonian Talmud, The, ed. Isidore Epstein, many vols, London: Soncino Press, 1978.

Biblia Pauperum: Faksimileausgabe des Vierzigblättrigen Armenbibel-Blockbuches ..., Hanau/Main: Werner Dausien, 1967.

Calvin, John, *Commentaries on the Four Last Books of Moses, Arranged in the Form of a Harmony*, tr. Charles William Bingham, 4 vols, Edinburgh: Calvin Translation Society, 1852–55.

—— *Institutes of the Christian Religion*, tr. Henry Beveridge, London: James Clarke, 1953; Edinburgh: Calvin Translation Society, 1845.

—— 'On the Law and Commandments', in Brown, *Ten Commandments*, pp. 100–5.

Luther, Martin, *The Large Catechism* (Penn State Electronic Classics Series), Pennsylvania State University, 2000, quoted from http://www2.hn.psu.edu/faculty/jmanis/m~luther/mllc.pdf (accessed 4 February 2013).

—— 'How Christians Should Regard Moses', in Brown (ed.), *Ten Commandments*, pp. 68–77, and in *Luther's Works*, vol. 35, pp. 161–74.

—— *Luther's Works*, vol. 35: *Word and Sacrament* 1, ed. E. Theodore Bachmann, Philadelphia, PA: Muhlenberg, 1960.

Maimonides, Moses, *The Guide for the Perplexed*, tr. M. Friedländer, New York: Dover, 1956 (1904).

Mekilta de-Rabbi Ishmael, ed. with tr. by Jacob Z. Lauterbach, 2 vols, Philadelphia, PA: Jewish Publication Society, 1933.

Melito of Sardis, *On Pascha: With the Fragments of Melito and Other Material Related to the Quartodecimans*, tr. Alistair Stewart-Sykes, Crestwood, NY: St Vladimir's Seminary Press, 2001.

Midrash Rabbah, The, tr. and ed. H. Freedman and Maurice Simon, vol. 1: Genesis, London: Soncino Press, 1977 (1939).

Mishnah, The, tr. Herbert Danby, Oxford: Oxford University Press, 1933.

[Origen] Origène, *Homélies sur l'Exode*, ed. and tr. Marcel Borret, Paris: Cerf, 1985.

Passover Haggadah, The, ed. Nahum N. Glatzer, New York: Schocken Books, 1953.

Pentateuch, with Targum Onkelos, Haphtaroth and Prayers for Sabbath and Rashi's Commentary, tr. and ed. M. Rosenbaum and A. M. Silbermann, vol. 1: Genesis, London: Shapiro, Valentine, 1929.

Philo of Alexandria, *The Works of Philo*, tr. C. D. Yonge, Peabody, MA: Hendrickson, 1993.

Purvis, J. S., *The York Cycle of Mystery Plays: A Complete Version*, London: SPCK, 1962.

Shutt, R. J. H., 'Letter of Aristeas', in James H. Charlesworth, *The Old Testament Pseudepigrapha*, vol. 2, London: Darton, Longman & Todd, 1985, pp. 7–34.

Vermes, Geza, *The Complete Dead Sea Scrolls in English*, rev. edn, London: Penguin Books, 2004.

General

This includes all other works referred to in the footnotes or in 'Further reading'.

Abbott, H. Porter, *The Cambridge Introduction to Narrative*, 2nd edn, Cambridge: Cambridge University Press, 2008.

Ackerman, James S., 'The Literary Context of the Moses Birth Story', in Kenneth R. R. Gros Louis (ed.), *Literary Interpretations of Biblical Narratives*, Nashville, TN: Abingdon Press, 1974, pp. 74–119.

Albertz, Rainer, *A History of Israelite Religion in the Old Testament Period*, 2 vols, London: SCM Press, 1994.

—— 'Exodus: Liberation History against Charter Myth', in J. W. van Henten and A. Houtepen (eds), *Religious Identity and the Invention of Tradition*, Assen: Royal Van Gorcum, 2001, pp. 128–43.

Alt, Albrecht, 'The Origins of Israelite Law', in *Essays on Old Testament History and Religion*, Oxford: Blackwell, 1966; reprinted Sheffield: JSOT Press, 1989, pp. 79–132. Published originally in 1934.

Alter, Robert, *The Art of Biblical Narrative*, London: Allen & Unwin, 1981.

Anderson, Gary, *Genesis of Perfection: Adam and Eve in Jewish and Christian Imagination*, Louisville, KY: Westminster John Knox Press, 2001.

Assmann, Jan, *Cultural Memory and Early Civilization: Writing, Remembrance and Political Imagination*, Cambridge: Cambridge University Press, 2011 (original 1992).

Baden, Joel S., *The Composition of the Pentateuch: Renewing the Documentary Hypothesis*, New Haven, CT: Yale University Press, 2012.

Baker, David L., *Tight Fists or Open Hands? Wealth and Poverty in Old Testament Law*, Grand Rapids, MI: Eerdmans, 2009.

Bal, Mieke, *Lethal Love: Feminist Literary Readings of Biblical Love Stories*, Bloomington, IN: Indiana University Press, 1987.

—— *Narratology: Introduction to the Theory of Narrative*, 2nd edn, Toronto: University of Toronto Press, 1997.

Baltzer, Klaus, *The Covenant Formulary in Old Testament, Jewish and Early Christian Writings*, Philadelphia, PA: Fortress Press and Oxford: Blackwell, 1971.

Bar-Efrat, Shimon, *Narrative Art in the Bible*, Sheffield: Almond, 1989.

Barr, James, *The Concept of Biblical Theology: An Old Testament Perspective*, London: SCM Press, 1999.

Barton, John, *The Cambridge Companion to Biblical Interpretation*, Cambridge: Cambridge University Press, 1998.

—— *The Nature of Biblical Criticism*, Louisville, KY: Westminster John Knox Press, 2007.

Berlin, Adele, *Poetics and Interpretation of Biblical Narrative*, Sheffield: Almond, 1983.

Bible and Culture Collective, The, *The Postmodern Bible*, New Haven, CT: Yale University Press, 1995.

Blenkinsopp, Joseph, *Ezra–Nehemiah: A Commentary* (OTL), London: SCM Press, 1988.

—— 'The Judaean Priesthood during the Neo-Babylonian and Achaemenid Periods: A Hypothetical Reconstruction', *CBQ* 60 (1998), pp. 25–43.

—— *The Pentateuch: An Introduction to the First Five Books of the Bible*, London: SCM Press, 1992.

—— *Wisdom and Law in the Old Testament*, rev. edn, Oxford: Oxford University Press, 1995.

—— 'An Assessment of the Alleged Pre-exilic Date of the Priestly Material in the Pentateuch', *ZAW* 108 (1996), pp. 495–518.

Bockmuehl, Markus, *Jewish Law in Gentile Churches: Halakhah and the Beginning of Christian Public Ethics*, Edinburgh: T & T Clark, 2000.

Booth, Wayne C., *The Rhetoric of Fiction*, Chicago, IL: University of Chicago Press, 1961.

Brenner, Athalya, 'An Afterword: The Decalogue – Am I an Addressee?', in Brenner (ed.), *A Feminist Companion to Exodus to Deuteronomy*, pp. 255–8.

Brenner, Athalya (ed.), (ed.), *A Feminist Companion to Genesis* (The Feminist Companion to the Bible 2), Sheffield: Sheffield Academic Press, 1993.

—— (ed.), *A Feminist Companion to Exodus to Deuteronomy* (The Feminist Companion to the Bible 6), Sheffield: Sheffield Academic Press, 1994.

—— (ed.), *Genesis* (A Feminist Companion to the Bible [Second Series] 1), Sheffield: Sheffield Academic Press, 1998.

—— *Exodus to Deuteronomy* (A Feminist Companion to the Bible [Second Series] 5), Sheffield: Sheffield Academic Press, 2000.

Brenner, Athalya, and Carole Fontaine (eds), *A Feminist Companion to Reading the Bible: Approaches, Methods and Strategies*, Sheffield: Sheffield Academic Press, 1997.

Brett, Mark G., *Decolonizing God: The Bible in the Tides of Empire*, Sheffield: Sheffield Phoenix Press, 2008.

Briggs, Richard S. and Joel N. Lohr (eds), *A Theological Introduction to the Pentateuch: Interpreting the Torah as Christian Scripture*, Grand Rapids, MI: Baker Academic, 2012.

Brown, William P., *The Ethos of the Cosmos: The Genesis of Moral Imagination in the Bible*, Grand Rapids, MI: Eerdmans, 1999.

Brown, William P. (ed.), *The Ten Commandments: The Reciprocity of Faithfulness*, Louisville, KY: Westminster John Knox Press, 2004.

Brueggemann, Walter, 'Pharaoh as Vassal: A Study of a Political Metaphor', *CBQ* 57 (1995), pp. 27–51.

—— *Theology of the Old Testament: Testimony, Dispute, Advocacy*, Minneapolis, MN: Fortress Press, 1997.

Burgess, John P., 'Reformed Explication of the Ten Commandments', in Brown, *Ten Commandments*, pp. 78–99.

Carmi, T. (ed. and tr.), *The Penguin Book of Hebrew Verse*, London: Penguin, 1981.

Carr, David M., *Reading the Fractures of Genesis: Historical and Literary Approaches*, Louisville, KY: Westminster John Knox Press, 1996.

—— *Writing on the Tablet of the Heart: Origins of Scripture and Literature*, New York: Oxford University Press, 2005.

—— *The Formation of the Hebrew Bible: A New Reconstruction*, New York: Oxford University Press, 2011.

Childs, Brevard S., *Biblical Theology of the Old and New Testaments: Theological Reflection on the Christian Bible*, London: SCM Press, 1992.

Choi, John H., *Traditions at Odds: The Reception of the Pentateuch in Biblical and Second Temple Period Literature*, New York and London: T & T Clark International, 2010.

Clements, Ronald E., *Old Testament Theology: A Fresh Approach*, London: Marshall, Morgan & Scott, 1978.

Clifford, Richard J., 'The Tent of El and the Israelite Tent of Meeting', *CBQ* 33 (1971), pp. 221–7.

Clines, David J. A., 'God in the Pentateuch: Reading against the Grain', in *Interested Parties*, pp. 187–211.

—— *Interested Parties: The Ideology of Writers and Readers of the Hebrew Bible*, Sheffield: Sheffield Academic Press, 1995.

—— *The Theme of the Pentateuch*, 2nd edn, Sheffield: Sheffield Academic Press, 1997.

Coats, George W., 'The King's Loyal Opposition: Obedience and Authority in Exodus 32—34', in Coats and Burke O. Long (eds), *Canon and Authority: Essays in Old Testament Religion and Theology*, Philadelphia, PA: Fortress Press, 1977, pp. 91–109.

—— *Genesis: With an Introduction to Narrative Literature*, Grand Rapids, MI: Eerdmans, 1983.

Cohen, Jeremy, *'Be Fertile and Increase, Fill the Earth and Master It': The Ancient and Medieval Career of a Biblical Text*, Ithaca, NY: Cornell University Press, 1989.

Cohn, Norman, *Noah's Flood: The Genesis Story in Western Thought*, New Haven, CT: Yale University Press, 1996.

Collins, John J., 'Marriage, Divorce and Family in Second Temple Judaism', in Leo G. Perdue et al., *Families in Ancient Israel*, Louisville, KY: Westminster John Knox Press, 1997, pp. 104–62.

Common Worship: Services and Prayers for the Church of England, London: Church House Publishing, 2000.

Cone, James H., *God of the Oppressed*, rev. edn, Maryknoll, NY: Orbis Books, 1997.

Cook, Stephen L., *The Social Roots of Biblical Yahwism*, Atlanta, GA: Society of Biblical Literature, 2004.

Cowley, A. E., *Aramaic Papyri of the Fifth Century B.C.*, Oxford: Clarendon Press, 1923.

Crawford, Sidnie White, 'The Use of the Pentateuch in the *Temple Scroll* and the *Damascus Document* in the Second Century B.C.E.', in Knoppers and Levinson, *Pentateuch*, pp. 301–17.

Croatto, J. Severino, *Exodus, a Hermeneutics of Freedom*, Maryknoll, NY: Orbis Books, 1981.

Cross, Frank Moore, *Canaanite Myth and Israelite Epic*, Cambridge, MA: Harvard University Press, 1973.

—— *From Epic to Canon: History and Literature in Ancient Israel*, Baltimore, MD: Johns Hopkins University Press, 1998.

Crüsemann, Frank, *The Torah: Theology and Social History of Old Testament Law*, Edinburgh: T & T Clark, 1996.

Damrosch, David, *The Narrative Covenant: Transformations of Genre in the Growth of Biblical Literature*, Ithaca, NY: Cornell University, 1987.

Davies, G. I., *Hosea* (NCB), London: Marshall Pickering and Grand Rapids, MI: Eerdmans, 1992.

——'The Composition of the Book of Exodus: Reflections on the Theses of Erhard Blum', in Michael V. Fox et al. (eds), *Texts, Temples and Traditions: A Tribute to Menahem Haran*, Winona Lake, IN: Eisenbrauns, 1996, pp. 71–85.

—— 'Introduction to the Pentateuch', in John Barton and John Muddiman (eds), *The Oxford Bible Commentary*, Oxford: Oxford University Press, 2001, pp. 12–38.

—— 'Genesis and the Early History of Israel: A Survey of Research', in A. Wénin (ed.), *Studies in the Book of Genesis: Literature, Redaction and History*, Leuven: Leuven University Press and Peeters, 2001, pp. 105–34.

—— 'Was there an Exodus?', in John Day (ed.), *In Search of Pre-Exilic Israel*, London and New York: T & T Clark International, 2004, pp. 23–40.

Davies, Philip R., *Memories of Ancient Israel: An Introduction to Biblical History – Ancient and Modern*, Louisville, KY: Westminster John Knox Press, 2008.

Davis, Ellen F., *Scripture, Culture and Agriculture: An Agrarian Reading of the Bible*, Cambridge: Cambridge University Press, 2009.

Day, John, *Yahweh and the Gods and Goddesses of Canaan*, Sheffield: Sheffield Academic Press, 2000.

—— 'Why does God 'Establish' rather than 'Cut' Covenants in the Priestly Source?', in A. D. H. Mayes and R. B. Salters (eds), *Covenant as Context: Esays in Honour of E. W. Nicholson*, Oxford: Oxford University Press, 2003, pp. 91–109.

Delaney, Carol, 'Abraham and the Seeds of Patriarchy', in Brenner (ed.), *Genesis*, pp. 129–49.

Douglas, Mary, *Purity and Danger: An Analysis of Concepts of Pollution and Taboo*, London: Routledge, 1966.

—— *Natural Symbols: Explorations in Cosmology*, 2nd edn, London: Routledge, 2003.

Dozeman, Thomas B., 'The Commission of Moses and the Book of Genesis', in Dozeman and Schmid, *Farewell*, pp. 107–29.

Dozeman, Thomas B. (ed.), *Methods for Exodus* (Methods in Biblical Interpretation), New York: Cambridge University Press, 2010.

Dozeman, Thomas B. and Konrad Schmid (eds), *A Farewell to the Yahwist? The Composition of the Pentateuch in Recent European Interpretation*, Atlanta, GA: Society of Biblical Literature, 2006.

Dozeman, Thomas B., Konrad Schmid and Baruch J. Schwartz (eds), *The Pentateuch: International Perspectives on Current Research*, Tübingen: Mohr, 2011.

Driver, S. R., *An Introduction to the Literature of the Old Testament*, 7th edn, Edinburgh: T & T Clark, 1898.

Dumbrell, William J., *Covenant and Creation: An Old Testament Covenantal Theology*, Exeter: Paternoster, 1984.

Dunn, James D. G., *The Partings of the Ways between Christianity and Judaism and their Significance for the Character of Christianity*, 2nd edn, London: SCM Press, 2006.

Eichrodt, Walther, *Theology of the Old Testament*, 2 vols, London: SCM Press, 1961, 1967.

Eissfeldt, Otto, *The Old Testament: An Introduction*, Oxford: Blackwell, 1965.

Emerton, J. A., 'The Origin of the Promises to the Patriarchs in the Older Sources of the Book of Genesis', *VT* 32 (1982), pp. 14–32.

Eskenazi, Tamara C. and Andrea L. Weiss, *The Torah: A Woman's Commentary*, New York; URJ Press, 2007.

Exum, J. Cheryl, '"You shall let every daughter live": A study of Exodus 1.8–2.10', in Brenner (ed.), *Exodus to Deuteronomy*, pp. 37–61.

———'Second Thoughts about Secondary Characters: Women in Exodus 1.8–2.10', in Brenner (ed.), *Exodus to Deuteronomy*, pp. 75–87.

——— *Fragmented Women: Feminist (Sub)versions of Biblical Narratives*, Sheffield: Sheffield Academic Press, 1993.

———'The Hand that Rocks the Cradle', in *Plotted, Shot and Painted: Cultural Representations of Biblical Women*, Sheffield: Sheffield Academic Press, 1996, pp. 80–100.

Faust, Avraham, *Israel's Ethnogenesis: Settlement, Interaction, Expansion and Resistance*, London: Equinox, 2006.

——— 'The Archaeology of the Israelite Cult: Questioning the Consensus', *BASOR* 360 (2010), pp. 23–35.

Fewell, Danna Nolan, and David M. Gunn, *Gender, Power and Promise: The Subject of the Bible's First Story*, Nashville, TN: Abingdon Press, 1993.

Finkelstein, Israel, *The Archaeology of the Israelite Settlement*, Jerusalem: Israel Exploration Society, 1988.

Fischer, Irmtraud and Mercedes Navarro Puerto (eds), *Torah*, The Bible and Women, 1.11, Atlanta, GA: Society of Biblical Literature, 2011.

Fishbane, Michael, *Biblical Interpretation in Ancient Israel*, Oxford: Clarendon Press, 1985.

Fitzpatrick-McKinley, Anne, *The Transformation of Torah from Scribal Advice to Law*, Sheffield: Sheffield Academic Press, 1999.

Fohrer, Georg, *Introduction to the Old Testament*, London: SPCK, 1976.

Fokkelman, J. P., *Narrative Art in Genesis*, 2nd edn, Sheffield: JSOT Press, 1991.

Fox, Michael V., *Proverbs 1—9* (Anchor Bible 18A), New York: Doubleday, 2000.

Frei, Peter, 'Persian Imperial Authorization: A Summary', in Watts, *Persia and Torah*, pp. 5–40.

Fretheim, Terence E., *God and World in the Old Testament: A Relational Theology of Creation*, Nashville, TN: Abingdon Press, 2005.

Fried, Lisbeth S., *The Priest and the Great King: Temple–Palace Relations in the Persian Empire*, Winona Lake, IN: Eisenbrauns, 2004.

Friedman, Richard Elliott, *Who Wrote the Bible?*, new edn, New York: HarperOne, 1997.

Frymer-Kensky, Tikva, 'Deuteronomy', in Newsom and Ringe, *Women's Bible Commentary*, pp. 52–62.

Gertz, Jan Christian, 'The Transition between the Books of Genesis and Exodus', in Thomas B. Dozeman and Konrad Schmid (eds), *A Farewell to the Yahwist? The Composition of the Pentateuch in Recent European Interpretation*, Atlanta, GA: Society of Biblical Literature, 2006.

Gertz, Jan Christian, Konrad Schmid and Markus Witte (eds), *Abschied vom Jahwisten: Die Komposition des Hexateuch in der jüngsten Diskussion*, Berlin: de Gruyter, 2002.

Goldingay, John, *Old Testament Theology*, Downers Grove, IL: InterVarsity Press, vol. 1: *Israel's Gospel*, 2003, vol. 2: *Israel's Faith*, 2007, vol. 3: *Israel's Life*, 2009.

Goodman, Martin, *Rome and Jerusalem: The Clash of Ancient Civilizations*, London: Penguin, 2007.

Gottwald, Norman K., *The Tribes of Yahweh: A Sociology of the Religion of Liberated Israel, 1250–1030* B.C.E., London; SCM Press, 1979.

Gottwald, Norman K. and Richard A. Horsley (eds), *The Bible and Liberation: Political and Social Hermeneutics*, Maryknoll, NY: Orbis Books and London: SPCK, 1993.

Gowan, Donald E., *Theology in Exodus: Biblical Theology in the Form of a Commentary*, Louisville, KY: Westminster John Knox Press, 1994.

Grabbe, Lester L., 'The "Persian Documents" in the Book of Ezra: Are They Authentic?', in Lipschits and Oeming, pp. 531–70.

—— 'The Law of Moses in the Ezra Tradition: More Virtual than Real?', in Watts, *Persia*, pp. 91–114.

—— *Judaism from Cyrus to Hadrian*, London: SCM Press, 1994.

—— *A History of the Jews and Judaism in the Second Temple Period*, vol. 1: *Yehud: A History of the Persian Province of Judah*, London and New York: T & T Clark International, 2004.

—— *Ancient Israel: What Do We Know and How Do We Know It?*, London and New York: T & T Clark, 2007.

Grossman, Avraham, 'The School of Literal Jewish Exegesis in Northern France', *HBOT* I:2, pp. 321–71.

Guest, Deryn, Robert E. Goss, Mona West and Thomas Bohache (eds), *The Queer Bible Commentary*, London: SCM Press, 2006.

Gunkel, Hermann, *The Stories of Genesis*, Vallejo, CA: BIBAL Press, 1994 (tr. from the 1910 edn of his commentary on Genesis).

Gunn, David M., 'The "Hardening of Pharaoh's Heart": Plot, Character and Theology in Exodus 1—14', in David J. A. Clines, David M. Gunn and Alan J. Hauser (eds), *Art and Meaning: Rhetoric in Biblical Literature*, Sheffield: JSOT Press, 1982, pp. 72–96.

—— 'Reading Right: Reliable and Omniscient Narrator, Omniscient God, and Foolproof Composition in the Hebrew Bible', in David J. A. Clines, Stephen E. Fowl and Stanley E. Porter (eds), *The Bible in Three Dimensions: Essays in celebration of forty years of Biblical Studies in the University of Sheffield*, Sheffield: Sheffield Academic Press, 1990, pp. 53–64.

—— 'New Directions in the Study of Biblical Hebrew Narrative', *JSOT* 39 (1987), pp. 65–75.

Gunn, David M. and Danna Nolan Fewell, *Narrative in the Hebrew Bible*, Oxford: Oxford University Press, 1993.

Habel, Norman C., 'The Form and Significance of the Call Narratives', *ZAW* 77 (1965), pp. 297–323.

—— *The Birth, the Curse and the Greening of the Earth: An Ecological Reading of Genesis 1—11* (The Earth Bible Commentary Series, 1), Sheffield: Sheffield Phoenix, 2011.

Habel, Norman C. (ed.), *Readings from the Perspective of Earth* (The Earth Bible, 1), Sheffield: Sheffield Academic Press, 2000.

Habel, Norman C. and Shirley Wurst (eds), *The Earth Story in Genesis* (The Earth Bible, 2), Sheffield: Sheffield Academic Press, 2000.

Habel, Norman C. and Peter Trudinger (eds), *Exploring Ecological Hermeneutics*, Atlanta, GA: Society of Biblical Literature, 2008.

Halbwachs, Maurice, *On Collective Memory*, ed. Lewis A. Coser, Chicago, IL: University of Chicago Press, 1992 (originals 1925 and 1941).

Haran, Menahem, *Temples and Temple Service in Ancient Israel: An Inquiry into Biblical Cult Phenomena and the Historical Setting of the Priestly School*, Winona Lake, IN: Eisenbrauns, 1985.

Harrison, Kenneth, *An Illustrated Guide to the Windows of King's College Chapel, Cambridge*, Cambridge: King's College, 1953.

Harrison, Peter, 'Subduing the Earth: Genesis 1, Early Modern Science and the Exploitation of Nature', *Journal of Religion* 79 (1999), pp. 86–109.

Hayes, John H. (ed.), *Dictionary of Biblical Interpretation*, 2 vols, Nashville, TN: Abingdon Press, 1999.

Hayes, John H. and F. Prussner, *Old Testament Theology: Its History and Development*, London: SCM Press, 1985.

Hendel, Ronald S., *Remembering Abraham: Culture, Memory and History in the Hebrew Bible*, New York: Oxford University Press, 2005.

Hoffmeier, James K., *Israel in Egypt: The Evidence for the Authenticity of the Exodus Tradition*, New York: Oxford University Press, 1997.

——— *Ancient Israel in Sinai: The Evidence for the Authenticity of the Wilderness Tradition*, New York: Oxford University Press, 2005.

Horrell, David G., *The Bible and the Environment: Towards a Critical Ecological Biblical Theology*, London: Equinox, 2010.

Hort, Greta, 'The Plagues of Egypt', *ZAW* 69 (1957), pp. 84–103, and 70 (1958), pp. 48–59.

Houston, Walter J., *Purity and Monotheism: Clean and Unclean Animals in Biblical Law*, Sheffield: Sheffield Academic Press, 1993.

——— 'Foods, Clean and Unclean', in *Dictionary of the Old Testament: Pentateuch*, Downers Grove, IL: Inter-Varsity Press, 2003, pp. 326–36.

———'The Character of YHWH and the Ethics of the Old Testament: Is *Imitatio Dei* Appropriate?', *JTS* n.s. 58 (2007), pp. 1–25.

——— *Contending for Justice: Ideologies and Theologies of Social Justice in the Old Testament*, 2nd edn, London and New York: T & T Clark, 2008.

——— *Justice – the Biblical Challenge*, London: Equinox, 2010.

——— 'Justice and Violence in the Priestly Utopia', in Matthew J. M. Coomber (ed.), *Bible and Justice: Ancient Texts, Modern Challenges*, London: Equinox, 2011, pp. 93–105.

——— 'Sex or Violence? Thinking Again with Genesis about Fall [*sic*] and Original Sin', in Nathan MacDonald, Mark W. Elliott and Grant Macaskill (eds), *Genesis and Christian Theology*, Grand Rapids, MI and Cambridge: Eerdmans, 2012, pp. 140–51.

——— 'The Scribe and His Class: Ben Sira on Rich and Poor', in Thomas Römer and Philip R. Davies (eds), *Writing the Bible*, Durham: Acumen, 2013.

——— 'Between Salem and Gerizim: The Context of the Formation of the Torah Reconsidered', *Journal of Ancient Judaism*, forthcoming.

Hurvitz, Avi, 'The Evidence of Language in Dating the Priestly Code', *Revue Biblique* 81 (1974), pp. 24–56.

Jackson, B. S., 'Ideas of law and legal administration: a semiotic approach', in R. E. Clements (ed.), *The World of Ancient Israel: Sociological, Anthropological and Political Perspectives*, Cambridge: Cambridge University Press, 1989, pp. 185–202.

——— *Wisdom-Laws: A Study of the Mishpatim of Exodus 21:1—22:16*, Oxford: Oxford University Press, 2006.

————'Response to Roger Tomes: Home-Grown or Imported?', *ZAR* 14 (2008), pp. 525–31.

Jennings Jr, Theodore, W., *Jacob's Wound: Homoerotic Narrative in the Literature of Ancient Israel*, New York: Continuum, 2005.

Jenson, Philip P., *Graded Holiness*, Sheffield: JSOT Press, 1992, pp. 89–114.

Jeppesen, Knud and Benedikt Otzen, *The Productions of Time: Tradition History in Old Testament Scholarship*, Sheffield: Almond, 1984.

Johnstone, William, 'The Decalogue and the Redaction of the Sinai Pericope in Exodus', *ZAW* 100 (1988), pp. 361–85; reprinted with modifications in Johnstone, *Chronicles*, pp. 168–97.

———— *Chronicles and Exodus: An Analogy and its Application*, Sheffield: Sheffield Academic Press, 1998.

Kaminsky, Joel S., *Yet I Loved Jacob: Reclaiming the Biblical Concept of Election*, Nashville, TN: Abingdon Press, 2007.

Kartveit, Magnar, *The Origin of the Samaritans*, Leiden: Brill, 2009.

Kaufmann, Yehezkel, *The Religion of Israel: From its Beginnings to the Babylonian Exile*, tr. and abridged M. Greenberg, London: Allen & Unwin, 1961 (original 1937–48).

Kent, Charles Foster, *Israel's Laws and Legal Precedents*, London: Hodder & Stoughton, 1907.

King, Thomas J., *The Realignment of the Priestly Literature: The Priestly Narrative in Genesis and its Relation to Priestly Legislation and the Holiness School*, 102, Eugene, OR: Pickwick, 2009.

Kirk-Duggan, Cheryl A., 'Let My People Go!: Threads of Exodus in African American Narratives', in Sugirtharajah (ed.), *Voices from the Margin*, pp. 258–78.

Kirkpatrick, Patricia G., *The Old Testament and Folklore Study*, Sheffield: JSOT Press, 1988.

Kissling, Paul J., *Reliable Characters in the Primary History: Profiles of Moses, Joshua, Elijah and Elisha*, Sheffield: Sheffield Academic Press, 1996.

Klauck, H.-J. et al. (eds), *The Encyclopedia of the Bible and its Reception*, 30 vols, Berlin: de Gruyter, 2010–.

Knauf, Ernst Axel, 'Bethel: The Israelite Influence on Judean Language and Literature', in Lipschits and Oeming (eds), *Judah*, pp. 291–349.

Knierim, Rolf P., *Text and Concept in Leviticus 1:1–9*, Tübingen: Mohr, 1992.

———— 'The Composition of the Pentateuch', in *The Task of Old Testament Theology*, pp. 351–79.

———— *The Task of Old Testament Theology: Substance, Method and Cases*, Grand Rapids, MI: Eerdmans, 1995.

Knight, Douglas A., *Law, Power and Justice in Ancient Israel*, Louisville, KY: Westminster John Knox Press, 2011.

———— *Rediscovering the Traditions of Israel: The Development of the Traditio-historical Research of the Old Testament*, Missoula, MN: Society of Biblical Literature, 1975.

Knohl, Israel, *The Sanctuary of Silence: The Priestly Torah and the Holiness School*, Minneapolis, MN: Fortress Press, 1995.

———— 'Who Edited the Pentateuch?', in Dozeman, Schmid and Schwartz, *Pentateuch*, pp. 359–67.

Knoppers, Gary N., 'Parallel Torahs and Inner-Scriptural Interpretation: The Jewish and Samaritan Pentateuchs in Historical Perspective', in Dozeman, Schmid and Schwartz, *Pentateuch*, pp. 507–31.

Knoppers, Gary N. and Paul B. Harvey Jr, 'The Pentateuch in Ancient Mediterranean Context; The Publication of Local Lawcodes', in Knoppers and Levinson, *Pentateuch*, pp. 105–41.

Knoppers, Gary N. and Bernard M. Levinson (eds), *The Pentateuch as Torah: New Models for Understanding its Promulgation and Acceptance*, Winona Lake, IN: Eisenbrauns, 2007.

Koch, Klaus, 'Is there a Doctrine of Retribution in the Old Testament?', in James L. Crenshaw (ed.), *Theodicy in the Old Testament*, Philadelphia, PA: Fortress Press and London: SPCK, 1983, pp. 57–87.

Kratz, Reinhard G., *The Composition of the Historical Books of the Old Testament*, London: T & T Clark, 2005 (original 2000).

—— 'Temple and Torah: Reflections on the Legal Status of the Pentateuch between Elephantine and Qumran', in Knoppers and Levinson, *Pentateuch*, pp. 77–103.

Kurle, Stefan, *The Appeal of Exodus: The Characters God, Moses and Israel in the Rhetoric of the Book of Exodus*, Milton Keynes: Authentic Media, 2013.

Lampe, G. W. H., 'The Reasonableness of Typology', in G. W. H. Lampe and K. J. Woollcombe, *Essays on Typology*, London: SCM Press, 1957.

Lang, Bernhard, 'The Yahweh-Alone Movement and the Making of Jewish Monotheism', in *Monotheism and the Prophetic Minority: An Essay in Biblical History and Sociology*, Sheffield: Almond Press, 1983, pp. 13–59.

Langston, Scott M., *Exodus through the Centuries* (Blackwell Bible Commentaries), Oxford: Blackwell, 2006.

Larsson, Göran, *Bound for Freedom: The Book of Exodus in Jewish and Christian Traditions*, Peabody, MA: Hendrickson, 1999.

Lash, Nicholas, 'What Might Martyrdom Mean?' in William Horbury and Brian McNeil (eds), *Suffering and Martyrdom in the New Testament*, Cambridge: Cambridge University Press, 1981, pp. 183–98; reprinted in Nicholas Lash, *Theology on the Way to Emmaus*, London: SCM Press, 1986, pp. 75–94.

LeFebvre, Michael, *Collections, Codes and Torah*, New York: T & T Clark International, 2006.

Lemche, Niels Peter, 'Israel, History of – Premonarchic Period', *ABD*, vol. 3, pp. 526–45.

Levenson, Jon D., *Creation and the Persistence of Evil: The Jewish Drama of Divine Omnipotence*, Princeton, NJ: Princeton University Press, 1988.

——*The Death and Resurrection of the Beloved Son: The Transformation of Child Sacrifice in Judaism and Christianity*, New Haven, CT: Yale University Press, 1993.

—— *The Hebrew Bible, the Old Testament, and Historical Criticism: Jews and Christians in Biblical Studies*, Louisville, KY: Westminster John Knox Press, 1993.

Levinson, Bernard M., *Deuteronomy and the Hermeneutics of Legal Innovation*, New York: Oxford University Press, 1998.

Lienhard, Joseph T., *Exodus, Leviticus, Numbers, Deuteronomy* (ACCS), Downers Grove, IL: InterVarsity Press, 2001.

Lindström, Fredrik, *God and the Origin of Evil: A Contextual Analysis of Alleged Monistic Evidence in the Old Testament*, Lund: CWK Gleerup, 1983.

Lipschits, Oded and Manfred Oeming, *Judah and Judeans in the Persian Period*, Winona Lake, IN: Eisenbrauns, 2006.

Liverani, Mario, *Israel's History and the History of Israel*, London: Equinox, 2005.

Lohfink, Norbert, *Theology of the Pentateuch: Themes of the Priestly Narrative and Deuteronomy*, Edinburgh: T & T Clark, 1994.

Louth, Andrew, *Genesis 1—11* (ACCS), Downers Grove, IL: InterVarsity Press, 2001.

MacDonald, Nathan, *Deuteronomy and the Meaning of 'Monotheism'*, Tübingen: Mohr, 2003.

Magen, Yitzhak, 'The Dating of the First Phase of the Samaritan Temple on Mount Gerizim in Light of the Archaeological Evidence', in Oded Lipschits, Gary N. Knoppers and Rainer Albertz, *Judah and the Judeans in the Fourth Century* B.C.E., Winona Lake, IN: Eisenbrauns, 2007, pp. 157–211.

Malamat, Abraham, 'The Proto-History of Israel: A Study in Method', in Michael P. O'Connor and Carol L. Meyers (eds), *The Word of the Lord Shall Go Forth: Essays in Honor of David Noel Freedman in Celebration of his Sixtieth Birthday*, Winona Lake, IN: Eisenbrauns, 1983, pp. 303–13.

Mann, Thomas W., *The Book of Torah: The Narrative Integrity of the Pentateuch*, Atlanta, GA: John Knox Press, 1988.

Matthews, Victor H., Bernard M. Levinson and Tikva Frymer-Kensky, *Gender and Law in the Hebrew Bible and the Ancient Near East*, Sheffield: Sheffield Academic Press, 1998.

Mayes, Andrew D. H., 'Pharaoh Shishak's Invasion of Palestine and the Exodus from Egypt', in Bob Becking and Lester L. Grabbe (eds), *Between Evidence and Ideology*, Leiden: Brill, 2010, pp. 129–44.

McCarthy, Dennis J., *Old Testament Covenant: A Survey of Current Opinions*, Oxford: Blackwell, 1972.

—— *Treaty and Covenant: A Study in Form in the Ancient Oriental Documents and in the Old Testament*, 2nd edn, Rome: Pontifical Biblical Institute, 1984.

McKeating, Henry, 'Sanctions against Adultery in Ancient Israelite Society, with Some Reflections on Methodology in the Study of Old Testament Ethics', *JSOT* 4 (11) (April 1979), pp. 57–72.

McKenzie, Steven L., *Covenant*, St Louis, MO: Chalice Press, 2000.

Mendenhall, G. E., 'Covenant Forms in Israelite Tradition', *Biblical Archaeologist* 17 (1954), pp. 50–76.

—— 'The Census Lists of Numbers 1 and 26', *JBL* 77 (1958), pp. 52–66.

Meyers, Carol L., *Discovering Eve: Ancient Israelite Women in Context*, New York: Oxford University Press, 1988.

Middlemas, Jill, *The Troubles of Templeless Judah*, Oxford: Oxford University Press, 2005.

Milgrom, Jacob, 'The Antiquity of the Priestly Source: A Reply to Joseph Blenkinsopp', *ZAW* 111 (1999), pp. 10–22.

Millard, Alan R. and Donald J. Wiseman, *Essays on the Patriarchal Narratives*, Leicester: InterVarsity Press, 1980.

Miller, J. Maxwell, and John H. Hayes, *A History of Ancient Israel and Judah*, 2nd edn, Louisville, KY: Westminster John Knox Press, 2006.

Miller, Patrick D., *The Ten Commandments*, Louisville, KY: Westminster John Knox Press, 2009.

Miranda, José Porfirio, *Marx and the Bible: A Critique of the Philosophy of Oppression*, London: SCM Press, 1977.

Moberly, R. W. L., *At the Mountain of God: Story and Theology in Exodus 32—34*, Sheffield: JSOT Press, 1983.

────── *The Old Testament of the Old Testament: Patriarchal Narratives and Mosaic Yahwism*, Minneapolis, MN: Fortress Press, 1992.

──────*The Bible, Theology, and Faith: A Study of Abraham and Jesus*, Cambridge: Cambridge University Press, 2000.

────── *The Theology of the Book of Genesis*, Cambridge: Cambridge University Press, 2009.

Moltmann, Jürgen, *The Church in the Power of the Spirit*, London: SCM Press, 1977.

Moor, Johannes C. de, *The Rise of Yahwism: The Roots of Israelite Monotheism*, rev. edn, Leuven: Leuven University Press and Peeters, 1997.

Moran, W. L., 'The Ancient Near Eastern Background of the Love of God in Deuteronomy', *CBQ* 24 (1963), pp. 77–87.

Mosala, Itumeleng J., *Biblical Hermeneutics and Black Theology in South Africa*, Grand Rapids, MI: Eerdmans, 1989. Pp. 13–42 are reprinted in Gottwald and Horsley, *Bible and Liberation*, pp. 51–73.

Newsom, Carol A. and Sharon H. Ringe (eds), *The Women's Bible Commentary*, London: SPCK, 1992.

Nicholson, E. W., 'The Decalogue as the Direct Address of God', *VT* 27 (1977), pp. 422–33.

────── *The Pentateuch in the Twentieth Century: The Legacy of Julius Wellhausen*, Oxford: Clarendon Press, 1998.

────── *God and His People: Covenant and Theology in the Old Testament*, Oxford: Clarendon Press, 1986.

Niditch, Susan, *Oral World and Written Word*, Louisville, KY: Westminster John Knox Press, 1996.

Nielsen, Eduard, *The Ten Commandments in New Perspective: A Traditio-Historical Approach*, London: SCM Press, 1968.

Nihan, Christophe, *From Priestly Torah to Pentateuch: A Study in the Composition of the Book of Leviticus*, Tübingen: Mohr, 2007.

────── 'The Torah between Samaria and Judah: Shechem and Gerizim in Deuteronomy and Joshua', in Knoppers and Levinson, *Pentateuch*, pp. 187–223.

────── 'Israel's Festival Calendars in Leviticus 23, Numbers 28—29 and the Formation of "Priestly" Literature', in Thomas Römer (ed.), *The Books of Leviticus and Numbers*, Leuven: Peeters, 2008, pp. 177–231.

──────'The Priestly Covenant, its Reinterpretations, and the Composition of "P"', in Shectman and Baden, *Strata*, pp. 87–134.

Noth, Martin, *The Deuteronomistic History*, Sheffield: JSOT Press, 1981 (original 1943).

────── *A History of Pentateuchal Traditions*, Chico, CA: Scholars Press, 1981 (original 1948).

Olson, Dennis T., *The Death of the Old and the Birth of the New; The Framework of the Book of Numbers and the Pentateuch*, Chico, CA: Scholars Press, 1985.

Opitz, Peter, 'The Exegetical and Hermeneutical Work of John Oecolampadius, Huldrych Zwingli and John Calvin', *HBOT* II, pp. 407–51.

Otto, Eckart, 'The Holiness Code in Diachrony and Synchrony in the Legal Hermeneutics of the Pentateuch', in Shectman and Baden, *Strata*, pp. 135–56.

Patrick, Dale, *Old Testament Law*, London: SCM Press, 1985.

Pixley, George V., *On Exodus: A Liberation Perspective*, Maryknoll, NY: Orbis Books 1987 (original 1983). A few pages reprinted in Gottwald and Horsley, *Bible and Liberation*, pp. 86–91.

Polzin, Robert, *Late Biblical Hebrew: Towards an Historical Typology of Biblical Hebrew Prose*, Missoula, MN: Scholars Press, 1976.

Porten, Bezalel and Ada Yardeni, *Textbook of Aramaic Documents from Ancient Egypt*, vol. 1: *Letters*, Jerusalem: Hebrew University, 1986.

Presbyterian Church (USA), *Study Catechism*, 1998, http://www.presbyterianmission.org/ministries/theologyandworship/catechism/

Pressler, Carolyn, *The View of Women Found in the Deuteronomic Family Laws*, Berlin: W. de Gruyter, 1993.

Prior, Michael, *The Bible and Colonialism: A Moral Critique*, Sheffield: Sheffield Academic Press, 1997.

Puckett, David L., *John Calvin's Exegesis of the Old Testament*, Louisville, KY: Westminster John Knox Press, 1995.

Pummer, Reinhard, 'The Samaritans and their Pentateuch', in Knoppers and Levinson, *Pentateuch*, pp. 237–69.

Pury, Albert de, 'The Jacob Story and the Beginning of the Formation of the Pentateuch', in Dozeman and Schmid, *Farewell*, pp. 51–72.

Rad, Gerhard von, 'The Form-critical Problem of the Hexateuch', in *The Form-critical Problem of the Hexateuch and Other Essays*, London: SCM Press, 1984, pp. 1–78. Original 1938.

——— *Old Testament Theology*, 2 vols, London: SCM Press, 1975 (original 1957, 1960).

Raeder, Siegfried, 'The Exegetical and Hermeneutical Work of Martin Luther', *HBOT* II, pp. 363–406.

Redford, Donald B., 'Exodus I 11', *VT* 13 (1963), pp. 401–18.

——— *A Study of the Biblical Story of Joseph (Genesis 37—50)*, Leiden: Brill, 1970.

——— 'The So-Called "Codification" of Egyptian Law under Darius I', in Watts, *Persia*, pp. 135–59.

——— *Egypt, Canaan and Israel in Ancient Times*, Princeton, NJ: Princeton University Press, 1992.

Rendtorff, Rolf, *The Problem of the Process of Transmission in the Pentateuch*, Sheffield: JSOT, 1990 (original 1977).

——— *The Covenant Formula: An Exegetical and Theological Investigation*, Edinburgh: T & T Clark, 1998.

——— *The Canonical Hebrew Bible: A Theology of the Old Testament*, Leiden: Deo, 2005.

Reventlow, Henning Graf, *History of Biblical Interpretation*, 4 vols, Atlanta, GA: Society of Biblical Literature, 2009–10.

Robertson, David A., *Linguistic Evidence in Dating Early Hebrew Poetry*, Missoula, MN: Society of Biblical Literature, 1972.

Rogerson, J. W., *According to the Scriptures? The Challenge of Using the Bible in Social, Moral and Political Questions*, London: Equinox, 2007.

——— *A Theology of the Old Testament: Cultural Memory, Communication and Being Human*, London: SPCK, 2009.

Rogerson, J. W. and Judith M. Lieu (eds), *The Oxford Handbook of Biblical Studies*, Oxford: Oxford University Press, 2006.

Römer, Thomas C., *The So-Called Deuteronomistic History: A Sociological, Historical and Literary Introduction*, London and New York: T & T Clark International, 2005.

Sæbø, Magne (ed.), *Hebrew Bible/Old Testament: The History of its Interpretation*, vol. 1: From the Beginnings to the Middle Ages (until 1300), Part 1: Antiquity, Göttingen: Vandenhoeck & Ruprecht, 1996, Part 2: The Middle Ages, 2000, vol. 2: From the Renaissance to the Enlightenment, 2008 (=*HBOT*).

Sailhamer, John H., *The Pentateuch as Narrative: A Biblical–Theological Commentary*, Grand Rapids, MI: Zondervan, 1992.

Sanders, E. P., *Paul and Palestinian Judaism*, London: SCM Press, 1977.

—— *Jesus and Judaism*, London: SCM Press, 1985.

Sanders, Seth L., *The Invention of Hebrew*, Urbana, IL: University of Illinois Press, 2009.

Schluter, Michael and Roy Clements, 'Jubilee Institutional Norms: A middle way between creation ethics and kingdom ethics as the basis of Christian political action', *EQ* 62 (1990), pp. 37–62.

Schmid, Konrad, 'The Persian Imperial Authorization as a Historical Problem and as a Biblical Construct: A Plea for Distinctions', in Knoppers and Levinson, *Pentateuch*, pp. 23–38.

—— *Genesis and the Moses Story: Israel's Dual Origins in the Hebrew Bible*, Winona Lake: Eisenbrauns, 2010 (original 1999).

—— *The Old Testament: A Literary History*, Minneapolis, MN: Fortress Press, 2012 (original 2008).

Scholz, Susanne, *Introducing the Women's Hebrew Bible*, London and New York: T & T Clark International, 2007.

Setel, Drorah O'Donnell, 'Exodus', in Newsom and Ringe, *Women's Bible Commentary*, pp. 26–35.

Shectman, Sarah, *Women in the Pentateuch: A Feminist and Source-critical Analysis*, Sheffield: Sheffield Phoenix, 2009.

Shectman, Sarah and Joel S. Baden (eds), *The Strata of the Priestly Writings: Contemporary Debate and Future Directions*, Zürich: Theologischer Verlag, 2009.

Sheridan, Mark, *Genesis 12—50* (ACCS), Downers Grove, IL: InterVarsity Press, 2002.

Siegert, Folker, 'Early Jewish Exegesis in a Hellenistic Style', *HBOT* I:1, pp. 130–98.

Ska, Jean-Louis, *Introduction to Reading the Pentateuch*, Winona Lake, IN: Eisenbrauns, 2006 (original 2000).

Smith, Morton, *Palestinian Parties and Politics that Shaped the Old Testament*, 2nd edn, London: SCM Press, 1987.

Sneed, Mark R. (ed.), *Concepts of Class in Ancient Israel*, Atlanta, GA: Scholars Press, 1999.

Soggin, J. Alberto, *Introduction to the Old Testament: From its Origins to the Closing of the Alexandrian Canon*, 3rd edn, Louisville, KY: Westminster John Knox Press, 1989.

Spencer, Nick, *Darwin and God*, London: SPCK, 2009.

Spiegel, Shalom, *The Last Trial: On the Legends and Lore of the Command to Abraham to Offer Isaac as a Sacrifice: The Akedah*, New York: Behrman, 1979.

Stackert, Jeffrey, 'Distinguishing Innerbiblical Exegesis from Pentateuchal Redaction: Leviticus 26 as a Test Case', in Dozeman, Schmid and Schwartz, *Pentateuch*, pp. 369–86.

Stendahl, Krister, 'Biblical Theology, Contemporary', in *IDB* 1 (1962), pp. 418–32; reprinted in Heikki Räisänen et al. (eds), *Reading the Bible in the Global Village: Helsinki*, Atlanta, GA: Society of Biblical Literature, 2000, pp. 67–106.

Sternberg, Meir, *The Poetics of Biblical Narrative: Ideological Literature and the Drama of Reading*, Bloomington, IN: Indiana University Press, 1985.

Stone, Ken, *Practicing Safer Texts: Food, Sex and Bible in Queer Perspective*, New York and London, T & T Clark International, 2005.

Sugirtharajah, R. S., *Postcolonial Criticism and Biblical Interpretation*, Oxford: Oxford University Press, 2002.

Sugirtharajah, R. S. (ed.), *Voices from the Margin: Interpreting the Bible in the Third World*, 3rd edn, Maryknoll, NY: Orbis Books, 2006.

Tawney, R. H., *Religion and the Rise of Capitalism*, Harmondsworth: Penguin, 1938 (1926).

Thompson, Thomas L., *The Historicity of the Patriarchal Narratives*, Berlin: W. de Gruyter, 1974.

Toesca, Pietro, *San Vitale of Ravenna: the Mosaics*, plates by Annibale Belli, London: Collins, 1954.

Tomes, Roger, 'Home-grown or Imported? An Examination of Bernard Jackson's Wisdom-Laws', *ZAR* 14 (2008), pp. 443–62.

Toorn, Karel van der, 'The Exodus as Charter Myth', in J. W. van Henten and A. Houtepen (eds), *Religious Identity and the Invention of Tradition*, Assen: Royal Van Gorcum, 2001, pp. 113–27.

Tov, Emanuel, *Textual Criticism of the Hebrew Bible*, Minneapolis, MN: Fortress Press and Assen: Royal Van Gorcum, 2001.

Trible, Phyllis, 'Depatriarchalizing in Biblical Interpretation', *JAAR* 41 (1973), pp. 30–48.

—— *God and the Rhetoric of Sexuality*, Philadelphia, PA: Fortress Press, 1978.

—— *Texts of Terror: Literary-feminist Readings of Biblical Narratives*, Philadelphia, PA: Fortress Press, 1984.

Tucker, G. M., *Form-criticism of the Old Testament*, Philadelphia, PA: Fortress Press, 1973.

Turner, Laurence A., *Announcements of Plot in Genesis*, Sheffield: JSOT Press, 1990.

Van Seters, John, *Abraham in History and Tradition*, New Haven, CT: Yale, 1975.

—— *In Search of History: Historiography in the Ancient World and the Origins of Biblical History*, New Haven, CT: Yale University Press, 1983.

—— *Prologue to History: The Yahwist as Historian in Genesis*, Louisville, KY: Westminster John Knox Press, 1992.

—— *The Life of Moses: The Yahwist as Historian in Exodus–Numbers*, Kampen: Kok Pharos, 1994.

—— 'The Geography of the Exodus', in J. Andrew Dearman and M. Patrick Graham (eds), *The Land that I will Show You: Essays on the History and Archaeology of the Ancient Near East in Honor of J. Maxwell Miller*, Sheffield: Sheffield Academic Press, 2001, pp. 255–86.

—— *A Law Book for the Diaspora: Revision in the Study of the Covenant Code*, New York: Oxford University Press, 2003.

Vansina, Jan, *Oral Tradition as History*, Madison, WI: University of Wisconsin Press and London: James Currey, 1985.

Vaux, Roland de, *The Early History of Israel*, 2 vols, London: Darton, Longman & Todd, 1978 (original 1971).

Walsh, Jerome T., *Old Testament Narrative: A Guide to Interpretation*, Louisville, KY: Westminster John Knox Press, 2009.

Waltke, Bruce K., *The Book of Proverbs Chapters 1—15* (NICOT), Grand Rapids, MI: Eerdmans, 2004.

Walzer, Michael, *Exodus and Revolution*, New York: Basic Books, 1985.

Warrior, Robert Allen, 'A Native American Perspective: Canaanites, Cowboys, and Indians', in Sugirtharajah, *Voices from the Margins*, pp. 235–41.

Washington, Harold C., '"Lest He Die in the Battle and Another Man Take Her": Violence and the Construction of Gender in the Laws of Deuteronomy 20—22', in Matthews et al., *Gender and Law*, pp. 185–213.

Watts, James W., *Reading Law: The Rhetorical Shaping of the Pentateuch*, Sheffield: Sheffield Academic Press, 1999.

—— 'The Torah as the Rhetoric of Priesthood', in Knoppers and Levinson, *Pentateuch*, pp. 319–31.

—— *Ritual and Rhetoric in Leviticus: From Sacrifice to Scripture*, Cambridge: Cambridge University Press, 2007.

Watts, James W. (ed.), *Persia and Torah: The Theory of Imperial Authorization of the Pentateuch*, Atlanta, GA: Society of Biblical Literature, 2001.

Weinfeld, Moshe, *Deuteronomy and the Deuteronomic School*, Oxford: Clarendon Press, 1972.

Wellhausen, Julius, *Prolegomena to the History of Ancient Israel*, Gloucester, MA: Peter Smith, 1973 (original 1878).

Westermann, Claus, *What Does the Old Testament Say about God?*, London: SPCK, 1979.

White, Lynn, Jr, 'The Historic Roots of Our Ecological Crisis', *Science* 155 (1967), 10 March, pp. 1203–7.

Whybray, R. Norman, *The Making of the Pentateuch: A Methodological Study*, Sheffield: JSOT Press, 1987.

Wijk-Bos, Johanna W. H. van, *Making Wise the Simple: The Torah in Christian Faith and Practice*, Grand Rapids, MI: Eerdmans, 2005.

Williamson, H. G. M., *Word Biblical Commentary 16: Ezra, Nehemiah*, Waco, TX: Word Books, 1985.

Wright, Christopher J. H., *Old Testament Ethics for the People of God*, Leicester: InterVarsity Press, 2004.

Wright, David F., 'Augustine: His Exegesis and Hermeneutics', *HBOT* I:1, pp. 701–30.

Wright, David P., *Inventing God's Law; How the Covenant Code of the Bible Used and Revised the Laws of Hammurabi*, New York: Oxford University Press, 2009.

Yee, Gale A., 'Postcolonial Biblical Criticism', in Dozeman, *Methods for Exodus*, pp. 193–233.

Yoreh, Tzemah L., *The First Book of God*, Berlin: de Gruyter, 2010.

Zimmerli, Walther, *Man and his Hope in the Old Testament*, London: SCM Press, 1971.

—— *Old Testament Theology in Outline*, Edinburgh: T & T Clark, 1978.

Index of biblical references

Bold figures indicate a major discussion of the passage

Selective index of post–biblical
and modern authors

Only authors whose work is discussed or quoted, not merely referred to, are indexed, and only where they are discussed or quoted. The 'further reading' sections are not covered.

Index of subjects

'God' or 'YHWH' is mentioned on almost every page. Generally only the major discussions are listed in these entries, and details on the activities of God (creation, blessing, promise, etc.) should also be sought under the specific activity. The entry '*Elohim*' gives all the places where that word is mentioned.

Bold figures elsewhere indicate a major discussion or definition.

INDEX OF SUBJECTS

exile 22, 77, 101, 102, 108, 110, 111, 114, 128, 133, 141, 142, 155, 211

exodus, the 3, 19, 27, 28, 45, 67, 78, 97, 99, 106–8, 114–5, 134–5, 140–2, 152–5, 163, 166, 169, 175–6, 176–7, 178–9, 188–9, 191, **196–9**, 200, 212, **220–2**

Ezra (the man) 130–1

faith, faithfulness 20, 26, 28, 30–1, 34, 39–40, 52, 74, 80, 83, 101, 106, 141, 166, 168, 171, 172, 174, 175, 179, 209–10, 211, 214, 219–20, 222–4, 228

Flood, the 3, 16, 25, 29. 31, 38, 71, 75–6, 90, 174, 188, 216, 217, 218

folktale 147

forgiveness 20, 26, 28, 31, 80, 82, 166, 221

fragmentary hypothesis 93, 98, 101

genealogy 14, 15, 17, 146, 147, 153

genre 13–18, 40, 41, 43, **54–60**, 90, 131, 147

Gerizim, Mt 44, 46, 123, 124, 129, 143

God
  appearance to Jacob 104–6
  appearance to Moses 20, 106–8
  as covenant-maker 71–2, 75–83, 218–20, 222–4
  as creator 216–8
  as one 215–6
  as protagonist 18–21
  as teacher (lawgiver) 43–54
  names of 4, 19, 25, 47, 78, 89, 92, 94, 98, 99, 104, 106–7, 114, 151, 215
  promises of 29–30, 36–7, 75–8, 218–20
  tests Abraham 32–5
  See also Elohim, YHWH

golah 128, 132, 133, 134, 135

haggadah 163, **166**, 168
halachah **163–5**, 171
Hellenistic period 120–2, 127, 135–6, 167–8
hermeneutic of suspicion 187–8, 190, 196, 198, 201, 214, 215
Hexateuch 97, 106, 124, 133–4, 209, 212–3
historicity 13, **138–58**, 213–4, 215
historiography **13–14**
history **89–158**, 173–6, 192, 211–3
holiness 49, 50–52, 113, 116, 152, 162–3, 164, 180, **226–7**
Holiness Code or H **51–2**, 59, 82, 94, **96**, 102–3, **112–4**, 116, 128, 131, 132, 135, 195, 225
Horeb 52, 53, 72, 79, 81, 97, 101, 106, 113, 140, 155, 178, 213, 225

ideology 21, 134, 156, **186–7**, 188–9, 191–2, 195, 196–7, 200, 202, 205, 223, 228
idolatry, images 28, 45, **46**, 48, 61, 80, 81, 141, 166, 215, 224, **225–6**
imperial authorization 125, 126, 130–2, 134–5, 136, 137
implied author 12, 24, 31, 41, 187
implied reader 12, 21–2, 23, 24, 33, 35, 43, 44
irony 34
Isaac 19, 22–3, 29, 32–5, 40, 73, 82, 89, 106, 114–5, 142, 149, 150, 152, 168, 174, 175, 177, 193, 218, 219
Israel, Israelites
  internal to the text 19–20, 23, 24, 26–7, 28, 29–31, 36–40, 43–54, 58, 64, 71–3, 77–83, 90, 113–4, 114, 116, 122, 128, 134, 153, 166, 167, 170, 175, 179–80, 182, 188–9, 193, 196, 198, 200,

201, 210, 211–2, 212, 214,
218–28
external to the text 2–3, 5, 6–8,
22, 33, 41, 43, 55–7, 63, 64, 66,
75, 78, 84, 91–2, **94–6**, 97–8, 99,
100, 108, 110, 115, 120, 121,
127, 134, **138–44**, 144–5,
149–50, 151, 152, 153, 155,
156, 162, 164, 169, 170, 176,
179–80, 195, 197, 211–2, 212,
213
northern kingdom 95, 97, 105,
110, 112, 114, 115, 141–2, 157

J (Yahwist) **94**, 95–6, 97, 98, 99,
100–2, 103, **104–8**, 114, 133,
151, 197, 218
Jacob 2, 19, 23, 26, 29, 40, 73, 82,
89, 90, 99, **104–6**, 106, 114,
142, 143, 147, 149, 150, 152,
175, 177, 195, 218, 219, 221
Jerusalem 14, 35 n. 65, 44, 46 n. 4,
76, 111, 115, 119, 123, 125,
127, 128, 129, 130, 141, 142,
143, 156, 164
Jesus Christ 1, 3, 32, 35, 163,
170–82, 209–10, 220
Jews, Jewish, Judaism 1–3, 6–8,
13, 19, 32, 35, 44–6, 50, 67, 69,
74, 91, 95, 112, 118–9, 123–5,
131, 135–6, 138, 140, 141,
162–70, 171, 184, 197, 208,
210, 211, 220, 226
  in Christianity 177, 178, 179,
180, 182
Judah, Judaeans, Yehud 63 n. 41,
64, 75, 91, 95, 98, 99, 100, 101,
114–6, 119, 122–5, 127–32, 133,
136, 142, 152, 156, 157
judgment 38, 196
justice 1, 23, 25, 27, **48, 49,** 56–7,
58, 60, 61, **62–3,** 63–7, 120, 131,
167, 168, 177, 181, 182, 183,
191, **199–200,** 201–2, 207, 214,
215, 220, 221–2, 225, **227–8**

law(s) 1–6, 11, 15, 16, 17–18, 20,
21, 22, 23, 25, 30, 37, 38–40,
42–69, 71, 80–3, 84, 90, 96–7,
97, 102, 107, **108–14,** 115,
118–22, 124–5, 126–7, 130–2,
134, **135–6,** 141, 152, 162,
163–5, 166–7, 167, 170–2,
179–83, 193–4, 195, 197,
199–200, 205, 211, 213, 220,
224–8.
See also commandment(s)
liberation, deliverance, etc. 19, 28,
78, 141, 175, 176, **195–8,** 201,
202, 220–2
love 1, 26, 52, 84, 127, 166, 172,
181, 216, 223, 227, 228

midrash 165, 168, 169, 170, 184
Miriam 27, 153, 191
Mishnah 163, 164, 165
monarchy, monarchic period 6, 66,
68, 95, 98, 99, 100, 106, 113,
115, 141, 142, 145, 152, 155,
197, 211
monotheism 155, 215–6, 220
moral law 1, 3, 5, 19, 25, 30, 40,
45–8, 49, 51–2, 53–4, 57–8, 59,
60, **63–7,** 108–12, 115, 164,
171–2, 179–83, 199–200, 213,
224–5, 227–8
Moses 15, 24, 32, 119, 120, 174,
179, 191, 195, 211, 212, 215
  as author of Torah 1, 92, 109,
130, 136, 164, 167
  as judge 56
  as liberator 3, 19, 29
  as mediator of covenants 78–80,
81
  as priest 50
  as prophet 99, 125
  as recipient of revelation 19, 28,
30, 45, 48–52, 77, 109, 111,
115, 152, 163, 166, 167, 177,
211, 213, 215, 226
  as YHWH's representative 19, 23,